Eight Items or Less Cookbook

fine food in a hurry

Ann Lovejoy

SASQUATCH BOOKS

Library of Congress Cataloging-in-Publication Data

Lovejoy, Ann, 1951–
    Eight items or less cookbook.

    Includes index.
    1. Cookery. I. Title.
TX652.L63 1988 641.5   88.4513
ISBN 0-912365-43-9

Design by Heckler Associates
Illustrations by Glenn Garner
Cover design by Karen Schober

Typeset in Century by Weekly Typography & Graphic Design

Hearty thanks to Michael Teer of Pike & Western Wine Shop, Seattle,
for reviewing the wine suggestions throughout the book.

Sasquatch Books
1931 Second Avenue
Seattle, Washington 98101
(206) 441-5555

Contents

1   Introduction

5   Using the New Supermarket

13   How to Use this Book

15   Fish

53   Seafood

89   Poultry

115   Pork, Rabbit, and Veal

149   Beef and Lamb

167   Cured and Smoked Meats

189   Eggs and Cheese

213   Vegetables and Fruits

237   Tips and Techniques

241   Index

$\mathcal{I}$ntroduction

Real food. Food made from fresh, whole ingredients without recourse to a can opener. There is nothing like it. In fact, there are few sustained pleasures to equal those of savoring, smelling, and preparing real food. The scent of fresh garlic sizzling in a fruity, golden olive oil is every bit as enticing, in its way, as the perfume of an unfolding rose. Lots of people claim that sex is a chocolate substitute, but surely a thick piece of warm homemade bread, with a melting pat of fresh butter. . .well, perhaps we won't pursue that but you get the idea. However you slice it, real food is one of life's great enduring pleasures.

For me the revelation came in Italy, where the creed of Real Food is practically holy. Even at midday, the entire family gathered and the meal was served, course by time-consuming course. It drove me crazy—who has time for this? Let's just grab a sandwich! Fortunately, politeness demanded participation. At the first bite into a meatball—hot with garlic and peperoncini, fragrant with cinnamon and nutmeg, light with egg and herbed bread crumbs—the scales fell from my eyes. This was It, the art to pursue. Here was yet another new language to learn, as unfamiliar and rewarding as the idiomatic dialect the Perugini speak. Even the salads were full of ingredients I had never tasted: young spring weeds (field greens) with biting snippets of radicchio. Fingerling beans; fuzzy, milky, infant almonds; fingerling carrots. Plates of ruby-stained blood oranges, sliced with sweet onions, sprinkled with minced basil. Dressings of balsamic vinegar, garlic, citrus juices, always with silky, aromatic olive oil. I had gone to Italy as an art-and-language student, intending to stay for three months. I ended up staying for three years, coaxing lessons from every great cook I encountered—and there were plenty. I learned more than recipes; I learned an attitude about food, about people, about taking time to live graciously.

Introduction

Back then, these were foreign concepts. Now America is learning the same language. We are in the heady throes of a love affair—lusty, passionate, and fraught with strife. We are infatuated with real food. The whirlwind courtship is a blast, but trouble lies ahead, implicit in our attitudes and assumptions about daily life. As a nation, we are geared to instant gratification. Life in the fast lane has taken on an absurd importance, an unholy glamour that blinds us to the impoverished quality of instant living.

Nowhere is this more obvious than in the supermarket. Foods and products we would scorn in restaurant fare are willingly, even proudly, used at home. Microwavable, prefab gourmet grazings. Little pots of stabilized garlic emulsion. Nondairy cheese spread in eight epicurian flavors. If there's no time to cook, there's no time to savor, which is just as well, for most of these little shortcuts are fairly unsavory. Yet as much as we would like to, few of us can afford to eat at fine restaurants very often, and certainly not for each and every meal. Bridging the gap between the heavenly food we pay the earth for at such places and the regrettable quickies we can thaw and eat in under twelve minutes at home can seem impossible. In fact, it is simple, as simple as taking a closer look next time you jet through the supermarket.

American supermarkets of the 1980s may be our greatest national achievement. The grocery stores of my childhood were neighborhood places, where shoppers knew the butcher, the checkers, the produce man, the bag boys, and the manager personally. My mother expected service and got it, but as grocery stores grew into supermarkets, the big-is-better sterility of mass marketing captured the consumer's fancy. Convenience was everything. Shoppers wanted wide aisles, cheap prices, and fast processing; shopping was no longer a social experience. The grocery industry as a whole was hard-hit by a number of societal postwar trends. Mom-and-pop grocers couldn't begin to compete with supermarket pricing, and for a long, dry stretch in American consumer history, service, their only drawing card, was devalued. Few people were willing to pay the difference, and small stores were forced to close their doors or turn into high-priced convenience stores.

Now the supermarkets themselves are coming of age and looking back to their homely roots for direction. The new buzzword in the supermarket industry is, once again, service. Today, the lucky consumer can enjoy both personal service and good prices as the supermarkets develop and perfect a synthesis of old and new. The butcher is back in the meat department, fish departments are proliferating, in-store delis make pizza to order. Ethnic food sections are standard even in the boonies. Produce sections boast dozens of fresh things in any season. For the educated consumer, it is food heaven.

Walk into my local grocery store, a relatively small branch of a modest regional chain. On the right is bread, over twenty kinds: whole grain or wheat free, airbread or local brands baked in imported European brick ovens. Variety breads abound: pitas, fresh crumpets, bagels in three sizes, focaccio, and challah. Hamburger buns, too—pay 79¢ for a dozen of the store brand, or nearly $3 for eight hand-built ones made of seven organically raised, stone-ground grains. On the left? Tall bins of coffee, locally roasted, with a do-it-yourself grinder alongside. Dozens of teas and tisanes, and wines imported from all over the world, as well as regional microbrewed beers.

Move on to the produce department. On an ordinary autumn day, one can buy cactus pads, baby artichokes, or mushrooms from enoki to oyster, with local chanterelles and morels in season. Next, an array of citrus fruits surrounds a juicing machine. Here, too, are star fruit, both sweet and sour, feijoa and custard apples, muscat and champagne grapes, bitter melon, kumquats. In the salad area, choose radicchio or white radishes, fringed endive or escarole. Bundles of fresh watercress, baby dill, basil, and cilantro share shelf space with wildflower salads, purple potatoes, and romanesco broccoli. This is the New American Supermarket, and there is nothing like it in the world.

For some of us, however, wider choices complicate life by making shopping harder than ever. It is tough enough to think about cooking after—or during—a busy work week. It is demoralizing to search through rows of foods you have never heard of, thankfully seizing upon something, anything, familiar. Experimentation doesn't feel like fun when you are always in a hurry. Tomatillos and tamarinds, kiwis and kumquats seem to cloud the real issue—what on earth can you cook tonight without having to make a big production out of it? You hastily grab a handful of old favorites, carry them home, and make the same old stuff, true but tried a few times too many. This is reflex shopping, an easy pattern to adopt. Carry this ritual to an extreme, and you don't even need a shopping list; you just keep buying and cooking the same few foods.

This book began as a newspaper column called "Eight Items or Less." It was designed to counteract that repetitive impulse, to convince busy people to slow down and smell the garlic. Our goal was Real Food, fast. The object, always, was to use familiar foods in uncommon ways and to introduce some less familiar foods in flavorful combinations that might inspire the reluctant or inexperienced cook to further exploration and happy experimentation. The recipes featured quick, unfussy entrées with few ingredients, enabling the shopper to zip through the express line on the way home, whip through the preparation, and still sit down to a decent, civilized meal made from fresh, seasonal foods.

Developing additional recipes for this book was tremendous fun. Some of them are streamlined classics, others echo exotic cuisines, and many are simple home-cooking with a twist and an emphasis on the best possible ingredients. All bring you fine food in a hurry. Given the format and restrictions, this cooking challenge was much like writing a series of food sonnets, kitchen poetry on small, defined themes.

In a perfect world, none of us would be too busy to cook and savor a fine meal. As it stands—or runs in place—it is a point of pride with us all to be as busy as possible, all the time, and both our cooking and our enjoyment of the results can suffer. In *Eight Items or Less,* you can have your piccata and eat it too, even on the run.

Ann Lovejoy

$\mathcal{U}$sing the New Supermarket

Shopping for a Supermarket

Not sure how to find certain ingredients? Want to know what's freshest in the meat or produce department? Curious about which foods are locally raised, where the exotic fruits come from, whether the apples are waxed or the vegetables are free of pesticides? Ever wonder how old the fish is, who catches the squid and digs the clams? If you really want to know, just ask. Today's supermarket personnel will know the answers, and will gladly pass the information on to you.

Asking questions helps you, the consumer, to make informed food choices while getting acquainted with the people who work with the food you buy and eat. You will quickly learn who decides what's on the shelves, and the buyers will become aware of your wants and needs. This give-and-take benefits both consumers and the supermarkets. Next time you see an unfamiliar item on the shelf, inquire about it. When you can't find an unusual item you want to try, ask for it. Ask the stock clerks, ask the department heads, ask the manager if necessary. The staff will either show you where to find it (some specialty items are practically hidden) or offer to special order it for you. Customer service ought to mean a lot to them; if it doesn't, shop around for a supermarket that features less common foods.

By showcasing fresh herbs and chiles, jícama and blue corn tortillas, gingerroot and black bean sauce, supermarket managers are demonstrating faith in their customers' willingness to try new things. Many stores make it a policy to try to satisfy any and all consumer requests. The best stores go out of their way to introduce uncommon foods to their customers. Such progressive supermarkets frequently provide descriptive information and recipes for new items. They realize that, although some of us might try star fruit or enoki mushrooms once out of curiosity, we won't buy them regularly unless we learn how to fit them into our daily menus. Tasting opportunities, how-to demonstrations, in-store video cooking lessons, guest-chef appearances, and similar educational events smooth the assimilation process. These clever folks have discovered an old truth: the best customer is an informed one.

If your favorite supermarket delivers the goods without such

---

backup information on how to use them, ask. Be equally vociferous in your praise when the information is delivered, to keep it coming. Supermarket buyers sincerely want to know how best to serve you; consumer questions are valuable marketing tools that clarify the areas in which promotional support will effectively boost sales. Never be shy about requesting more information; even in the short run, everybody benefits—you, your fellow shoppers, the supermarket, the food distributors, and the farmers.

Using Uncommon Ingredients

So what's the best way to learn how to use these strange and wonderful foods? In practical terms, try just one or two new things at a time and make a point of using the item as soon as possible—especially fish, seafood, or produce—while it is still in its prime. To get started, combine unfamiliar ingredients with familiar ones: top hamburgers with a fresh relish made of chopped Thai basil, cilantro, and green onions, or serve baked chicken with a sauce of tomatillos, fresh chiles, and sour cream. Accompany an unfamiliar fish with your favorite seafood sauce, substitute rabbit in your usual chicken recipe, or spoon that exotic Oriental sauce over roasted game hens.

Some recent offerings are familiar friends in new clothes; fresh herbs have similar flavors to their dried counterparts, yet they are distinctly different, with both over- and undertones not found in the dried versions. Fresh herbs can be used more generously and are more versatile—for example, fresh sages can be minced into a honey-yogurt dressing for fruit salad or added to a blueberry-garlic vinaigrette, but dried sage would not give the same effect at all in either instance. With unfamiliar herbs or old standbys alike, it's worth taking a minute to evaluate them thoughtfully (this goes for spices, too). Choose one and smell it. Taste a bit of it, see what it reminds you of, what suggests itself to you.

This exploratory model holds true for all flavoring agents. Try adding one teaspoon (or less) of a spice, herb, or condiment to your usual recipe for cheese sauce or salad dressing, to a simple casserole, or to hamburger meat. A chile, some capers, or green peppercorns can't transform an ordinary dish into haute cuisine, but it can give you a good idea of what flavor principle is involved. Trying new things in old contexts (and vice versa) can spark untapped kitchen creativity, stimulating new ideas about the food we usually eat, and suggesting ways to expand our cooking vocabulary. It helps to recognize that these exotic ingredients are as common as chicken or peanut butter to cooks in other parts of the world. For stable ingredients—things like olive oil and sun-dried tomatoes—using them at once is not an issue. Still, since quality and flavor can vary enormously, though not necessarily in relation to price, it is wise to buy small amounts until you find the brands you favor. If your store offers a great range of brands and prices, ask around before buying. Ask the store staff, your friends, even favorite restaurants, which brands they use, and start your search with those. Certain oils, especially the nut ones, are best stored in the refrigerator, but most can sit on the pantry shelf for several months without developing off-flavors or getting stale.

Produce

Perhaps the most remarkable changes are evident in supermarket produce departments. Until quite recently, most seasonal foods—soft fruits like strawberries and cherries; tender greens such as sorrel and watercress; fresh herbs—were available for as little as a month each year. Out of season, such things, though tired past freshness, cost the earth. Today, we can find Chilean asparagus and peaches at Thanksgiving, fresh Californian basil and artichokes in January, and although the prices reflect the length of their trip to the market, such foods are no longer exorbitant. Moreover, the quality can be amazingly fine, though not, of course, the equal of produce fresh from local farms. As cooks, we naturally want to take advantage of all this bounty whenever possible. Happily, the more we request and buy such foods, the more common and more reasonably priced they will become.

There is no need for daily salads to be dull, now that supermarkets offer all sorts of lettuces nearly year-round. Pairing lettuces of different qualities gives character to a basic salad. Butterhead types contrast well with the crisper oakleaf lettuces, ruffled red loose heads with crunchy romaine. Less common greens are rapidly gaining American recognition. Sorrel, for one, has been hybridized by the gastronomically brilliant French from a lowly weed, rank and wrenchingly sour,

---

into an angelic, sublime green with a moderate, stirringly tangy sourness—heavenly in omelets and soups, as well as in salads. The whole great class of Oriental greens, collectively called "mustard greens," is sometimes too hot for Western palates; however, recently developed strains are as mild, even as sweet, as young spinach. Some have peppery or onionlike overtones, but this is far from unpleasant in a salad. To experiment, buy small bundles of several kinds and sample a few leaves at a time in salads made chiefly of ordinary lettuces. Challenging new flavors are most acceptable in small doses and when accompanied by the familiar. When you find greens that you enjoy eating, incorporate them more wholeheartedly.

A second group of Oriental vegetables is the choys, cabbage-family relatives that range from the crunchy sweetness of crinkle-leaved Chinese or Napa cabbage to the slightly bitter, peppery flavor of the celerylike bok choy. These bitter-sweet and bitter-peppery elements are appreciated far more in other cultures than in ours, but again, restraint in the initial encounters can lead to a greater enjoyment for the piquant touch these greens bring to salads and stir-fries. Certain European salad greens—radicchio (chicory), arugula (rocket), and escarole —share these qualities in varying degrees. Few people will immediately be drawn to eating an entire head of radicchio, however young it may be, though for all these darker-flavored greens, it is true that the younger they are, the less the bitter quality predominates.

Dairy

There is a lot more in the dairy case than brick cheese these days. Imports abound: sharp Italians such as Asiago, pecorino, Romano and true, aged Parmesan are available coarsely shredded, finely grated, or by the chunk with the authenticating waxy rind still intact. Any of these cheeses will surprise palates accustomed to the characterless, salty stuff in those familiar cylindrical boxes. English Cheddar is flanked by Wesleydale, Gloucester, Stilton, and Cheshire. France sends us creamy goat cheeses and delicately veined bleus, as well as the ubiquitous Brie. Switzerland, Sweden, Norway, Germany are among the dozens of countries now represented on our supermarket shelves. American specialty cheeses can hold their own in this noble array: Tillamook or Vermont Cheddars, fresh mozzarellas from San Francisco or New York, aged or fresh California jack, and Oregon goat cheeses match anything the Continent has to offer.

The observant shopper will notice not one but half a dozen brands of ricotta, sour cream, yogurt, cream or cottage cheeses, among which the "natural" home-style types, made in small batches using genuine dairy ingredients, are outstanding. Nancy's and Alta Dena are brands to watch for, though some supermarkets are putting out their own lines of unadulterated dairy items, thanks to the increasing appreciation for their flavors, textures, and cooking qualities. Crème fraîche, once virtually impossible to buy in America, is now distributed nationally by several companies. Tofu, once similarly obscure, is now omnipresent.

Newcomers to the dairy section are the many nut butters. Here we find peanut butter in its finest form, without added hydrogenated fats, sugars, or even salt. Almond, cashew, and hazelnut butters may be discovered as well, along with tahini, the sesame paste used extensively in non-Western cookery, often in multiple flavors. Look here, too, for fresh, home-style salsas, pestos, soups, and pasta sauces, many of which are locally made and delivered on a daily basis. In my supermarket, one dairy department case is filled with small cuts of variety cheeses, bottles of microbrewery beers from around the world, and half-sized bottles of fine regional wines.

Fish and Seafood

The big news in the fish department is that there is one. As consumers become more knowledgeable, the supermarket response is to hire seafood specialists to oversee the buying and—perhaps even more important—the storage and presentation of these fragile foods. Many places routinely date shrink-wrapped fish and all cooked seafood. Watch for this and don't buy any precooked items that are more than a day or two old.

In the Northwest, certain fishermen, known for their advanced storage-and-freezing techniques, can command top dollar for their entire catch. Salmon bearing price tags labeled "Bruce Gore caught" practically swim out of the stores, proving that plenty of people are willing to pay for excellence. If you have no such guaranteed product, stick with the basics;

fresh fish and seafood smell pleasantly of the sea, perhaps with a faint whiff of seaweed, but never like ammonia. Fish scales should be glossy, tightly attached, and lie flat. Fish eyes should be intact, unstained, and protruding—though shrink-wrapped fish may have damaged eyes because the wrapping is so tight. When all other signs are good, you can consider buying such a fish anyway, but tell the fish person that you want to feel and smell the fish first. The flesh of fillets or whole fish, alike, ought to be firm and resilient; gentle pressure ought to leave no lasting mark.

For inlanders, it can be difficult to find seafoods that have not been frozen and given a sulfite rinse (this information must legally be on the package). Happily, as modern flash-freezing techniques improve, the quality of prefrozen seafood keeps getting better, though the cost may reflect the expense of these techniques. For all fish and seafood, prices vary markedly with supply and season. It makes sense to enjoy such foods most often when they are abundant, fresh, and reasonably priced.

Buy shellfish live whenever possible; many shellfish gatherers identify their catch with name tags, which assures good quality or at least some level of accountability. If this is not so in your area, buy cautiously and in small quantities until you find a source you can trust. Again, use your nose to evaluate freshness, and if in doubt, don't eat any seafood or fish raw—it is simply asking for trouble, perhaps even serious illness. If the fish department is not run by a specialist (often the meat buyer will also order fish), if all the fish and seafood is shrink-wrapped, frozen, or precooked, tell the department manager that you intend to buy your fish from a specialty fish store until the supermarket gets serious about selling fish—and stick to your word.

Meat

Fortunately, we don't have to be quite so militant in the meat department. Here, we will find much the same assortment of meats that our mothers did, but with a twist. Most meats are leaner than they were even ten years ago, many traditional cuts have been trimmed of extra fat, and smaller portions are packaged, reflecting our national obsession with food and fitness. There are other changes as well; pork, which

used to be considered hearty, heavy, and full of fat, is now
heralded as the new white meat. Once sold mainly in big,
slow-cooking cuts like roasts, chops, and hams, it is now lean,
tender, and offered in small, often boneless, cuts. The new
pork is mildly flavorful, low in fat, and may be broiled, stir-
fried, or grilled in just minutes. The same is true for lamb,
and here, too, these lean little cuts can be prepared very
quickly.

A couple of oldtimers have recently emerged from the
freezer compartment. Rabbit is now appearing fresh in the
supermarkets—try substituting rabbit in your favorite chicken
recipes, though it may need to cook a little longer. Farm-raised
animals are more tender and milder in flavor than wild rabbits
(less disease prone, as well), and usually require shorter cooking times. Turkey is no longer a winter holiday visitor. It is on
the scene year-round, fresh, and in many guises: as breasts to
bake whole or grill in thick slices, as hindquarters to roast or
stew, and ground, smoked, or stuffed into sausages.

"Organic" meats of all kinds represent a healthy return to
traditional husbandry practices. The animals are raised without steroids, fed grains grown without pesticides, and allowed
to roam free (rather than being kept in pens). The meat is at
least equal to the mass-produced kind, and often is distinctly
superior in flavor and texture (feed and animal health can
greatly affect both of these qualities).

Specialty Foods

Supermarkets all over the country have delis, ethnic-food
sections, and bulk-food areas, all good places to check for new
foods, especially condiments, sauces, and spices.

The selection of both dried and fresh herbs and spices is
greatly improved; we now find a choice of brands where last
year we found none at all. Spices and condiments often can be
the most expensive ingredients you buy. Keep in mind, however, that one jar of saffron, or capers, or cardamom pods will
play a part in numerous meals. Unless it is an item you plan
to use a good deal of, buy spices in the smallest possible quantities or divide and freeze the extra amount. It is far better to
buy relatively small amounts several times a year, even at
greater cost, and be assured of having fresh, potent flavorings
to work with. Dusty, musty old herbs and spices can't possibly

improve a dish, yet they can actively harm it.

Dried chiles—the small, dark red peperoncini beloved of the Italians; darker, almost black Thai red-hots; slender red Japanese dried chiles—can be used interchangeably, though each has its particular qualities. A little experimentation will help you discover which have the flavor and heat intensity you enjoy. If you buy several kinds, freeze what you won't use soon, tightly wrapped in several plastic bags (or the odors will penetrate the entire freezer) or share with your friends, for dried peppers, like most spices, can taste tired if they sit on the shelf too long.

Again, consider these uncommon ingredients when you plan your next meal. Chutneys and sauces based on peanuts and garlic, or fermented black beans and hot chiles, dried shrimp or lemon grass can elevate plain, grilled chicken to an extraordinary level. Fruity olive oil, fruit vinegars, and specialty mustards give homemade salad dressing unrivaled savor and snap.

Supermarkets—even those you think you know well—are worth a closer look, even prolonged exploration. Some have in-store bakeries that sell chunks of fresh yeast, others provide sourdough starter, fresh puff pastry in blocks or party shapes, whole-wheat pie crusts or braided challah. Wine and beer sections may feature local or regional brews. Take another look at the lowly pasta. Where once we found four or five shapes, now there might be thirty, flavored with squid ink, rosemary, lemon peel, or wild mushrooms. This Panglossian profusion is to be found in cities and towns all over the country, gathered under one roof: that of the American supermarket.

Every book has its underlying assumptions. With
cookbooks, in particular, it is nice to know exactly what they
are. Before you begin cooking from this book, take a minute
to review this section, so that when mealtime comes around,
all the surprises will be pleasant ones.

Quantities

Unless otherwise stated, all recipes will serve two
moderate eaters, without leftovers. This reflects national
trends, visible both in restaurants and in the home, for
lighter, smaller meals. In line with this, the sauce proportions
are generally modest, rather than lavish. Should you prefer
more generous helpings, or saucier food, you can easily
double either the whole recipe or just the sauce portions.

Salt

I don't cook with salt, and none of the recipes call for it.
Partly this was done because the ingredients lists were
intended to be quick shopping guides, and few of us need to
buy salt each time we cook. Also, we wanted to keep the
'Eight Item' theme practical; it is a challenge to make good,
even great food using so few things, and each ingredient must
carry its weight. By presuming that people would add salt to
their own taste, we allowed a bit more scope for recipe
development. Those interested in reducing the amount of
salt in their diets may find that these recipes give them
valuable ideas, and just for curiosity's sake, the skeptical
might try a few just as they are written, and see if they aren't
surprisingly flavorful.

Oils, Fats, and Sweating Foods

Again reflecting national trends, these recipes call for
relatively small amounts of fats, especially of the saturated
kinds. Unfortunately, those are often the tastiest, so rather
than eliminating them entirely, we have tried to use them in
moderate, but effective, amounts. The recipes rely chiefly on
mono-saturated fats (chiefly olive oil), which add significant
flavor without hiking cholesterol. Cooking with reduced lipids
can require close attention and one technique—that of
"sweating" food—will be invaluable. To do this, you quickly
sear or brown a food, whether meat or vegetable, in a small

amount of oil, then cover the pan, at least partially, and continue cooking over moderate heat. In effect, this steam-fries the food, using juices which would be lost through evaporation in an open pan. In any case, where you find that a recipe tends to be dry (this can depend on the relative heat of each oven or stovetop), you can either increase the liquids called for, or try sweating it (perhaps someone will invent a less indelicate term one day soon).

Substitutions

Most of the recipes which call for unusual or strictly seasonal ingredients—satsumas, sorrel, Stilton—also offer suggestions for substitutions in the introduction paragraph. Where you dislike a key ingredient—perhaps fresh cilantro, or mussels—you can use any of the suggested foods, or choose other substitutions which you prefer. Naturally, it won't be the same entrée but the point is to please yourself.

Specific substitutions are also listed in the 'ingredients' section at the beginning of this book. For some foods, substitutions won't greatly affect the recipe—blue corn tortillas are great, but any kind and size could be used. In a few cases, substitution is impossible, and where this is so, it is duly noted.

Should it become necessary to substitute more than one or two items, it might be wise to choose another recipe. In fact, one good way to use this book is to carry it with you while shopping; if something tempting catches your eye—baby artichokes, rabbit, purple potatoes—you can quickly look it up and buy whatever you need to complete the meal.

Timing and Equipment

Nearly all of these recipes take under an hour to prepare and cook. Most have fairly short preparation times, especially if you use a food processor. About a third are very quick indeed, no matter how few kitchen gadgets you own. Though a food processor can speed things up, the fanciest machine any of these recipes actually requires is a blender. We do assume that you own decent knives—one big, one small—and ordinary pots and pans, as well as a baking sheet, something to roast in (sheet cake pans work perfectly well), and casserole dishes in quart, 1½ quart, and individual sizes. Custard cups, do fine for the smaller things, and Pyrex dishes with lids are very inexpensive and endlessly useful for marinating as well as cooking.

#

17 Grilled Tuna Lampedusa

18 Broiled Tuna with Pine Nuts and Dill

19 Fresh Tuna with Fennel

20 Tuna Noodle Casserole

21 Masked Salmon

22 Baked Eggs with Smoked Salmon

23 Salmon with Herbed Mustard Sauce

24 Butterflied Coho Salmon with Herbed Barbecue Sauce

25 Salmon Butter and Peas with Fettucine

26 Fresh Salmon Salad

27 Smoked Salmon Sandwiches

28 Sole Veronique

29 Sole in Rosé Sauce

30 Sole with Spinach and Curried Cashews

31 Sole with Shrimp Meringue

32 Gold Fish

33 Sole and Green Tomatoes in Cornmeal

34 Red Snapper in Salsa Verde

35 Red Snapper Poached in Orange Juice

36 Green Snapper

37 Stars and Stripes Snapper

38   Honey-glazed True Cod
39   Black Cod with Chinese Mustard Sauce
40   Black Cod in Pine Nut Sauce
41   Black Cod Muscadet
42   Fish Chowder

43   Saffron Haddock
44   Halibut Mixed Grill
45   Fresh Tomato Curry with Halibut
46   Fish Sticks

47   Trout with Green Sauce
48   Flaming Trout
49   Perch with Currants and Walnuts
50   Poached Perch with Chervil
51   Catfish with Three Butters
52   Catfish in Cornmeal with Black Butter

Grilled Tuna Lampedusa

The tiny island of Lampedusa, once part of the holdings of
the great Sicilian family of that name, lies closer to the coast
of Tunisia than to the Italian mainland. Clear-cut during the
last world war, it remains a scrubby, plain place, where aban-
doned fields are edged with crumbling walls, and inhabited
caves hang above white beaches and an impossibly blue-green
sea. Fisher friends made this stunningly aromatic dish daily,
pulling the boat up to the nearest beach, gleaning herbs from
the hillsides. Olive oil and wine were always in the boats,
along with excellent bread, olives, salty cheese, and rough
wine (that's cheap red, of course).

Fresh tuna *or* black cod steaks
1 bunch fresh oregano, 1 tablespoon chopped
1 bunch fresh thyme, 1 tablespoon chopped
Olive oil
3 cloves garlic, 1 thinly sliced, 2 mashed
Loaf unsliced bread

●Start coals in grill. Rinse tuna, pat dry. Brush lightly with
oil on both sides. Sprinkle chopped herbs and sliced garlic
over fish. Slice bread thickly, drizzle one side of each slice
with olive oil, and spread with mashed garlic. Place sprigs of
herbs on grill. Place tuna on top and grill, allowing 5 to 7
minutes for each side, until fish is opaque. When you turn
tuna, put bread slices on grill, oil-side down, for 2 to 3 minutes, until crisp and lightly brown. Give each person some
tuna and some bread. This is supreme but messy finger food,
and the use of forks and plates is acceptable, if inauthentic.

Broiled Tuna with Pine Nuts and Dill

The only tuna that regularly frequents American waters is albacore, light in color and mild in flavor, the tuna that makes its way into millions of cans. In the Northwest, albacore steaks are fresh in the markets from July through October. Both yellowfin and bluefin are deep ocean fish, which prefer warmer waters. They are flown in daily from Hawaii, Mexico, and sometimes California, but the bulk of the catch goes to Japan, where the demand for these oilier, dark-fleshed fish is insatiable. Any city with a sizeable Asian community is likely to get regular air shipments of these prized tunas, though high prices reflect the care required to keep them in good shape. If you find fresh tuna in your market, this is a wonderful way to savor it. Since tuna steaks can be quite large, one will often serve two people. Cod or salmon can be substituted, as can thick fillets of perch. The garlicky dill sauce, crunchy with pine nuts, rich with cheese and sour cream, complements practically any fish or seafood dish. Serve with rice or fresh rolls, romanesco broccoli with herb butter, and a bright Chablis or weissbier.

1¼ pounds tuna steaks (1 or 2 pieces)
1 to 2 teaspoons olive oil
1 ounce grated pecorino *or* Parmesan cheese
¼ cup sour cream
1 tablespoon chopped fresh dill *or*
   1 teaspoon dried
1 tablespoon chopped fresh flat Italian parsley *or*
   1 teaspoon dried
3 cloves garlic, pressed
2 tablespoons pine nuts, toasted

●Preheat broiler. Rinse tuna, pat dry. Brush lightly with olive oil on both sides and put on broiler pan. Blend cheese with sour cream, add herbs and 1 clove garlic; stir. Spread more garlic over tuna, and broil 4 to 6 minutes. Turn, spread remaining garlic over tuna, and broil for another 4 to 6 minutes. Add pine nuts to cheese sauce, spoon over fish, sprinkle on herbs for garnish, and broil another 2 to 3 minutes.

Fresh Tuna with Fennel

Thick steaks of fresh tuna become smoky and even more flavorful when cooked with anise-flavored fennel, chunky leeks, and garlic greens. Young garlic tips from the garden or the produce department of enlightened supermarkets are invaluable additions to spring salads, as well as sauces like this one. (Mustard greens or shredded arugula can be substituted.) If you find that yogurt gets runny when heated, try some of the alternative brands. Once found exclusively in health food stores and coops, they are increasingly popular in supermarkets as consumers discover the delights of genuine dairy products. Look for brands without carrageenan, fillers, gums, or agar-agar, or labels that describe the culture used to make the yogurt (this holds equally true for sour cream). Many of these are of superior quality and flavor, and the texture holds up particularly well to heat. Have herbed rice, a salad with mustard vinaigrette, and a robust ale.

---

1 cup yogurt
½ teaspoon freshly ground pepper
1 tablespoon olive oil
1 small bulb Florence fennel, thinly sliced
1 leek, cut into 1-inch slices
1 bunch garlic tips *or* mustard greens, chopped
1 pound thick-cut tuna steaks
1 ounce pecorino cheese, grated

●Blend yogurt with pepper; set aside. In a large frying pan, heat oil over medium heat. Add fennel, leek, and garlic tips and sauté for 3 to 5 minutes. Add tuna and cook for 4 to 6 minutes on each side until just opaque. Remove tuna and vegetables (leaving juices in pan) to warm plates and hold in warm oven. Cover pan and boil juices for 3 to 5 minutes until reduced by nearly half; stir in yogurt and cook for 2 to 3 minutes until hot through. Pour sauce around tuna, sprinkle with cheese, and serve hot.

Tuna Noodle Casserole

Every cookbook has to have one, right? Still, I doubt very
much whether your Mom used this recipe, or anything faintly
like it. Chunks of tuna are mounded on fresh fettuccine, drizzled with lime juice, then covered with a silky green peppercorn sauce and broiled to a fast finish. If you happen to have
leftover fish on hand, it will certainly outshine canned tuna,
but there are some fine brands of the canned stuff out there
that are more than respectable. Try buying different brands
until you find one that suits your taste. This needs only the
support of a little salad, perhaps rolls or warm sourdough
slices sprinkled with garlic and dill. Drink an Orvieto or a
weissbier on the side.

8 ounces fresh fettuccine *or*
  4 ounces dry
1 6½-ounce can tuna fish in water or olive oil, drained
1 lime, quartered
1 to 2 teaspoons olive oil
4 green onions, thinly sliced on diagonal
2 teaspoons green peppercorns in vinegar
½ teaspoon dried dill
3 to 4 tablespoons crème fraîche *or* sour cream

●In saucepan, bring water to boil. Add fettuccine and cook
until al dente. Drain and heap into 2 lightly oiled individual
casserole dishes. Mound tuna on top of noodles, keeping fish
in good-sized chunks. Squirt 1 wedge lime over each dish. In a
frying pan, heat oil over medium heat. Add onions and sauté
quickly. Stir in peppercorns and their vinegar, dill, and crème
fraîche; blend. Spoon over tuna to cover fish and noodles completely and broil for 3 to 5 minutes until golden brown. Serve
very hot.

green onion brooms, slivers, diagonals

Masked Salmon

Who is that masked salmon? Any firm-fleshed fish will benefit from baking beneath a smooth, tangy coating, and salmon
is particularly succulent when treated in this way. If yogurt
sounds like diet food, use sour cream and double the lemon
juice; the tangy contrast provides balance to the richness of
the fish. Arranged on a bed of spinach and topped with this
mustard and honey mask, the fish cooks to moist tenderness.
Serve with spinach noodles sprinkled with poppyseeds, steamed
baby carrots and snap beans sprinkled with balsamic vinegar,
and a gentle yet full-bodied white Côtes du Rhône.

---

1 pound salmon fillet, skinned and boned
1 bunch fresh spinach, chopped
1 medium red onion, chopped
⅔ cup yogurt
1 tablespoon Dijon mustard
1 teaspoon honey
1 teaspoon chopped dill
½ small lemon, juiced

●Rinse salmon, pat dry. Put spinach and onion in baking dish.
Place salmon on top of spinach and onion. Blend yogurt, mustard, honey, dill, and lemon juice; smooth over salmon. Bake in
350 degree oven for 20 to 25 minutes, until salmon is opaque
and flakes easily.

Baked Eggs with Smoked Salmon

In much of the world, smoked salmon means lox, the soft, smooth stuff found in delis. In the Northwest, hard-smoked salmon is a regional specialty, sometimes made in brittle sticks like the pemmican of East Coast American Indians. Any firm-smoked salmon or lox may be used in this extravagant little dish, which elevates baked eggs into a small but sumptuous evening meal or a satisfying brunch entrée. It is quickly assembled in small casseroles or ovenproof serving dishes, especially if the smoked salmon is presliced—buy the thinnest slices you can or cut whole fillets with a very sharp knife. Have tiny hot rolls, sweet butter curls, asparagus, or steamed artichokes with orange and caper butter. Green salad and a Chablis or dry gewürtztraminer will complete the meal in style.

---

1 to 2 tablespoons butter
3 tablespoons soft bread crumbs
2 eggs
1 fat clove garlic, pressed
2 ounces cream cheese
2 ounces sliced smoked salmon
2 ounces aged sharp Cheddar cheese, grated
1 ripe tomato, thickly sliced

●Butter casseroles (custard cups work well). Press 2 to 3 teaspoons bread crumbs on bottom and sides of each. Blend remaining crumbs with 1 tablespoon butter; reserve. Break an egg into each dish. Mash garlic with cream cheese and gently place over eggs. Add smoked salmon, folding long strips as needed. Grate Cheddar and sprinkle over salmon. Put 1 fat tomato slice (from middle of tomato) on each dish (dice the rest for salad). Crumble half the crumbs over each dish and bake in 350 degree oven for 8 to 15 minutes (depending on how you enjoy your eggs), then broil for 2 to 3 minutes, until tops are browned and slightly crisp. Serve at once.

Salmon with Herbed Mustard Sauce

Velvety herb mustard sauce adds snap to the smooth richness
of buttered and broiled salmon steaks. The mustard can be a
sharp Dijonaise or a milder sort from Provence, or even the
grainy pub kind with a few minced leaves of tarragon and
chives stirred in. Sour cream can get runny when heated, but
the "natural" types stay splendidly thick. Asparagus spears,
tied with a strip of red pepper and sprinkled with crumbled
bleu cheese, make a pleasant contrast, and tiny croissants or
dinner rolls will round out the meal lightly. A Bordeaux Graves
or an icy Alsatian riesling will stand up to these complex
flavors without overpowering them.

---

1 tablespoon mustard
1 teaspoon chopped fresh chives *or*
  ½ teaspoon dried
1 teaspoon chopped fresh tarragon *or*
  ½ teaspoon dried
2 tablespoons sour cream
2 salmon steaks (1 pound total)
1 tablespoon butter, melted

●Blend mustard, herbs, and sour cream; set aside. Preheat
broiler. Rinse salmon, pat dry. Brush lightly with melted butter and broil for 5 to 7 minutes on each side. Top each steak
with mustard sauce, broil for another 2 to 3 minutes, and
serve at once.

Butterflied Coho Salmon with Herbed Barbecue Sauce

Sharp and citrusy, fragrant with chopped herbs, this light barbecue sauce smells as if you are brushing on summer itself. The basic recipe is given here, but it can be varied to suit practically anything you grill, and since leftover sauce keeps well when refrigerated, you can experiment freely. Start with about a teaspoon of each herb, adjusting amounts upward to taste, and keep notes about what you like (or dislike). In the Northwest, where salmon is grilled nearly as often as chicken, small cohos, split by the fishmonger, are a beloved seasonal delicacy. Fat steaks from larger salmon work equally well, but try tuna steaks, thick fillets of true cod, or eastern bluefish as well as chicken or veal chops. Serve with a salad of young lettuces and coarsely grated radishes dressed with a cilantro vinaigrette. Add a fresh baguette, sliced local toma-toes, and a dry Frascati for a simple but satisfying meal.

---

1 clove garlic, pressed
¼ cup olive oil
1 teaspoon freshly ground black pepper
½ orange, juiced plus ½ teaspoon grated peel
½ lemon, juiced plus ½ teaspoon grated peel
1 tablespoon chopped fresh fennel leaves *or*
　½ teaspoon dried
1 tablespoon chopped fresh dill leaves *or*
　½ teaspoon dried
2 coho salmon steaks or fillets (about 1 pound each),
　butterflied

●Start coals in grill. In a jar, mix garlic, oil, pepper, fruit juices, peels, and herbs. Close top tightly and shake well. Brush lightly over both sides of salmon. Grill for 6 to 8 minutes, basting and turning several times, until fish is opaque and flakes easily. Serve hot or cold.

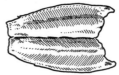

butterflied fillet

Salmon Butter and Peas with Fettuccine

Smoky salmon butter and tiny new peas combine in a satiny, peppery sauce made right on the serving platter, like noodles Alfredo. Smoked salmon is a staple in many Northwestern kitchens, and when fresh peas arrive in the markets, this is a splendid way to savor both delicacies. Tender lox or slightly smoked salmon fillets work better in this recipe than the crunchy, dry kind that comes in sticks. Italian pecorino is an Umbrian cheese traditionally made of sheep's milk. Piquant and sharp, it has a distinctive salty tang. A chunk of aged Romano will do nicely as well. Serve with a salad of tender baby greens tossed with garlic tips and raspberry vinaigrette, and a dry Chablis or a muscadet.

---

4 ounces smoked salmon, skinned, boned, and chopped
2 tablespoons butter
½ cup heavy cream
2 tablespoons grated pecorino cheese
8 ounces fresh peas, shelled
8 ounces fresh fettuccine *or*
  4 ounces dry
½ teaspoon green peppercorns

●Start water for pasta. Mash smoked salmon with butter to a smooth paste. Put a shallow serving dish in warm oven and put salmon butter, cream, and cheese in dish. Steam peas for 2 to 3 minutes until barely tender, and add to serving dish. Cook pasta, drain but do not rinse, and toss at once with salmon butter mixture. Add the green peppercorns and serve at once.

Fresh Salmon Salad

Fresh fish can be hard to find these days, but it's still worth the effort. If you aren't sure how to assess fish, the points to remember are fortunately fairly obvious: fresh fish do not smell "fishy" or ammonia-like, though they may have a faint and not unpleasant sea smell. Fresh fish look fat and sassy— they are still plump, not flaccid, the gills are a clear scarlet color, the scales glossy, flat, and snug fitting, the eyes still bright and rounded. If you find one like that, bring it home and grill it. Use the leftovers in this quick and unusual salad. (It could, of course, be made with canned tuna or salmon, but it is far tastier when made with the real thing.) For variety, toss this fish salad with pasta, serve it with rice or rolls, stuff it into pita bread pockets, or heap it on mixed greens. Tuna or swordfish steaks are also wonderful when treated in this manner.

---

1 pound cooked fresh salmon *or* tuna
1 teaspoon minced fresh dill (3 sprigs) *or*
  ½ teaspoon dried
1 teaspoon minced fresh tarragon (2 to 3 leaves) *or*
  ½ teaspoon dried
3 tablespoons olive oil
2 cloves garlic, pressed
½ teaspoon freshly ground white pepper
4 plum tomatoes, diced
¼ cup walnuts, toasted

●Skin and bone salmon; flake into good-sized chunks. Add dill and tarragon to oil. Add garlic and at least 1 teaspoon pepper; stir to blend. Toss tomatoes with salmon in the dressing. Cover and chill. Before serving, bring salad to room temperature for best flavor. Add toasted walnuts to salad when you take it out of the refrigerator; this keeps the nuts crunchy but lets the flavors mix a bit.

Smoked Salmon Sandwiches

These hot, open-faced sandwiches reflect the Scandinavian influences still strongly evident in the Pacific Northwest. The effect is quite salty, so you may want to try this with just half an anchovy fillet the first time. Use black rye bread, dense extrasour sourdough, a robust pumpernickel, or a combination for extra character. Have the smoked salmon thinly sliced at the deli, or use a very sharp knife to get the wafer-thin pieces needed. Drink dopple-bok.

6 to 7 slices bread (dark rye or extrasour sourdough)
1 tablespoon sweet butter
1 anchovy fillet
1 clove garlic, pressed
4 ounces smoked salmon
1 bunch asparagus
4 ounces fontina *or* Gruyère cheese, thinly sliced

●Thinly spread bread with butter, allowing several pieces for each person. Remove crusts from an additional piece and crumble bread into fine bits. Mash butter with anchovy fillet. Add garlic and mash well to blend. Rub in bread crumbs; set aside. Snap asparagus spears to trim, discarding thick bases. Steam in wire basket for 4 to 6 minutes until tender but still crisp. To assemble sandwiches, put several strips of salmon on each piece of bread, arrange 2 to 3 stalks of asparagus on top, and layer on cheese, letting asparagus tips show. Sprinkle on bread crumbs and broil for 3 to 5 minutes until browned and bubbly.

Sole Veronique

There are many versions of this classic dish, the simplest of which are generally the best. Purists will insist that only muscat grapes—silvery, aromatic, and full of sweet juice—are worthy of inclusion in the true dish. However, fresh, ripe grapes of all persuasions may be used, whether white, green, or red. Seedless ones speed things up considerably, and the results are wonderful, authentic or no. A plate of steamed butter clams and a crisp, dry raspberry ale (the true lambic ale is worth springing for) make a splendid appetizer on a warm summer evening. Some fresh rolls with sweet butter, a salad of young greens with a curried vinaigrette, and a cool pinot noir make an unbeatable follow-up—unless you prefer a muscadet.

½ cup grapes, cut in half lengthwise and seeded
8 ounces sole fillets
¼ cup dry white wine
2 green onions, thinly sliced
1 tablespoon butter
1 tablespoon whole wheat pastry flour
¼ cup heavy cream
1 teaspoon freshly ground black pepper

●Preheat broiler. Rinse fillets and set them in a wide, shallow pan to poach (a large iron frying pan works well). Scatter on onions, pour wine and 2 tablespoons water over them. Bring to a boil over high heat; reduce heat to very low, cover pan, and simmer most gently for 5 to 6 minutes. In a small, heavy saucepan, melt butter over medium heat. Stir in flour and cook for 1 minute. Add cream and pepper; stir well. Add wine stock from fish to cream mixture. Remove fish to ovenproof platter. Spoon sauce over fish, arrange grapes all around, cut-sides up, then broil for 2 to 3 minutes until bubbling. Serve at once.

Sole in Rosé Sauce

This rosy sauce gets its ineffable flavor from ripe tomatoes cooked very slowly in butter, a method invented by Edouard de Pomiane—the results are purest synergy. The white fish, flecked with green, floats in the fragrant pink sauce of tomatoes, making a lovely presentation. Grenache rosé may be replaced with any dry rosé or blush wine, and what you don't use in the sauce, you can sip at dinner. Serve with long grain or basmati rice, steamed beans with savory, or zucchini spears with basil and orange zest.

2 tablespoons butter
4 tomatoes, halved
8 ounces sole fillets
4 sprigs fresh dill, chopped (reserving 1 sprig for garnish) *or*
  1 teaspoon dried
¼ cup grenache rosé
3 to 4 tablespoons heavy cream

•In a heavy frying pan, melt 1 tablespoon butter over low heat. Add tomatoes to butter, cut-side down. Make a few small cuts in their skins and let them cook for 5 minutes; turn. In another pan, heat 2 teaspoons butter until foamy. Add dill to butter. Rinse fish, pat dry, and slide into butter. Add wine and simmer for 5 to 6 minutes, until sole is cooked at thickest point. While sole is cooking, turn tomatoes again. Add cream to tomato juices and stir gently. Increase heat to medium. As soon as cream is hot through and beginning to simmer, remove from heat. Put sole on each plate, garnish with a few bits of fresh dill, spoon sauce around each piece (not on top), and serve at once, very hot.

Sole with Spinach and Curried Cashews

On the West Coast, delicate little sand dabs are the sole of choice, but any fish in the family, whether Rex, Dover, or petrale, has a subtle flavor, requiring gentle cooking and moderate, thoughtful seasoning. This is the way an Indian friend prepares sole. It is a beautiful and fascinatingly flavorful dish in which curried cashews provide textural contrast to the mousselike spinach sauce. The raw spinach is cooked only by the heat of the fish and the oniony, light-bodied sauce of cooked spinach, sour cream, and lemon juice. Despite the apparent complexity, this entrée goes together quickly, yielding impressive results in under half an hour. Hot corn muffins or onion bread, and ale or a glass of dry Chablis will complete the meal pleasantly.

---

8 ounces sole fillets
2 bunches spinach, trimmed
2 tablespoons cashews
1 lemon, juiced plus grated peel
2 to 3 tablespoons butter
½ onion, finely chopped
1 to 2 tablespoons sour cream
¼ teaspoon hot curry powder

●Preheat oven to warm. Rinse fish, pat dry. Finely chop 1 bunch spinach. Remove stems and any large central ribs from the other bunch and arrange leaves on 2 plates. In a heavy pan, melt 1 teaspoon butter over medium heat. Stir in onion and cook for 2 to 3 minutes. Add chopped spinach; cover and cook another 6 to 8 minutes until limp. While it cooks, melt 1 to 2 teaspoons butter in sauté pan, slide sole in, and sprinkle with 1 teaspoon grated lemon peel. Cook for 3 to 4 minutes, turn fillets, and reduce heat to low. When spinach is done, add 1 tablespoon or more lemon juice and sour cream; remove from heat. When sole is done, slide onto fresh spinach and hold in warm oven. In fish pan, cook cashews and curry powder for 2 to 3 minutes over high heat, stirring often. To serve, pour a wide ribbon of spinach sauce over sole, sprinkle cashews and pan juices over top.

Sole with Shrimp Meringue

This unusual topping, an airy, fluffy shrimp and egg concoction, owes something to the dessert meringue of the pastry shop and a bit more to a certain appetizer popular in the fifties, in which mounds of mayonnaise and grated cheese were mixed with whole tiny shrimp and broiled on toast rounds. This version is subtle enough to suit sole, which has a smooth, gentle flavor easily destroyed by hasty seasoning or harsh cooking. To succeed with sole, use moist and moderate heat and remove the fish from the pan the moment it is done—often sooner than you think. Fresh fillets of sole are translucent and may require as little as one or two minutes cooking on each side. They can be held for a couple of minutes on a warm plate while you finish a sauce, but prolonged waiting makes them tough and tasteless. This entrée is easiest if made in a dish that travels from stovetop to oven (even an iron frying pan will work). Drizzle steamed zucchini spears with balsamic vinegar and chopped chives and serve long grain rice or herbed wheat rolls and a glass of stout or a dry pear wine.

---

8 ounces sole fillets
3 to 4 ounces cooked shrimp
1 teaspoon butter
1 medium onion, sliced into rings
1 red sweet pepper, sliced into strips
1 egg
2 tablespoons yogurt *or* sour cream
2 to 3 teaspoons grated Parmesan cheese

●Preheat broiler. Rinse sole and shrimp, pat dry. Chop shrimp in small bits. In a frying pan, heat butter over low heat until foamy. Add onion and pepper to pan and cover. Cook slowly over medium heat for 4 to 5 minutes until soft. Slide sole on top of vegetables; cover pan and cook for 6 to 8 minutes, until sole is opaque. While sole is cooking, separate egg; whip egg white until stiff but still glossy. Fold in yogurt, cheese, and shrimp. Mound this sauce over sole as soon as it is done, then transfer entire pan to oven; broil 3 to 4 minutes until browned. Serve at once.

Fish

Gold Fish

These golden fillets are tender, with barely crisped edges and an underlying buttery smoothness. Whole wheat pastry flour gives both richer color and flavor than regular flour, and the white peppercorns add a gentle, not overpowering nip of warmth. An Italian breading technique makes the coating subtle—a silken wrap rather than a muffling overcoat. Round out this meal with steamed green beans and tiny red new potatoes boiled in their thin spring jackets. Toss them in butter with snippets of fresh fennel, and use another feathery sprig of fennel and a generous slice of lemon to garnish each plate. A Bordeaux Graves or sauvignon blanc will support this menu pleasantly.

¼ cup whole wheat pastry flour
2 tablespoons grated pecorino *or* Parmesan cheese
½ teaspoon freshly ground white pepper
8 ounces sole fillets
2 eggs, lightly beaten
2 tablespoons butter
1 lemon, juiced plus peel cut into strips
1 teaspoon capers

●Blend flour, cheese, and pepper. Rinse sole, pat dry. Lightly dredge sole on both sides in flour mixture, then in egg. In a frying pan, heat 2 tablespoons butter over medium heat until foamy. Add sole, cooking one fillet at a time for 2 to 3 minutes on each side; transfer to warm plates. When sole is cooked, add remaining butter to pan, heat until foamy with 3 strips of lemon peel and capers. Add lemon juice to taste. Remove and discard peel. Pour sauce over fish, and serve at once.

Sole and Green Tomatoes in Cornmeal

The simplest coating of egg and cornmeal makes a crunchy jacket for thick slices of green tomatoes. Tasty tarragon, pepper, and cheese add a savory flavor. A cornmeal coat does equally good things for fillet of sole, a good combination with which to commemorate summer's end. Add a chunky salad of late vegetables with garlic dressing, a fumé blanc, apples and nuts, a piece of Stilton, and you have a memorable meal.

---

8 ounces sole fillets
2 eggs
½ teaspoon minced fresh tarragon (3 to 4 leaves) *or*
   ¼ teaspoon dried
½ cup finely ground cornmeal
½ teaspoon black peppercorns, cracked
1 to 2 ounces grated Parmesan cheese
1 to 3 tablespoons butter
2 to 3 green tomatoes, sliced into wheels

●Rinse sole, pat dry. In a deep, flat dish or pie pan, beat eggs with a fork. Add tarragon to eggs. In another flat dish, blend cornmeal with peppercorns and cheese. In a cast-iron skillet, heat 1 tablespoon butter over medium heat until foamy. Preheat oven to warm. Dip slices of tomato (both sides) first into egg, then into cornmeal for a light coating (if a few spots get missed, it doesn't matter). Put them to cook in butter, allowing 3 to 5 minutes a side. When done, transfer to a platter in warm oven. Repeat dipping steps with sole (you may need to add more butter, heating it until foamy again), and cook 3 to 4 minutes on each side just until golden, then serve.

Red Snapper in Salsa Verde

Pumpkin seeds turn up often in Mexican recipes, adding their distinctively grainy texture and nutty flavor to many sauces. Here, hulled seeds (green ones) puff up like little crisp pillows when they are toasted. They add crunch and body to the softer vegetables in the sauce. If you don't live in a city with a substantial Mexican population, look for pumpkin seeds in health food stores or coops or substitute sunflower seeds. The salsa provides moderate to definite heat, depending on how much you use. The sour-sweet tang of the tomatillos gives the sauce a special twist. Serve with rice or hot rolls on the side, a green salad with an orange-chile dressing, and cold beer.

½ to 1 pound red snapper fillets
1 teaspoon olive oil
8 to 10 tomatillos, husked, well rinsed, and quartered
1 medium onion, sliced into thin wheels
1 orange, juiced plus thin slices of peel
1 to 3 tablespoons green salsa
2 tablespoons hulled pumpkin seeds

●Rinse snapper, pat dry. In a heavy frying pan, heat oil over medium-high heat. Toss in tomatillos, onion, and 2 to 3 slices orange peel. Cover pan and reduce heat to medium low. Cook until vegetables are soft, about 10 minutes. Add orange juice and salsa; stir, then slide in snapper. Cover and poach snapper in simmering sauce until opaque and flaky, about 12 minutes. Serve with a generous spoonful of sauce. Garnish with pumpkin seeds.

tomatillos

Red Snapper Poached in Orange Juice

Lemon thyme has a citrusy, Mediterranean flavor, which makes this sauce especially fragrant. It shows up only occasionally on grocery shelves, generally at a premium price. Fortunately, it is among the easiest of herbs to grow, usable year-round where winters are mild. Regular thyme, with its pleasant, woodsy flavor, can always be substituted. In this recipe, the herb adds depth to the poaching sauce. You could serve parsley rice or warm onion rolls, a medley of steamed green and golden wax beans, or chunks of winter squash lightly sauced with more orange juice and lots of pepper. To drink, have more of the wine you use for the fish: a muscadet, Chablis, or dry blush would be good choices.

---

2 tablespoons walnuts, toasted and chopped
¼ cup white wine
2 fat shallots, peeled and sliced
1 teaspoon chopped fresh lemon thyme *or*
  ½ teaspoon dried
2 oranges, juiced plus 3 1- x 2-inch slices peel
1 carrot, coarsely grated
1 to 2 tablespoons crumbled Roquefort cheese
8 ounces red snapper fillets

●Rinse snapper, pat dry. In a sauté pan, combine wine, shallots, thyme, orange juice, peel, and carrot over medium-high heat. Bring to a boil; reduce heat, slide in snapper, partially cover pan, and simmer gently for 8 to 10 minutes, or until snapper is opaque and flakes easily. To serve, transfer snapper to warm plates, top each piece with walnuts and Roquefort, and return to warm oven. Quickly reduce sauce by half. Spoon a bit over each piece of snapper and pass the rest in a bowl.

Green Snapper

This is a wonderful way to deal with the last of the green tomatoes, but it's equally tasty if made with ripe ones. Potato pancakes are in keeping with the Scandinavian overtones of this dish, as would be a bowl of warm applesauce (homemade or not, slightly warming it changes the character completely). Have a green salad with julienne beets and a few walnuts, hard cider, or a pleasant ale.

½ pound red snapper fillets
1 to 2 teaspoons butter
2 green tomatoes, chopped (yielding about 1 cup)
1 teaspoon chopped fresh dill *or*
    ½ teaspoon dried
½ teaspoon freshly ground pepper
3 tablespoons yogurt *or* sour cream (or a combination)

●Rinse snapper, pat dry. In a sauté pan, melt butter over medium heat until foamy. Slide in tomatoes, sprinkle in dill; stir and cook for 6 to 8 minutes, until tomatoes are soft. Reduce heat to medium low, slide in snapper. Add half the pepper; cook for 3 to 5 minutes on each side, or until snapper is opaque and flakes easily. Transfer snapper only to warm plates and hold in warm oven. Increase heat, bring tomato sauce to gentle boil, and reduce quickly until thickened. Reduce heat, stir in yogurt, heat through, and spoon around snapper. Add more pepper, serve at once.

Stars and Stripes Snapper

This is a natural for the Fourth of July, featuring red snapper fillets, Florence fennel and garlic yogurt (both white, you will notice), and blue corn tortillas—could anything be more patriotic? Perhaps this should be our new national dish. Serve corn on the cob, grilled in the husks, thickly sliced fresh tomatoes lavishly sprinkled with basil and drizzled with a garlic vinaigrette, and wonderful beers from both Americas for an international gesture.

½ to 1 pound thick red snapper fillets
1 to 2 teaspoons olive oil
1 large bulb Florence fennel with leaves
3 cloves garlic, pressed
1 cup yogurt
1 to 2 fresh red chiles, seeded and thinly sliced
1 bunch fresh cilantro, trimmed and chopped
1 package large blue corn tortillas

●Start coals in grill. Rinse snapper, pat dry, and brush lightly with oil on both sides. Chop fennel leaves, but leave bulb whole. Brush bulb lightly with oil on both sides. Spread 1 clove garlic on each side of snapper, then scatter half the fennel leaves on each side. Press remaining garlic into yogurt; stir in chiles, 2 to 3 tablespoons cilantro, and remaining fennel leaves. Loosely wrap in foil as many tortillas as you can eat, set at edge of grill to warm. Grill snapper and fennel bulb, allowing 4 to 6 minutes per side for each. Snapper is done when opaque and flakes easily. Fennel should be tender crisp and warm through (the grill marks gold rather than black). To serve, cut fennel bulb into thin strips and fish into chunks. Put some of each in a tortilla and top with yogurt sauce. Fireworks!

Florence fennel

Honey-glazed True Cod

This thin teriyakilike glaze sizzles with garlic and fresh ginger mellowed by honey and the smooth sesame seed paste called tahini. Shoyu, the Japanese soy sauce, which is less salty and more complex in flavor than the Chinese kind, adds deep color to the combination. Brush it over fish steaks, boneless chicken fillets, or pork or beef cubes for a lovely glaze of intense flavor. When time allows, fill a plastic zip-lock bag with boned chicken or turkey chunks (tofu, even) and marinate them in the glaze for at least an hour, or even overnight. Thread the meat on skewers and grill, basting often with the marinade; the meat will be moist and flavorful inside, glazed and crispy outside. Serve balls of sticky rice, a salad of chopped Swiss chard, mustard greens, and cashews in a garlic vinaigrette, and small bowls of toasted sesame seeds to dip the fish into for extra crunch. Drink a cold lager or hot tea.

¼ cup rice vinegar
2 teaspoons honey
2 tablespoons shoyu (Japanese soy sauce)
1 teaspoon sesame oil
1 tablespoon sesame tahini
3 cloves garlic, minced
2 inches gingerroot, peeled and minced
2 true cod steaks *or*
  1 pound thick fillet

●Start coals in grill. In a small, heavy saucepan, combine and heat all ingredients except cod, stirring until honey and tahini are melted into sauce. Brush cod lightly with glaze and grill or broil for 6 to 8 minutes total on each side, basting and turning several times.

Black Cod with Chinese Mustard Sauce

Long summer evenings lure us out-of-doors, and it's fun to find excuses to stay there. A meal like this can be quickly readied, then cooked and eaten outside. Black cod has a mild yet distinctive flavor that stands up well to the intensity of both sesame oil and mustard. When you grill, throw a few small chunks of green alder or maple wood on with your briquettes for a wonderful smoky flavor. Better yet, use a fire made entirely of seasoned and green alder together; this makes marvelous, even coals, and needs no foul smelling (and tasting) charcoal lighter. Have a glass bowl full of shredded bok choy, red cabbage, and carrots dressed with mirin and shoyu, hot or cold rice (cold balls of sticky rice is a traditional accompaniment), and a pale ale.

---

2 tablespoons shoyu (Japanese soy sauce)
1 tablespoon honey
1 to 2 teaspoons dry mustard (powdered seeds)
1 tablespoon mirin *or* sake
8 ounces black cod steaks
2 teaspoons sesame oil

●Start coals in grill. Blend 1 tablespoon shoyu with honey, mustard, and mirin. Let sauce sit 15 minutes, then taste (add more mustard if you like it very hot). Brush cod on both sides with a mixture of sesame oil and 1 tablespoon shoyu. Place cod over medium hot coals and grill or broil for 7 to 8 minutes per side. Have mustard sauce in individual dipping bowls at each plate, unless you know each other well enough to share.

Black Cod in Pine Nut Sauce

Pine nuts are valued throughout the Americas; wherever the piñon pine grows, the birds and squirrels get stiff human competition for the succulent little nuts. They are highly regarded in Europe as well; the Italians gather them from the ubiquitous umbrella-topped stone pines. In India and North Africa, pine nuts are also used appreciatively, and we do well to take the hint. Here, they are the base of an aromatic, citrusy sauce, which is thickened with avocado. It works best to start the coals and assemble all the ingredients ahead, so that you can whip the sauce together while the fish grills. Whether you use thick steaks or plump fillets, the cooking time will be brief, so be prepared. Grill sweet corn in the husk at the same time and offer sour rye bread, salad greens with a mustard and garlic vinaigrette, a dry blush wine, or a flowery weissbier.

---

8 to 12 ounces black cod fillets *or*
  2 cod steaks
1 avocado, peeled and cut into slices
1 lemon, juiced plus grated peel
½ bunch fresh cilantro, trimmed
2 cloves garlic
¼ cup pine nuts
Olive oil
½ teaspoon freshly grated nutmeg

●Start coals in grill. Rinse cod, pat dry. Sprinkle avocado with 1 tablespoon lemon juice. Put avocado, cilantro, 1 tablespoon lemon juice, garlic, and pine nuts into blender or food processor; buzz to blend. Add 1 tablespoon olive oil if necessary. Stir in 1 teaspoon lemon peel and nutmeg; blend and pour onto 2 dinner plates. If using thick fillet, cut into 2 equal pieces. Brush both sides lightly with oil, then grill or broil for 4 to 6 minutes on each side until opaque. Place 1 piece of cod on each plate of sauce, sprinkle with a few leaves of cilantro, and serve.

Fish

Black Cod Muscadet

Once an obscure wine found only along the coasts of Normandy and Brittany, muscadet is now widely held to be the supreme wine to drink with seafood. It is made from melon de Bourgogne grapes, which the California growers have renamed pinot blanc. Big, pearly muscat grapes have a distinctive, intense flavor, and are the grape of choice for the classic Sole Veronique. It is a shame not to branch out a bit, as they are wonderful additions to many chicken, pork, and sausage dishes, and complement other fish as well, or better, than sole. Serve with rice or boiled, chunked potatoes rolled in parsley butter, steamed carrots, and snow peas with a tad of shoyu and pickled sushi ginger. To drink, finish the muscadet.

---

8 ounces black cod *or*
  2 cod steaks
1 tablespoon butter
1 medium yellow onion, thinly sliced into rings
1 teaspoon chopped fresh lemon thyme *or*
  ½ teaspoon dried
¼ cup muscadet
4 ounces muscat grapes, halved and seeded
½ teaspoon freshly ground white pepper

●Rinse cod, pat dry. In a heavy frying pan, melt butter over low heat. Add whole onion slices with thyme and cook slowly, until onions are soft. Turn them with a spatula, cook for 3 minutes. Increase heat to medium, add wine, and cook for 5 minutes. Slide in cod, cook for 3 minutes (fillets) or 4 to 6 minutes (steaks), turn. Add grapes and pepper, simmer for 4 to 5 minutes. Serve cod, spooning onions and grapes over each portion.

Fish Chowder

This New England classic is made for chasing away the cold. To be authentic, it really should be served with corn sticks, but fresh corn bread, baked in a hot, well-buttered iron skillet for that crispy, crunchy edge, will more than compensate. For those who can't abide certain traditional holiday fish dishes (lutefisk, perhaps?), but like the link with family history, this recipe might make an acceptable replacement. To brighten the presentation, garnish each soup plate with flat Italian parsley and a sprinkle of diced red sweet peppers. Serve with a salad of apples, toasted walnuts, and butterhead lettuce with a Gorgonzola dressing. To brighten your mood (and make the very little work lighter), try a chilled Chablis or pinot blanc.

---

8 ounces cod *or* haddock
2 unpeeled boiling potatoes, cut up
1 cup frozen corn
4 strips thick bacon
1 medium onion, diced
½ cup sliced mushrooms
2 cups half-and-half
1 to 2 teaspoons butter

●Skin and bone cod; rinse and pat dry. In saucepan, boil potatoes in salted water until just tender, 10 to 12 minutes. Add corn and let sit, covered, for 2 minutes; drain. In large pan or soup pot, cook bacon slowly, then drain on paper towels. Add cod, onion, and mushrooms to pan; cover and cook over low heat for 5 to 7 minutes, until cod flakes and becomes opaque. Add potatoes, corn, half-and-half, and butter. When butter melts, serve at once, topping each bowlful with crumbled bacon.

Fish

Saffron Haddock

Haddock has a full, distinctive flavor that can stand up to a complex sauce. Here, saffron, the golden powdered stigma of the saffron crocus, is used to gild and enrich a simple, buttery sauce. Saffron needs contact with moist heat to reconstitute properly—you will notice how the aroma blooms to fill the kitchen as the saffron softens. A little goes a long way, which is fortunate—saffron costs the earth, but then, it must be harvested by hand, and crawling around in a hot crocus field can't be stimulating work. In addition, it takes thousands of the stigma to make up a single ounce. Cilantro, the seed of the familiar cilantro or Chinese parsley, is often partnered with saffron, both in Indian and South American cooking (this recipe is adapted from a traditional Brazilian one). Tomato paste in tubes keeps indefinitely in the refrigerator and is handy in recipes that call for just a smidge. Serve this with rice, throwing in some lemon peel as it cooks. Toss up a salad of lettuce, mustard greens, and Niçoise olives, and pour out a glass of Frascati or a flowery, scented Chilean Canepa.

½ to 1 pound haddock fillets
⅛ teaspoon saffron threads
1 tablespoon butter
1 teaspoon coriander
2 teaspoons tomato paste
1 medium onion, sliced into wheels
1 small lemon, juiced plus large strips of peel

●Rinse haddock, pat dry. Soften saffron in 1 tablespoon boiling water. Mash butter, coriander, and tomato paste together. Layer half the onion slices with lemon peel in bottom of casserole. If you don't have a small casserole with a tight cover, use a large piece of foil. Put haddock on top. Smooth saffron paste over haddock, dot generously with butter mixture, layer on remaining onions, and pour lemon juice over all. Cover pan or close foil (set foil packet on baking sheet or inside another pan while haddock cooks) and bake in 350 degree oven for 25 to 30 minutes, or until haddock is opaque and flakes easily.

Halibut Mixed Grill

Lightly brushed with oil, the fresh tomatoes and peppers that make up the tangy, smoky sauce are grilled before the halibut. Thick halibut fillets or small steaks of any firm-fleshed fish work equally well, and either looks attractive nestled in circles of vivid sauce. The heavy cream carries the subtle but definite snap of garlic, and the chives add a spiky green note both flavorful and pretty. Serve a salad as a separate course, perhaps greens tossed with fresh mozzarella and chopped hazelnuts, with a garlicky tomato dressing to tie the two together. To drink, a verdicchio, a white Burgundy, or a weissbier.

---

6 ripe tomatoes
2 red sweet peppers
1 to 2 fresh chiles (jalapeños, pasillas, or other)
1 to 3 tablespoons olive oil
3 cloves garlic
2 tablespoons heavy cream
8 ounces halibut fillets *or*
  2 halibut steaks
1 small bunch fresh chives, chopped into 1-inch pieces

●Start coals in grill about half an hour before you plan to begin cooking. Rinse tomatoes, peppers, and chiles, dry well. Brush them lightly with oil and grill over very hot coals, turning so that all sides are blackened. Scrape or rub off skins, cut off stems, discard seeds, and toss vegetables into blender or food processor. Crush 1 garlic clove and put in a small bowl with heavy cream. Put the other 2 cloves in blender and buzz to liquify; the sauce should be quite thick, but you can add 1 tablespoon water if necessary. Pour sauce onto 2 dinner plates and put in a warm oven. Rinse halibut, pat dry. If using a thick fillet, cut into 2 equal pieces. Brush with oil. Grill 4 to 6 minutes on each side, depending on thickness. Halibut will be opaque when done. Set 1 piece of halibut on each plate. Remove and discard garlic from cream. Then pour cream over each halibut serving. Sprinkle chives sparingly over both halibut and sauce. Serve at once.

Fresh Tomato Curry with Halibut

Halibut has a lovely, firm consistency and a mild, slightly sweet flavor that is complemented rather than overwhelmed by this lively sauce. Whether made with ripe garden tomatoes or canned ones, it will taste fresh at any season. Fish curries are not often found on American menus, yet many seafoods take well to such a spicy, savory seasoning. The original Bombay recipe calls for ghee, the clarified butter often used in Indian cooking, but sweet butter works well, too. It's worth taking the time some Saturday to seek out the aromatic spice blends sold as garam masala in Indian and specialty food stores if it isn't on your supermarket shelf.

---

8 ounces halibut steaks
2 tablespoons sweet butter
2 cloves garlic, crushed
2 medium onions, sliced into thin wedges
1 fresh chile, trimmed and partially seeded
1 bay leaf
4 tomatoes, sliced into wedges *or*
  1 15-ounce can chopped tomatoes in sauce
1 to 2 teaspoons garam masala *or* curry powder

● Rinse halibut, pat dry. In a heavy skillet, heat 1 tablespoon butter over medium heat until foamy. Add garlic and brown on all sides; reduce heat, add remaining butter, then add onions, chile, and bay leaf. Cook, stirring several times, until onions are soft. Add tomatoes, cook for 3 minutes; add garam masala to taste. Slide halibut into bubbling sauce, partially cover pan, and poach until opaque and firm (this may take from 12 to 20 minutes, depending on thickness of steak). Remove and discard bay leaf and garlic. Serve halibut with sauce surrounding it.

Fish Sticks

Remember fish sticks, the ones the baby-sitter used to feed you? Well, this is a little different. Here lightly marinated swordfish grills with tart, tangy star fruit, a tropical fruit that looks like a pickle with wings. Star fruit is grown in Florida, as well as throughout the tropics. It appears in markets from late summer through the spring. Applewood skewers have a smoky sweet fragrance that's hard to beat, so if you or your friends have trees that need pruning, collect a handful of straight water shoots for future barbecues. All fruit trees are great for this, as is the sweet bay (*Laurus nobilis*), which adds pungent spicy smoke to the meal. If you plan ahead, the fish can marinate overnight, but even after half an hour, it acquires an herbal accent. Serve with warm pitas, a plate of baby vegetables to grill along with the fish, a salad with cilantro-salsa dressing, and some cold beer.

---

1 lemon, juiced plus grated peel
1 teaspoon minced fresh dill
1 teaspoon minced fresh rosemary *or*
  ½ teaspoon dried
¼ cup olive oil
1 pound swordfish, cut into 1-inch cubes
1 red sweet pepper, cut into chunks
1 star fruit, sliced into 1-inch stars

●Combine lemon juice with 1 teaspoon of grated peel, dill, rosemary, and oil in a large zip-lock bag. Add swordfish and marinate overnight or at least 30 minutes. Add pepper and star fruit and coat with marinade. Thread chunks of fish, pepper, and star fruit on skewers. Broil or grill for 4 to 6 minutes on each side, turning several times.

star fruit

Trout with Green Sauce

Fat little brookies are particularly delicious with this aromatic frothy sauce verte so deservedly beloved by the French. The tender, almost sweet trout is beautifully underscored by the herbs, which in concert have a savory, slightly woodsy tang. The bitterness of watercress and the aniselike sharpness of fresh tarragon are tempered by the sour cream, and the wine melds them all into a satisfying whole. Start the meal with ripe apricots stuffed with a mixture of ricotta, chives, and kasséri cheese served with a dry Belgian raspberry ale. Yellow wax beans and baby-finger carrots garnished with a bit of orange-zested mayonnaise, dense sourdough rolls and sweet butter, are simple and pleasant additions. Muscadet or a dry fumé blanc will help make this a summer meal par excellence, served hot or chilled.

---

2 small trout, about 1 pound each
½ cup sour cream
1 cup dry white wine
1 bunch fresh spinach, chopped
1 bunch fresh watercress, chopped
1 bunch fresh flat Italian parsley, chopped
1 tablespoon chopped fresh tarragon

●Rinse trout, then poach in ¾ cup wine with ¾ cup water; cover pan and simmer gently for 12 minutes for 2 small brookies, or 15 to 20 minutes for 1 larger trout. In a blender, combine remaining wine, sour cream, spinach, watercress, parsley, and tarragon. Buzz to a smooth paste, then pour out onto 2 plates. Drain trout and arrange on top. Garnish with a sprig or 2 of herbs and a ribbon of sour cream. Chill or serve at once.

Fish

Flaming Trout

When Mr. D served this at Seattle's Philoxenia restaurant, all the lights in the place were doused. This Greek treatment is delicious and different—the presentation as dramatic as you choose to make it. Dried herbs in half the amounts can be substituted for fresh, and any liqueur you have on hand can be used for the flaming. Don't begin to cook the trout until everything is ready and in place; it only takes a few minutes, and interruptions will spoil the spectacular effect. For a simple meal, include a fragrant rice pilaf and chunked, steamed vegetables drizzled with a lemon and oregano dressing. Or go all out with hot fan rolls, asparagus tips, and curried apricots. A fumé blanc or a dry, dry semillon will brighten the menu.

---

2 tablespoons chopped fresh oregano *or*
  1 tablespoon dried
2 tablespoons chopped fresh rosemary *or*
  1 tablespoon dried
2 tablespoons chopped fresh thyme *or*
  1 tablespoon dried
2 cloves garlic
1 lemon, sliced into thick wedges
1 thick slice bread, toasted and cubed
2 small trout (1 pound each), cleaned, head on
1 tablespoon triple sec or other liqueur

●Chop herbs, garlic, and half the lemon wedges together into a rough paste; mix with bread cubes, reserving 2 large cubes. Stuff half the mixture into each trout. Prop each trout's mouth open with toothpicks; broil for 4 to 6 minutes on each side. In a heavy saucepan, gently warm liqueur. Briefly soak remaining bread cubes in warm liqueur; replace toothpicks with bread cubes. Put cooked trout on a warm serving platter garnished with remaining lemon slices. Ignite bread cubes and serve at once.

Perch with Currants and Walnuts

In Morocco and throughout North Africa, fish is apt to be cooked with fruits, nuts, and spices in exotic combination. This is adapted from a traditional Moroccan recipe that shows European influences. Thick ocean perch fillets bake in a subtle white wine sauce, slightly sweetened with dried currants. Toasted walnuts make a gravelly, crunchy topping in rich contrast to the citrusy tang of the sauce. Walnut oil adds a delightful undertone. Serve it with a spinach salad, perhaps adding toasted nuts and some grated Asiago, rice or warm wheat rolls, and a glass of Vernaccia or a smooth Bardolino.

---

2 tablespoons walnuts, toasted and chopped
½ to 1 pound perch fillets
1 tablespoon walnut oil
1 teaspoon dried dill
1 clove garlic, thinly sliced
1 lime, halved plus grated peel
2 teaspoons dried currants
¼ cup dry white wine

●Put plates in warm oven. Rinse perch, pat dry. In sauté pan, heat oil over medium-high heat. Add dill, garlic, and perch; cook for 1 minute. Add juice from half the lime and ½ teaspoon peel; cook for 5 to 6 minutes on first side. Flip perch, cook an additional 5 minutes. Add currants and wine; reduce heat and simmer, partially covered, for 4 to 6 minutes, until perch is opaque and flakes easily. Remove perch to warm plates and hold in oven. Quickly reduce sauce by half, stirring constantly. Pour sauce over perch, top with walnuts, and serve at once.

Poached Perch with Chervil

Delicate and distinctive, chervil makes an unusual complement to the mild flavor of poached ocean perch. If fresh
chervil is not available, use flat Italian parsley and chives or
tarragon; the result will be different but equally good. Any of
the fuller-flavored fish need only a sprig or two of a single
herb in the poaching liquid. Julienne carrots and turnips add
gentle color and a touch of peppery sweetness to the dish;
most food processors julienne quickly, but it doesn't take long
to do just two vegetables by hand. Serve with buttery baby
beets, zucchini strips, or a fluffy green salad with a bit more
chervil snipped into the dressing. A dry pear wine is especially good with this.

8 ounces perch fillets
1 tablespoon butter
2 shallots, thinly sliced
1 carrot, cut into matchstick pieces
1 turnip, cut into matchstick pieces
1 tablespoon snipped fresh chervil
¼ cup dry white wine
½ teaspoon freshly ground pepper

●Rinse perch, pat dry. In a heavy skillet, heat butter over
medium heat until foamy. Add shallots, carrot, turnip, and
chervil; stir well. Add wine and simmer, partially covered, for
10 minutes. Slide in perch. Add at least ½ teaspoon pepper,
bring to a gentle boil, then reduce to a simmer. Poach perch
until opaque, 10 to 15 minutes depending on thickness. Serve
at once, with sauce spooned over perch.

Catfish with Three Butters

 F arm-raised catfish appears frequently in the supermarket these days. Fish farm conditions are better than those in the average river, and the succulent quality of this fine fish is now readily apparent. In this dish, it is topped by three butters in complementary flavors, which run together to make a savory, herbed sauce for grilled or baked fish. It is easiest to serve the butters in rough pats, but to be fancier, fill tiny paper cups with them, or pipe butter rosettes through an icing nozzle onto foil. The butters will set up quickly in the freezer, and may be placed artistically upon the fish at serving time. Serve with a salad of romaine, watercress, sliced kiwis, and avocados drizzled with walnut oil and orange juice, a basket of crusty, hot cornbread, and a vivid riesling.

3½ tablespoons butter
½ teaspoon grated orange peel
½ teaspoon white pepper
1 tablespoon chopped fresh cilantro *or*
  ½ teaspoon dried
½ teaspoon capers
½ teaspoon chopped fresh tarragon *or*
  ½ teaspoon dried
1 teaspoon chopped fresh chives *or*
  1 teaspoon dried
1 pound catfish fillets, skinned

●Divide 3 tablespoons butter in 3 pats. To the first, add orange rind and white pepper; to the second, add cilantro and capers; to the third, add tarragon and chives. Mash each, divide into 2 portions, and chill. Lightly brush catfish on both sides with melted butter. Grill or broil for 5 to 7 minutes on each side. Serve each portion with pats of each butter.

Catfish in Cornmeal with Black Butter

This recipe combines the haute with the down home; catfish in cornmeal with a spicy beurre noire. The results are splendid: the sauce is bold—warm with pepper, tangy with vinegar—and the succulent flavor of the fish wins through as it should. Cornbread is a classic accompaniment, and a side dish of black beans, smoky with bacon ends, is equally welcome. Quickly steam a panful of fresh greens—beets, poke salad, mustard, and spinach—and drizzle with vinegar for a tonic addition. A hoppy, bitter ale or a robust lager will taste fine here.

¼ cup finely ground cornmeal
1 teaspoon dried dill
1 pound catfish fillets, skinned
1 large egg, slightly beaten
4 tablespoons butter
1 dried chile
1 tablespoon balsamic vinegar
2 tablespoons olive oil

●In a pie pan or wide bowl, combine cornmeal and dill (and a shake of salt, if you like). Dip catfish into cornmeal, then into egg, then into cornmeal again, coating both sides. In a small, heavy saucepan, melt butter over low heat. Add chile and sauté until nearly black, but not burnt. Remove and discard chile. Add vinegar, stir to blend, and keep warm over lowest heat. In a heavy frying pan, heat oil over medium heat. Add catfish and fry for 4 to 6 minutes on each side, depending on thickness. Serve with black butter on each portion.

Seafood

55   *Prawns in Clam Clouds*

56   *Prawns in Black Bean Sauce*

57   *Prawns with Sushi Ginger*

58   *Prawns in Green Salsa*

59   *Prawn and Jícama Salad*

60   *Camarónes Bolivianos*

61   *Enoki Mushrooms with Shrimp and Sanbai-su*

62   *Aglio-Oglio with Bay Shrimp*

63   *Sorrel Soup with Shrimp and Bacon*

64   *Mexican Shrimp Salad*

65   *Crab and Clam Pie*

66   *Crab Casseroles*

67   *Grilled Dungeness Crab*

68   *Roquefort Crab with Green Peppercorn Sauce*

69   *Crab with Enoki Mushrooms*

70   *Red Peppers Stuffed with Crab*

71   *Crab Bisque*

72   *Crab Salad*

73   *Butter Clam Hash*

74   *Capelli d'Angelo with Clam Sauce*

75   *Clam Chowder*

76 Skewered Scallops

77 Scallops with Cardamom Orange Rice

78 Lemon Fettuccine with Scallops and Three Peppers

79 Hot Scallop Salad with Blood Oranges

80 Scallop and Feijoa Salad

81 Mussels Gratinée

82 Mussels in Pesto Sauce

83 Steamed Mussel Soup

84 Oyster Omelet

85 Oyster Stew

86 Squid in Gin and Ginger

87 Squid Rings with Rotini

88 Squid and Shrimp Salad

Prawns in Clam Clouds

Fat prawns lurk in nests of shredded green onions beneath the soft, cloudy clam topping in these elegant and simple little casseroles. If you can't find prawns, you may use cooked shrimp, crab, or even chicken, with a happy result. Similar recipes, popular back in the fifties, call for as much as half a cup of mayonnaise, but this slimmed-down version is actually tastier than the originals. Spark a simple green salad with shredded black radish, more green onions in tiny slivers, pumpernickel croutons, and a raspberry vinaigrette. Break out a dry gewürtztraminer or a noble stout.

½ teaspoon butter
4 green onions, shredded diagonally
6 cooked prawns, peeled
1 egg
1 to 2 tablespoons mayonnaise
¼ teaspoon freshly ground pepper
⅓ cup minced clams *or*
   canned

●Preheat broiler. Butter 2 individual casseroles or small ovenproof dishes. Line cups with grassy strips of onion. Nest prawns in onion "grass." Divide egg, reserving yolk for another dish. Whip egg white to soft peak, fold in mayonnaise and pepper. Drain clams and gently stir into egg mixture. Spoon egg mixture over prawns, set dishes under broiler, and cook 3 to 5 minutes until puffy and well browned.

Prawns in Black Bean Sauce

Ubiquitous in southern Chinese cuisine, black bean sauce is only now finding its ways onto American supermarket shelves. Fermented, sometimes aged in wooden casks much like whiskey, this sauce has a pungent, spicy bite which can take some getting used to, so start with a small amount. The most widely available kinds are chopped or minced and fairly mild, but the several brands that use whole beans are very salty and often hotter than the others. Briefly rinsing the whole-bean kind—most often found in authentic Asian markets—makes it more palatable to Western tastebuds. This showy entrée needs only the simplest accompaniment—steamed baby bok choy dressed with orange juice, shoyu, and rice vinegar, long grain rice, and some cold ale or hot tea.

---

2 teaspoons oil
1 onion, sliced into rings
2 carrots, 1 sliced into thin diagonals, 1 sliced lengthwise
    into curls for garnish
1 chile, thinly sliced
4 ounces snow peas
8 ounces peeled, cooked prawns
Shoyu (Japanese Soy sauce)
1 to 3 tablespoons black bean sauce

●In a frying pan, heat oil over medium heat. Toss in onions and carrots; stir-fry for 2 minutes. Add chile, snow peas, and prawns; stir-fry for another 2 minutes. Sprinkle with shoyu to taste. Add bean sauce to pan; stir-fry for 2 more minutes. Garnish with carrot curls and serve at once.

Prawns with Sushi Ginger

Pickled or sushi ginger is made from fresh gingerroot that is so finely sliced it is nearly transparent. The ginger is often mixed with the purple-black leaves of perilla, a basil-and-cinnamon-scented herb more often used in Asian cookery than in ours. (A surprising number of Americans grow this plant as an ornamental.) Rice vinegar is added, sometimes along with a bit of mirin or sweet sake. Sushi ginger is sold in plastic bags or packets, in jars, or frozen. The best sushi ginger can be purchased from sushi bars, where it is freshly made. To make it yourself, slice an inch of peeled fresh gingerroot into a tablespoon of rice vinegar and let it marinate for at least an hour. In this entrée, sushi ginger and bok choy, the crisp, peppery sweet Chinese cabbage, put prawns in a whole new light. Rice, a vegetable stir-fry, and a mild lager will make a satisfying combination.

½ to 1 pound prawns
2 teaspoons almond oil *or* vegetable oil
4 green onions, thinly sliced on diagonal
1 red pepper, sliced into thin strips
4 to 6 leaves bok choy, thinly sliced (including white bulb)
1 to 2 ounces pickled ginger in vinegar
1 to 2 teaspoons shoyu (Japanese soy sauce) to taste
¼ cup whole almonds, toasted

●Rinse prawns briefly, drain. In a heavy frying pan or wok, heat oil over medium-high heat. When hot, add prawns and cook, stirring for 2 minutes. Add vegetables; stir, cover, and cook for 2 to 3 minutes. Stir in ginger with vinegar and shoyu; simmer for 2 more minutes until very hot. Add almonds and toss. Serve at once.

bok choy

Prawns in Green Salsa

If you consider cleaning and deveining shrimp a chore, choose prawns; these fat creatures are far easier to handle. Nearly all prawns and shrimp are frozen on the boats—and often defrosted behind the scenes at the grocery store—so don't shun the frozen kind if that's all there is. When cooked, cleaned, and quickly frozen right on board the fishing vessel, both prawns and shrimp are every bit as good as what is sold as fresh. Here, each chubby prawn rolls up in a blue corn blanket with a dollop of hot green salsa to warm it up. Pass around a green salad, adding toasted peanuts or pumpkin seeds for crunch and tossing it with a sassy fresh chile vinaigrette. Pour out a cold lager, iced tea, or extradry hard cider and dig in.

---

1 package medium blue corn tortillas
8 cooked prawns
10 tomatillos, husked, well rinsed, and quartered
1 to 3 fresh chiles, seeded and thinly sliced
6 olives, pitted and sliced
1 teaspoon olive oil
2 to 3 tablespoons green salsa to taste
¼ cup sour cream *or* yogurt

●Loosely wrap in foil as many tortillas as you think you can eat, keep in warm oven. Rinse prawns briefly, drain. In a heavy frying pan, heat oil over medium-high heat. Add tomatillos, chiles, and olives. Stir in 2 to 3 tablespoons water; reduce heat and simmer, partially covered, until vegetables are soft, about 10 minutes. Add salsa and prawns; heat through. To serve, spoon a large prawn, some sauce, and a dollop of sour cream into a warm tortilla, roll up and eat!

Prawn and Jícama Salad

Jícama may not be a glamour vegetable—it looks like a knobby, misshapen, beige beet—but it definitely has potential. In Mexico, sliced jícama is marinated in lime juice or vinaigrette, then eaten as an appetizer or tossed in a salad. It has been an Asian staple for several centuries and is especially popular with the Chinese, who use it interchangeably with water chestnuts. The flesh is crisp, tender, and somewhat sweet, with an earthy flavor similar to potatoes. Choose small, firm tubers for best texture and flavor—big ones can get stringy and tough—and peel away the rough outer skin, which has a bitter flavor. Here, jícama and prawns meet under an unusual New Mexican sauce—lemon, cilantro, and fragrant, freshly grated nutmeg blended with tart yogurt, avocado, and salsa. Have a plate of small vegetables, more salsa and a creamy sauce for dipping, a big bowl of corn chips, or a stack of warm tortillas on the side. Cold cerveza, a Frascati, or fresh lemonade are all good drinks.

---

1 large avocado, peeled, halved, and thinly sliced
1 small lemon, juiced plus grated peel
8 ounces jícama, peeled and sliced into thin strips
8 prawns, cooked and peeled
½ bunch fresh cilantro, trimmed, reserving 2 sprigs
    for garnish
⅔ cup yogurt
2 to 4 tablespoons salsa to taste
½ teaspoon freshly grated nutmeg

●Sprinkle half the avocado slices with 1 tablespoon lemon juice. Toss gently with jícama and prawns, and divide on 2 salad plates. Put cilantro in blender or food processor with other half of avocado, 1 tablespoon lemon juice, and yogurt; buzz to blend. Stir in salsa, 1 teaspoon lemon peel, and nutmeg. Spoon sauce over salads, sprinkle on a few cilantro leaves, and serve.

Camarónes Bolivianos

This creamy, soufflelike casserole is characteristic of the savory South American cooking too seldom experienced north of the border. Here fresh corn and coconut milk meet blazing chiles (or a blend of medium-hot and sweet ones). Shrimp, raisins, and olives help temper the heat, and the peppery leaves of cilantro blend the flavors together. To make fresh coconut milk, crack a coconut and grate the meat (thin brown skin left on) in a food processor or put it in the blender with one-half cup of hot water. Strain the result through cheesecloth, pressing lightly. Strain again with another one-fourth cup of water. The two pressings should give you about a cup of milk. Fairly thick, rich, but not overly sweet, coconut milk is a common ingredient in foods of the Caribbean, South America, and even Thailand. A lot of grocery stores carry it canned or frozen, and either kind will work well.

---

2 ears uncooked fresh sweet corn (about 1 cup)
2 eggs, lightly beaten
⅔ cup coconut milk
2 tablespoons chopped fresh cilantro
1 to 3 fresh chiles (any combination of varieties), seeded
  and thinly sliced
8 green olives, pitted and chopped
8 ounces cooked shrimp
2 tablespoons golden raisins

●Cut or grate the corn off cobs into a bowl, reserving milky juice. In a large bowl, blend eggs, coconut milk, and corn. Stir in cilantro, chiles, olives, shrimps, and raisins. Pour mixture into a 1½-quart casserole and bake, uncovered, in 250 degree oven for 35 to 40 minutes until set and golden brown. Spoon out onto plates.

Enoki Mushrooms with Shrimp and Sanbai-su

This is a lovely dish; light but satisfying with flecks of pink, ivory, yellow, and soft green tossed like confetti over a bed of rice. A small packet of enoki mushrooms doesn't look like much, but they are tightly shrink-wrapped. Open the bag, and they begin to fluff up at once. They often have a blend of bran and sawdust clinging to them, so cut away the bottom inch or so of the entire clump to clean them. The stalks should be supple but firm and of a warm ivory white, the tiny caps unblotched. Sanbai-su, "three-taste dressing," is often found in supermarkets with an Asian food section. If you can't find it, combine equal parts rice vinegar, shoyu (Japanese soy sauce), and mirin or honey for a good facsimile. Serve with a light, crisp sauvignon blanc or sake over ice.

½ cup uncooked rice
8 ounces shrimp
1 teaspoon sesame oil *or* vegetable oil
8 to 10 yellow or green beans, sliced on diagonal
3 green onions, sliced on diagonal
3 to 4 ounces enoki mushrooms (1 package),
    bottom inch trimmed
1 tablespoon sanbai-su (see above)
2 green onions, trimmed like brooms

●Cook rice as directed on package. Rinse shrimp, pat dry. In a frying pan or wok, heat oil over medium heat. Add beans and onions; stir and cook for 2 minutes. Add shrimp and mushrooms; stir and cook for 2 to 3 minutes. Add sanbai-su; stir and cook for 1 more minute. Serve at once, spooned over rice and garnished with green onion brooms.

green onion brooms, slivers, diagonals

Aglio–Oglio with Bay Shrimp

Garlic (aglio) and olive oil (oglio) are among the most beloved foods in the Italian lexicon. Aglio-oglio is a dish to whip up in no time, a classic late-night entrée to serve after an evening at the opera or theater, or the perfect punctuation for a cozy midnight stroll. Use the fruitiest, most full-flavored oil you can muster, for it is a key ingredient here, and quality counts. Shrimp makes this a hearty dish, and the smoking undertone of heat from the peperoncini (dried red chiles) can be muted (use one pod) or escalated to fireworks (use three, four, or even more). If Italian peperoncini are unobtainable, substitute the small, dark red Japanese dried chiles (though really, any kind will do). Have a bowl of mixed greens in the refrigerator ready to toss with a citrusy vinaigrette, a crusty loaf to spread with sweet butter, and a bottle of Frascati chilling while you stroll.

---

2 tablespoons olive oil
2 cloves garlic, mashed
1 to 3 dried red chiles
10 ounces cooked, peeled shrimp
8 ounces fresh linguine *or*
   4 ounces dry
1 tablespoon shredded Asiago or Parmesan cheese

●Put pasta water on to boil. In a heavy frying pan, heat oil over medium heat. Add garlic and chile and cook until brown, then remove and discard. Add shrimp; reduce heat and stir to coat shrimp with oil. Cook pasta to taste, drain quickly but do not rinse. Toss at once with oil and shrimp. Serve very hot with a sprinkle of cheese on each portion.

Sorrel Soup with Shrimp and Bacon

In the Northwest and other mild winter areas, sorrel has two seasons, spring and fall. The epicurean French have elevated this humble meadow weed to the haute cuisine, taming the puckering, astringent quality of wild sorrel to a tingling, piquant sourness. In the best strains, young sorrel is mild enough to eat raw, snipped into spring salads. Here, sorrel's tartness is deliciously offset by crumbled bacon and sweet shrimp in a rich soup that is as bright and green as spring itself. Like spinach, sorrel cooks down a great deal, so although four bunches seems like a lot, it ends up being a modest amount. A salad of young lettuce and mustard greens dressed with a curried vinaigrette, hot rolls, a piece of aged cheese, and a glass of stout make this a delightful meal to enjoy indoors or out.

---

1 tablespoon butter
4 bunches (4 cups) sorrel, rinsed and trimmed
3 cups milk
2 strips bacon
6 ounces shrimp, cooked
2 tablespoons sour cream
1 green onion, sliced into thin circles

●In a heavy saucepan, melt half the butter over low heat. Add damp sorrel; cover and cook slowly until tender and limp, about 12 to 15 minutes. While sorrel is cooking, scald milk. In a frying pan, cook bacon over medium heat; drain off grease. When sorrel is done, add 1 cup scalded milk to saucepan (it will curdle), stirring well. Put in blender or food processor, and buzz until smooth. Return to saucepan, add remaining milk, butter, shrimp, and sour cream; heat until butter melts. Ladle into bowls, garnish with green onions and crumbled bacon. Serve at once.

Mexican Shrimp Salad

F at shrimp and chubby chunks of ripe avocado meet a spicy, tangy sauce of cilantro and lime (in one of the fastest recipes I know) with surprisingly complex results. Expand the usual salsa-and-chips appetizers with a plate of baby vegetables and chunks of cheese. If you have avoided blue corn chips, thinking them a trendy fad, try them; they are far more tasty than the average commercial stuff. Thick slices of oranges and Walla Walla sweet onions make a good salad if drizzled with vinaigrette. Either fresh tortillas or corn muffins go very well with this salad. Drink cold beer, of course, though a crisp Côtes du Rhône blanc will stand up to the strong flavors very well.

---

1 large lime, juiced
2 tablespoons olive oil
1 to 2 tablespoons fresh salsa
½ bunch cilantro, trimmed and chopped (to equal
    about ¼ cup), reserve 2 sprigs for garnish
1 large cucumber, diced
1 large avocado, cut into chunks
12 ounces cooked shrimp
2 bunches spinach, rinsed and trimmed

●Blend lime juice with olive oil, salsa, and cilantro. In a large bowl, gently toss cucumber and avocado with shrimp and salsa dressing. Pile lettuce on 2 large plates, mound shrimp salad on top, garnish cilantro sprigs.

Crab and Clam Pie
(Serves 4 to 6)

In the Northwest, seafood pie has been a longtime favorite, traditionally made with butter or razor clams, Dungeness or Alaska king crab. The cheese would be Cheddar, the excellent aged, sharp Tillamook or Cougar Gold, though a Vermont or New York Cheddar will work fine, too. Pie crusts may be found frozen or freshly made at a number of bakeries—or perhaps you are in the habit of making and freezing a few extras of your own. The ubiquitous green salad may be dressed up with chopped hazelnuts, a few sections of satsumas or oranges, and some shreds of arugula or mustard greens. A velvety stout or porter will complement this rich dish.

---

1 large onion, sliced into thin rounds
1 9-inch pie crust
½ cup grated sharp Cheddar cheese
1 cup crab meat
1 cup butter or razor clams
3 eggs
1 cup half-and-half
Freshly ground black pepper (at least ½ teaspoon)

●Scatter onion over pie crust and top with half the cheese, followed by the crab and clams. Beat eggs lightly; add half-and-half and a lot of pepper to eggs. Pour egg mixture over seafood, scatter remaining cheese on top, and bake (set pie on a baking sheet) in 350 degree oven for 45 to 50 minutes until set and golden. Let stand for 10 minutes before slicing, then serve hot or at room temperature.

Crab Casseroles

Winter is open season for crabs, and the fishermen are free to bring in all they can. The price is often lower, too, especially when the catch is good. If pre-cooked crab isn't dated, sniff it—it ought to smell faintly of the sea, but not at all of ammonia. It is worth the search to find a supermarket with an up-to-date, reliable fish department, for seafood is too fragile to withstand improper storage and handling. When you do find a good source, let them know how much you appreciate it—such places deserve enthusiastic encouragement from consumers. In these elegant casseroles, the sweet savor of the crab comes through the velvety richness of the tangy sauce. Slivered kohlrabi and beets tossed with lemon butter make an unusual and complementary side dish, and a loaf of rye bread and a dark, chocolatey stout go wonderfully with crab, odd as that may sound.

½ lemon, juiced plus grated peel
8 ounces cooked crab meat, shredded or cut into small pieces
1 ounce cream cheese
1 teaspoon chopped fresh chives
1 teaspoon green peppercorns
2 tablespoons bread crumbs
1 to 2 teaspoons butter
1 ounce shredded Gruyère cheese

●Drizzle lemon juice over crab; set aside. Mash cream cheese with chives, lemon peel, and peppercorns. Divide cream cheese mixture into 2 casseroles, custard cups, or other oven-proof dishes. Layer crab over cream cheese. Rub bread crumbs into butter and then crumble over crab in each dish. Top with cheese. Broil for 3 to 5 minutes until hot and bubbly, serve.

Grilled Dungeness Crab

During the summer months, the Dungeness crab comes close to shore to mate. Northwesterners scramble to catch the males, using rakes, shovels, or nets to scoop them out of the water. The shallows are full of people in hip boots waving dollar bills—the standard we measure by. If the bill is longer than the crab shell is wide, the crab gets a reprieve. Many of the captured are boiled, but grilled crab is an unbeatable treat. This is supposed to be performed on live crab (stick a skewer through the shell between the eyes before grilling), but the squeamish and the humane may prefer to grill already-cooked crab. In any case, the shell cuts easily with kitchen shears to let in the sauce. Any supermarket with a specialty fish buyer will date all cooked shellfish—if cooked crab is more than one day old or smells like ammonia, don't buy it. This is a quick meal that needs only a bold ale, a salad, a baguette of sourdough bread, and a lot of napkins to complete it.

---

1 whole Dungeness crab, cleaned, with shell cut in a cross
 (about 1 pound)
2 tablespoons butter
1 shallot, thinly sliced
1 lemon, cut into wedges

●Start coals in grill or preheat broiler. In a saucepan, melt butter over medium heat until foamy. Add shallots and sauté until pale golden, about 4 minutes. Squeeze in lemon juice, a slice at a time, until sauce is tangy but not overwhelmingly acid. Keep sauce warm over lowest possible heat. Place crab on grill or under broiler, cut-side up, and cook for 10 to 12 minutes (cooked crab) or up to 20 minutes (raw crab). Baste several times by tipping a teaspoon of sauce into shell through the cross. When done, the crab meat will be opaque and slightly firm, and the underside of the shell will be well browned. Cut crab in two (use scissors or shears) and pass any remaining sauce and the lemon wedges.

crab cut for basting

Roquefort Crab with Green Peppercorn Sauce

Whether baked in snazzy shell-shaped individual casseroles or Pyrex custard cups, this entrée is lovely to look at and splendid to eat. It takes only minutes to prepare, especially if the crab meat is precooked and cleaned. If you know of no local source of fresh crab, try the frozen kind. When thawed, it ought to have a firm, tender texture; a pleasant, mild scent; and a fresh flavor. Flaccid texture and tired taste may indicate poor storage practices. When you find a good brand, try this entrée. The glossy green peppercorn sauce puffs beneath the broiler, as light and cloudy as a soufflé. Slender wands of asparagus, bound with ribbons of red pepper and drizzled with blueberry vinaigrette, are a suitably elegant accompaniment, as is a salad sparked with shreds of radicchio and young sorrel, tiny hot rolls, and a glass of dark stout or a crisp chardonnay.

½ teaspoon butter
8 ounces *or* 1 cup cooked crab meat
1 to 2 ounces Roquefort cheese
1 egg
2 tablespoons yogurt *or* sour cream
2 to 3 teaspoons grated Asiago *or* Parmesan cheese
½ teaspoon green peppercorns

●Preheat broiler. Butter the dishes, then put half the crab into each. Sprinkle on Roquefort. Separate egg, reserving yolk for another dish. Beat or whisk egg white until stiff but not dry. Gently stir yogurt and cheese into egg white. Drain vinegar from peppercorns over crab. Fold peppercorns into egg white. Spoon sauce over crab, smoothing to cover crab meat completely. Broil for 4 to 6 minutes until puffed and browned. Serve hot.

Crab with Enoki Mushrooms

Northwesterners deeply appreciate their plentiful and succulent local shellfish, among which Dungeness crab is justly famous. The flavor is rich and delicate and faintly sweet, well complemented by the satiny, crisp enoki mushrooms. The buttery broth is plumped out with cream and warmed with the gentle bite of green peppercorns, which pop in vinegary little explosions as you eat them. Many bakeries offer freshly made puff pastry—you can find patty shells, swan cups, and other pleasant forms, though the frozen kinds are tasty too. Serve thick slices of ripe tomatoes, sprinkled with minced basil and drizzled with balsamic vinegar for a spicy-tart accompaniment. A dolcetto, one of the dry Orvieto whites, or a blush suit this meal.

---

2 to 4 puff pastry patty shells
1 tablespoon butter
3 shallots, thinly sliced
1 red sweet pepper, cut into thin strips
12 ounces cooked crab meat
1 teaspoon green peppercorns in vinegar
3½ ounces enoki mushrooms (1 packet), bases trimmed
1 teaspoon shoyu (Japanese soy sauce)

●Preheat oven to 425 degrees. Put patty shells on a baking sheet and bake for 20 minutes (or follow directions, if packaged). In a saucepan, melt butter over medium-high heat until foamy. Stir in shallots and peppers; cook gently for 5 minutes. Add crab and peppercorns (along with their vinegar); cover pan, reduce heat to medium, and simmer until bubbling hot. Remove patty shell tops and return shells to oven. Add enoki mushrooms to crab and cook for 1 minute, then add shoyu and heat until hot through. Fill patty shells with crab mixture and serve at once.

enoki mushrooms

Red Peppers Stuffed with Crab

When it's too hot to fire up the oven, this makes a beautiful summer salad—the red cups stuffed with pink crab, white rice flecked with herbs, and bits of olives. It is especially good made with wild rice; serve rice earlier in the week with salmon or game hens, and make enough extra to have leftovers for this dish. The strongly flavored Spanish or Greek olives do more for any dish than the bland, salty kind, especially if packed in good olive oil. Crusty rolls, some sharp cheeses, a bowl of fruit, and a pinot noir make a simple and refreshing meal.

---

2 large red sweet peppers
½ cup cooked rice *or*
   ¼ cup uncooked
4 ounces fresh mozzarella cheese, cubed
2 teaspoons fresh fennel leaves, minced
6 to 8 olives in their oil
1 lemon, juiced plus grated peel
8 ounces *or* 1 cup cooked crab meat
1 ounce grated Parmesan *or* pecorino cheese

●Slice off tops of peppers at the shoulder. Remove core and seeds. In a large pan, bring lightly salted water to boil. Add peppers and cook for 5 minutes; drain. If using uncooked rice, cook it. Put cooked rice into a mixing bowl. Add mozzarella to rice. Add fennel, olives and their oil, 1 teaspoon lemon peel, and 2 tablespoons juice to rice. Rinse crab meat briefly and toss with rice. Stuff peppers with the rice mixture, top with cheese. Place in steamer basket and steam for 20 minutes. Serve hot or at room temperature.

Crab Bisque

An unabashedly sumptuous soup, rich enough to be a whole, extravagant meal in itself. Don't use cooking sherry; splurge on the best sipping sherry you can find, and you will definitely notice the difference. You won't want much else at this feast, just a simple salad of romaine, butter lettuce, and green onions dressed up with herbed croutons and a vinaigrette seasoned with Dijon mustard. Drink a porter or stout, or an Orvieto.

---

2 to 3 teaspoons butter
1 red sweet pepper, seeded and cut into squares
1 medium onion, chopped
¼ cup slivered Florence fennel (1 small bulb),
    plus leaves for garnish
1 teaspoon green peppercorns
1 to 2 tablespoons dry oloroso sherry
1 pound cooked crab meat
1 cup heavy cream

●In a heavy saucepan, melt 2 teaspoons butter over medium heat. Add pepper, onion, and fennel; stir and cook for 5 to 6 minutes. Add 1 cup water, peppercorns, and sherry; simmer until vegetables are soft, about 15 minutes. Bring soup to boil, reduce heat, add crab, cream, and a bit of butter, heat through until just hot and butter is melted, but never let soup boil. Garnish with sprigs of fennel. Serve at once, very hot.

Florence fennel

Crab Salad

In the Northwest, the only way to get fresh crab in the summer is to catch it yourself. However, the quality and availability of flash-frozen crab is improving as consumer demand increases. Flash-freezing is a process by which crab and fish are coated with ice-water and frozen almost instantly; this seals in the flavor and keeps out odors. The result is high-quality texture and taste. This salad relies on Chinese greens for much of its snap. Though all are mustard greens, some, such as pak choy, are mild, crunchy, and slightly sweet, while joi choy has a gentle, peppery bite. Try small bunches of several types to get the combination you prefer. Have rolls, a dry chardonnay, or an ale of character to make a meal of it.

---

2 cups mustard greens, chopped
1 grapefruit, peeled and sectioned
1½ cups cooked crab meat
2 tablespoons light olive *or* vegetable oil
1 to 2 tablespoons rice vinegar
1 tablespoon mirin (sweet sake)
2 tablespoons pine nuts, toasted

●Arrange mustard greens in a salad bowl. Top with grapefruit sections and crab. Blend oil, vinegar, and mirin. Pour dressing over salad and toss gently. Sprinkle pine nuts over all and serve at once (at room temperature for best flavor).

Butter Clam Hash

This is something of a hybrid between the clam cakes of New England and the everlasting beef hash so often featured on pioneer menus. In the Northwest, we prefer the tender, slightly sweet, native butter clams, but any kind will do. A mixed salad of greens—shredded cabbage, radishes, and green onions—tossed with a citrusy dressing, and a glass of white Bordeaux or a smooth ale will round things out nicely.

---

2 potatoes, cut into 1-inch cubes
1 tablespoon butter
1 medium onion, chopped
1 cup clams
1 tablespoon chopped fresh flat Italian parsley *or*
   1 teaspoon dried
½ teaspoon freshly ground pepper or to taste
2 to 3 teaspoons tarragon *or* wine vinegar

●In a large saucepan, bring salted water to boil. Add potatoes and cook until tender, about 12 minutes; drain. In a small, heavy skillet, heat 1 tablespoon butter over medium heat until foamy. Add potatoes and onion; cook for 4 to 5 minutes until just soft. Add clams, parsley, and pepper. Cook over medium-low heat without stirring for 15 to 20 minutes, until golden crust forms on bottom of pan. Cut hash in half, slide onto plates, crust-side up, sprinkle with vinegar, and serve very hot.

Capelli d'Angelo with Clam Sauce

Capelli d'Angelo—angel's hair pasta—cooks in about two minutes when fresh, and only slightly longer when dry. Start the sauce first, using chopped fresh clams when available, or making do with clams canned in their own broth. Whipped cream (sometimes flavored with grated horseradish) is a traditional accompaniment to clam broth in New England. Here, white wine, parsley, and lovage (celery greens may be substituted) combine in the green-flecked, peppery broth, which thickens as the whipped cream melts. Freshly ground pepper makes a world of difference to this and nearly any recipe, for the hot aroma and pungent essence of pepper is largely missing from the preground stuff. Salad dressed with a shallot vinaigrette, warm garlic rolls, and a Soave or a sturdy ale will make a pleasant meal of it.

---

1 tablespoon butter
1 white onion, cut into thin half-moon slices
1 pint chopped clams in broth *or*
   6 to 8 ounces canned clams in clam broth
1 teaspoon freshly ground black pepper
¼ cup dry white wine
1 tablespoon chopped lovage *or* celery leaves
8 ounces fresh pasta *or*
   4 ounces dry
¼ cup heavy cream, whipped

●In a saucepan, heat butter over medium heat. Add onion and sauté for 3 to 5 minutes, until barely tender. Add clams and cook for 2 minutes. Stir in ⅓ cup broth, pepper, wine, and herbs; simmer briskly for 10 to 12 minutes, until sauce is reduced by about half. Cook pasta while sauce is simmering. Spoon some over each portion of pasta, top with whipped cream, and serve at once.

Clam Chowder

Digging clams is a pleasant summer pastime on both coasts—when the tides aren't red, the beaches aren't polluted, and the real world of the twentieth century is otherwise kept in abeyance. Raw or cooked and cleaned, clams are generally sold by the pint, and in their own juices, called clam liqueur or nectar. My father's traditional Cape Cod clam chowder started with a chunk of salt pork, neatly cubed and slowly fried until crisp—what New Englanders call "trying." Here, lean bacon replaces the salt pork, and the addition of mushrooms will equally horrify old-school cooks. Have corn on the cob, a salad, and pass a bowl of oyster crackers with the soup.

3 slices lean bacon, chopped
1 medium yellow onion, chopped
2 medium potatoes, diced
1 cup mushrooms, thickly sliced
1 cup clams, cleaned and chopped *or*
   1 7-ounce can chopped
2 cups milk
1 teaspoon freshly ground black pepper

●In a heavy 1½-quart saucepan, cook bacon over medium heat until crisp. Remove and drain bacon on paper towels, leaving drippings in pan. Add onions, potatoes, and mushrooms; stir to coat with drippings, cover pan, and cook until onions are soft, 5 to 6 minutes. Add clam nectar with enough water to equal ½ cup if needed. Bring to a boil, then reduce heat and simmer until potatoes are tender, 6 to 8 minutes. Add clams; stir and cook for 2 to 3 minutes. Add milk and pepper; cook over medium heat, stirring occasionally, until warmed through. Sprinkle bacon on each portion for garnish.

Skewered Scallops

Fresh or frozen, scallops ought to have a slight, almost sweet flavor and a firm, yielding texture. Tough or rubbery scallops may actually have been stamped out of skate (though skate can be tender, the quality is variable and seldom worth top dollar). The tiny calico scallops—there may be well over a hundred of them to the pound—are generally the most expensive. However, they are not markedly different from the little bay scallops or the heftier deep-sea scallops, especially after they have been frozen and thawed. The larger scallops are more convenient to use in recipes like this one, where they are threaded on skewers. Scallops quickly toughen and dry if cooked too long (more than a minute or two) or over too great a heat. Here, scallops are rolled in soft crumbs and interwoven with lean bacon strips to keep them moist and flavorful. Broil them in the oven or grill them on the hibachi for a fall picnic par excellence. Toss a bowl of mustard greens with a garlic-and-blueberry vinaigrette, pass a bowl of warm rice, and crack a bottle of chenin blanc or an ale to round things out.

---

1 slice soft bread, crumbed
1 tablespoon grated Romano *or* Parmesan cheese
½ teaspoon freshly ground white pepper
1 tablespoon olive oil
8 ounces sea scallops
6 slices lean bacon
12 cherry tomatoes

●In a bowl combine bread crumbs, cheese, and pepper. Pour oil into another small bowl or plate. Roll scallops in oil, then in crumb mixture. Stick skewer through one end of bacon strip, add a cherry tomato, pass bacon over and skewer it again, add a scallop, thread bacon again and so on, ending with bacon and tomato. Repeat with each strip of bacon for a total of six skewers. Broil or grill quite close to the heat for 1 to 2 minutes a side, turning several times. Serve at once, very hot.

skewered scallops

Scallops with Cardamom Orange Rice

This entrée will vie in fragrance with the garden flowers on a summery evening. It is as pretty as it is good—the rice flecked green, gold, and orange and studded with ivory scallops. Basmati rice, an Indian specialty, has a warm, nutlike aroma. When it is properly stored, the best qualities of basmati rice are intensified and refined, so aged basmati is highly prized and amazingly expensive. Gilded in butter, the raw grains toast to pale gold and the flavor, always more distinctive than that of ordinary rice, deepens as well. Serve this entrée with steamed fingerling carrots or infant beets dressed in cranberry vinaigrette and cupped in leaves of ruby lettuce. Chill a bottle of dry muscat or chenin blanc, and enjoy a highly civilized meal.

½ cup uncooked basmati rice
1 tablespoon butter
6 green or white cardamom pods
1 orange, juiced plus grated peel
1 tablespoon chopped fresh chives
8 ounces scallops
1 yellow sweet pepper, coarsely grated or finely chopped

●Rinse rice in a sieve, drain. In a heavy saucepan, melt 2 teaspoons butter over medium heat. Add 5 cardamom pods, 2 teaspoons orange peel, rice, and 2 teaspoons chives. Sauté 3 to 5 minutes until faintly golden. Then add 1¼ cups lightly salted water. Bring to a boil, cover pan, reduce heat, and simmer for 15 minutes. Remove cover and cook for another 10 minutes, while you prepare scallops. Rinse scallops and pat dry. In another frying pan, heat remaining butter over medium heat until foamy. Add pepper, remaining cardamom pod and remaining chives; sauté for 5 minutes. Add ½ teaspoon peel and all the orange juice. Bring to a quick boil; add scallops, and cook for 2 minutes until opaque. Spoon scallops and sauce over rice. Serve at once.

Lemon Fettuccine with Scallops and Three Peppers

There is a marvelous variety of pasta in the markets these days—dozens of shapes and flavors available fresh, dried, or frozen. In this recipe, lemon-flavored fettuccine is tossed with scallops and tricolored pepper confetti for a beautiful presentation. If you can't find lemon pasta, try adding several strips of lemon peel to the pasta water, or grate a teaspoon or so of lemon zest into the sauce. If you use regular chives, you might want to press a small clove of garlic into the sauce for that subtle bite. When using dried herbs, start with half the suggested amount and increase to taste. Serve with a mixed green salad enriched with mushrooms and pine nuts, warm garlic bread, and a glass of verdicchio, a soft Orvieto, or a golden pinot bianco.

---

8 ounces fresh lemon pasta *or*
 4 ounces dry
8 ounces scallops
2 to 3 teaspoons butter
½ yellow sweet pepper, cut into small dice
½ red sweet pepper, cut into small dice
½ purple or green sweet pepper, cut into small dice
2 teaspoons chopped fresh fennel leaves
1 tablespoon chopped fresh garlic chives

●Start pasta water.* Rinse scallops briefly; set aside. Heat half the butter over medium heat until foamy. Stir in pepper confetti and herbs; cook, partially covered, for 3 to 5 minutes until barely soft. Add scallops; cook and stir for 1 to 2 minutes. Drain pasta, toss with remaining butter, and top with sauce. Serve at once.
  *Fresh pasta takes only a few minutes to cook and should be added when you put the scallops in the pan; dried pasta will take a little longer, so adjust timing accordingly.

Hot Scallop Salad with Blood Oranges

Cut into a blood or moro orange and the juice will spurt out as red as blood. The fruit is highly prized in Italy, partly because the juice reminds the faithful of the blood of Christ, but also because it is exceptionally beautiful and tasty. The rind may show a faint marking or two—a sullen mottling of dark red—but the flesh of the fruit shimmers like stained glass, ruby, tawny port, amber, and auburn. Blood oranges are now grown in California and Florida, with more coming in from Chile during the winter, so they appear frequently in supermarkets. Here, sunset-toned orange fans add sparkle to a hot scallop dressing. (Tangerines, satsumas, or grapefruit also work.) Serve hot scones or herb rolls, a piece of Stilton or buttery Roquefort, some apples—Cox's orange pippins or Granny Smiths—and a gentle dolcetto or a distinctive ale.

---

1 head buttercrunch or any lettuce, torn into small pieces
1 tablespoon olive oil
2 shallot bulbs, peeled and thinly sliced
8 ounces scallops
8 ounces jícama, peeled and sliced into 1- x 2-inch strips
2 blood oranges, peeled and cut into fans
1 avocado, peeled and thinly sliced
2 tablespoons balsamic vinegar

●Spin or pat lettuce dry, tear into small pieces and arrange in a salad bowl. In a sauté pan or skillet, heat oil over medium heat. Add shallots and cook 3 to 4 minutes. Add scallops; stir and cook for 1 minute. Add jícama, oranges, avocado, and vinegar; cover and cook for 2 to 3 minutes just until hot through. Heap on top of lettuce, serve at once.

jícama

Scallop and Feijoa Salad

Tender, tiny scallops can be poached in about a minute, so this attractive, aromatic salad requires the barest minimum of cooking, a boon when hot weather makes the kitchen uninviting. Feijoa may be more familiar as pineapple guava (though it is related to neither and is now marketed almost exclusively under its own name). Feijoa (pronounced fay-HO-ah) looks like an undersized avocado and has the texture of a firm pear; when ripe, the center is like vanilla custard. Feijoa has a complex flavor; to my mind it is similar to strawberries with undertones of mint and overtones of lime. My husband disagrees, saying it tastes exactly like Ben-Gay. We agree that its fragrance is powerfully appealing. Here, slices of feijoa provide a tangy, tart counterpoint to a smooth, pale green dressing of mint and garlic thickened with crème fraîche. A baguette, ripe figs, and a glass of white Burgundy or dry riesling are all you need to add.

---

1 bunch mustard greens *or* spinach, chopped
2 feijoa, peeled and thickly sliced
⅓ cup dry white wine
2 cloves garlic, sliced
8 ounces scallops
2 tablespoons minced fresh mint
¼ cup crème fraîche *or* sour cream
¼ cup almonds, toasted and chopped

●Arrange mustard greens in a salad bowl. Heap feijoa on top. In a saucepan, bring wine and garlic to a boil over high heat. Add scallops; reduce heat to medium and simmer, turning once, for 1 to 2 minutes or until scallops are opaque. Remove scallops to the salad bowl using a slotted spoon. Pour cooking liquid into blender or food processor, add mint, crème fraîche, and 2 tablespoons of almonds; blend briefly. Pour dressing over salad, and top with remaining almonds. Serve at room temperature for fullest flavor.

Mussels Gratinée

Fresh or saltwater mussels are every bit as delicious as clams and oysters. The same health precautions must apply, since polluted waters and red tides are sadly common these days. By the time mussels hit the supermarket, they usually have been cleaned, but if not, scrub the shells with a stiff fingernail brush and pull off lingering bits of seaweed or beard. Live mussels, like clams, shut tightly when touched; limp or easily opened ones should be discarded. Whether presented in individual gratinée dishes, or custard cups, this browned and bubbling dish will make a satisfying entrée for shellfish fans. Endive and grapefruit salad with a shallot vinaigrette, hot rolls, and a glass of pale golden Soave make a pleasant, small feast.

---

24 live mussels, cleaned
1 tablespoon butter
1 slice bread, crumbled
1 shallot, chopped
½ teaspoon green peppercorns
2 teaspoons chopped fresh chives
1 teaspoon chopped fresh cilantro
1 tablespoon shredded Gruyère cheese

●Steam mussels for 6 to 8 minutes, discarding any that fail to open. Shell cooked mussels. Butter gratinée dishes and pile half the mussels in each. In a small pan, heat remaining butter over medium heat. Add bread crumbs and shallots and brown. Add peppercorns and herbs; toss together and spread over mussels. Sprinkle cheese on top and broil for 3 to 5 minutes until hot and browned. Serve at once.

Mussels in Pesto Sauce

Steamed mussels are usually far less expensive than other shellfish, and inland, local freshwater mussels may be available where seafood is unreliable. Happily, mussel farms are springing up in many parts of the country, ensuring a steady supply of wholesome, unpolluted mussels. Thanks to clever greenhouse growers, fresh basil may be had even in winter. Though it may lack the full, resonating savor of summer, it provides a lively, fresh flavor to such dishes as this. The sauce is thinner than most pestos, because it relies on dry white wine rather than lashings of olive oil. Use the finest, fruitiest oil you can afford, since even a small amount can contribute significant flavor if the quality is good. Steamed broad beans or spears of romanesco broccoli drizzled with warm blueberry vinegar and melted butter are outstanding adjuncts to this meal, as is a glass of crisp semillon or a brisk ale.

---

18 live mussels, cleaned
1 tablespoon plus 1 teaspoon olive oil
2 cloves garlic, chopped
1 bunch fresh basil, chopped
2 tablespoons grated Parmesan cheese
2 tablespoons pine nuts, toasted
½ cup dry white wine
8 ounces fresh shell pasta *or*
   4 ounces dry

●Steam mussels for 6 to 8 minutes, discarding any that fail to open. Start pasta water. In blender or food processor, combine 1 tablespoon olive oil, garlic, basil, 1 tablespoon cheese, 1 tablespoon pine nuts, and wine. Blend to a smooth, thin paste, adding up to ¼ cup water if needed. Add pasta to boiling water. As it cooks, heat shelled mussels in remaining oil for 3 to 4 minutes. Add pesto sauce and simmer gently until pasta is cooked to your taste. Drain pasta. Divide pasta onto plates, ladle sauce over each portion, and sprinkle remaining pine nuts and cheese over each. Serve at once.

Steamed Mussel Soup

The earliest settlers of the West Coast loved mussels, as evidenced by the ample shell heaps unearthed in every coastal archaeological dig. Later, immigrant Asians and transplanted Easterners combed western beaches for mussels, which found their way into scores of pioneer recipes. Modern beachcombers also know the joys of eating freshly gathered mussels. Steamed over an open fire, seasoned with garlic and wine, they are best savored with starlight and the swooshing surf for background. Here, steamed mussels decorate a robust soup, thick with rice and chunks of tomato and fragrant with fresh sage. Out of season, a can of diced tomatoes will give more and better flavor than pallid hothouse tomatoes. Serve this in broad, flat soup plates, so the dramatic blue-black shells contrast handsomely with the deep red tomatoes. Cornbread or wheat rolls, small salads with a garlicky vinaigrette, and a crisp ale or dry sauvignon blanc will make a splendid meal.

---

16 live mussels, cleaned
6 ripe tomatoes, diced
2 teaspoons olive oil
1 clove garlic, mashed
1 teaspoon chopped fresh sage *or*
  ½ teaspoon dried
½ cup dry white wine
3 tablespoons rice
½ teaspoon capers

●Steam mussels for 6 to 8 minutes, discarding any that fail to open. In a saucepan, heat oil over medium heat. Add tomatoes with their juice and cook until soft. Add garlic, sage, wine, and rice (and a shake of salt, if you wish); cover and simmer for 12 to 15 minutes, until rice is tender. Stir in capers. Spoon soup into bowls, dividing mussels equally between each bowl. Serve at once.

Oyster Omelet

Oyster omelets have been a San Francisco specialty for over a century, so popular that they contributed to the disappearance of the native oyster. Olympias have the best flavor, but any fresh oysters will do fine. This is a scaled-down version of the old classic, which called for more butter and cream than we are accustomed to eating at one sitting. But even in modified form, it will make lipid lovers happy while scandalizing ardent dieters. Have hot scones, a green salad with a citrus dressing, and a glass of Chablis or a young Beaujolais.

---

5 to 6 teaspoons butter
1 tablespoon whole wheat pastry flour
½ cup heavy cream
½ pint shucked fresh oysters
½ teaspoon pepper
1 to 2 teaspoons dry sherry
1 tablespoon grated Romano *or* Parmesan cheese
3 eggs

●In a heavy saucepan, melt 1 tablespoon butter over medium heat. Stir in flour and cook for 1 minute. Slowly add cream, stirring all the while. Continue cooking and stirring until thick (5 to 6 minutes). Add oysters with their liquid, pepper, sherry, and 2 teaspoons cheese. Stir and reduce heat to warm. Whisk eggs gently with 3 tablespoons water. In an omelet pan or heavy frying pan, heat butter over medium heat until foamy. Add eggs and reduce heat to medium low. Tilt pan and raise sides of omelet to let egg mixture run underneath, until omelet is barely set. Increase heat to medium, shaking pan to loosen omelet (add butter if it sticks), and cook for 2 minutes. Spoon the filling over the omelet, fold, sprinkle with remaining cheese, and serve.

Oyster Stew

To Nantucket folks, oyster stew means oysters poached in their own liqueur, then slid into a bath of warm heavy cream. Staunch traditionalists will probably pop a gusset at the thought of adding sweet vegetables, but this is really only a modification of an old friend—corn chowder. Fresh oysters are unbeatable when they are safe to eat (an awful thing to have to say). In the Northwest, pollution and overharvesting cause frequent shortages of our tiny (there are well over a hundred to a pint), native Olympia oysters—so delectable, many otherwise restrained people may unblushingly eat that same pint at one go. The giant Willapas, actually Japanese oysters first imported at the turn of the century, are more than a mouthful for the stoutest eater, for there may be as few as four in a pint. Many oysters, even canned oysters will do in this stew. Serve up some warm biscuits or cornbread, a simple salad and a mild lager with this one.

---

2 tablespoons butter
1 medium yellow onion, chopped
1 medium sweet potato, diced
½ cup fresh cut corn, cut from 1 large ear *or* frozen
1 pint oysters in their own juices (liqueur), chopped if large
2 cups milk *or* half-and-half
½ teaspoon black pepper
2 tablespoons shredded Asiago *or* Parmesan cheese

●In a saucepan, heat butter over medium heat until foamy. Add onion and potato; cook until soft, 5 to 6 minutes. Add oyster liqueur with enough water to cover vegetables. Bring to a boil, reduce heat, cover pan, and simmer until sweet potatoes are tender, about 6 to 8 minutes. Add corn and oysters and simmer for another 5 to 6 minutes, until the oysters' edges begin to curl. Pour in milk and add pepper. Heat through and serve at once, topped with cheese.

Squid in Gin and Ginger

Popular before the Second World War, this West Coast war horse still tastes fresh and sassy to modern palates. The overall influence is Asian, but given that California twist, it becomes a distinctly American hybrid. If the sesame flavor is too potent for your taste, use plain vegetable oil, adding just a tad of the sesame oil—it is an intense flavoring. A small mesh strainer or tea ball works well when it's time to separate the gin from the ginger—start by adding the smaller amount of gin and adjust to taste. Balls of sticky rice would be appropriate, and a salad of mustard greens, slivered cabbage, and radishes needs only a dressing of orange juice, sesame oil, and shoyu to tie it all together. Have cold beer or ale with this one.

---

8 ounces squid tubes
4 tablespoons gin
1 inch gingerroot, peeled and grated or minced
1 teaspoon sesame oil
12 snow peas, trimmed
3 green onions, sliced into large diagonals
1 to 2 teaspoons shoyu (Japanese soy sauce)

●Rinse squid tubes well, inside and out; pat dry. Cut in ¼-inch rings and marinate in gin. Add ginger to gin. In a heavy frying pan or wok, heat oil over medium-high heat. Toss in snow peas and onions and cook for 1 to 2 minutes. Drain marinade off squid; reserve. Add squid rings and ginger to vegetables. Cook and stir for 2 to 3 minutes. Add 1 to 2 tablespoons gin and shoyu; cook for 1 minute. Serve hot.

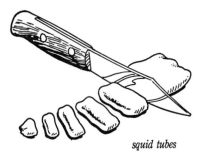

squid tubes

Squid Rings with Rotini

Well-cooked, squid is softly chewy and mildly flavored. When overcooked, it has all the textural appeal of a plate full of rubber bands. This happens so fast that first-time squid cookers are advised to pay careful attention, tasting every minute or so. Don't be put off, for once you have the hang of it, you will recognize the exact moment when squid achieves perfection; the pale flesh turns a flatter white, the edges begin to curl, and each band becomes slightly puffed. Try it for yourself a time or two before serving squid to guests—if the trial batch is a success, marinate it in olive oil, lemon juice, and minced garlic and serve it chilled as an antipasto. This Italian entrée is so quickly made that you can have it on the table in twenty minutes. Steamed or lightly sautéed green beans; a salad of greens, orange sections, and sweet onion rings; and garlic bread sticks round things out, as will a grignolino, a Gavi, or a bright Arneis.

---

8 ounces squid tubes
1 tablespoon olive oil
2 cloves garlic
1 small golden (summer) squash, sliced into thin wheels
1 large ripe tomato, dried (reserving juice)
2 sprigs fresh oregano, chopped *or*
  1 teaspoon dried
8 ounces fresh vegetable rotini *or*
  4 ounces dry
1 tablespoon shredded Parmesan cheese

●Heat water for rotini. Rinse squid tubes well, inside and out. Drain and pat dry. Slice into ½-inch rings; set aside. In a frying pan, heat oil over medium heat. Add whole garlic. Cook until golden brown, then remove and discard. As soon as pasta goes in boiling water, put squid rings in oil, stirring to coat. Add squash and cook for 1 minute. Add tomato with juice and oregano. Cook quickly (about 1 minute), stirring often, until hot through. When pasta is done, drain well and serve in bowls. Pour sauce over pasta, sprinkle on cheese, and serve.

Squid and Shrimp Salad

In Italy, this salad is served from the little cafés—often only a single table with an umbrella—that border the sandy beaches of Calabria. The usual accompaniment is a searing peperonata too stout for northern taste buds. It brings tears to all eyes; for the chef, tears are a sign of his tremendous amusement, for the partaker, they mean pain. Make a gentle peperonata out of three colors of sweet peppers, and offer panini (crusty round rolls) to sop up the sauces. Begin with thick slices of cantaloupe draped with thin cuts of prosciutto and end with a bowl of cherries, blueberries, and raspberries set over a larger bowl of crushed ice. Drink a luscious trebbiano, a Frascati, or a crisp verdicchio.

---

8 ounces squid tubes
2 tablespoons olive oil
1 lemon, juiced plus grated peel
1 tablespoon minced fresh basil
2 cloves garlic, pressed
2 medium tomatoes, diced to equal 1 cup (reserve juice)
4 ounces cooked shrimp
1 ounce grated Asiago *or* Parmesan cheese

●Rinse squid tubes well, inside and out. In a large pan, bring salted water to boil. Drop in squid and cook for 1 to 2 minutes until opaque and curling. Drain well and reserve. Blend oil, lemon juice, 1 teaspoon lemon peel, basil, and garlic in a bowl. Add tomatoes and their juice. Slice the cooled squid into ½-inch rings. Add squid and shrimp to dressing and toss. Sprinkle cheese over all, chill or serve at once.

$\mathcal{P}$oultry

91   Roasted Lemon Chicken

92   Mushroom-stuffed Chicken Breasts

93   Chicken Caribbe

94   Tomatillo Chicken

95   Thai Banana Chicken

96   Chicken in White Burgundy

97   Spicy Cardamom Chicken

98   Chicken with Plums and Ginger

99   Chicken in Cherry Ale

100   Chicken Orangerie

101   Chile Cream Chicken

102   Coconut Chicken with Two Corianders

103   Jícama and Chicken Soup

104   Liver, Shrimp, and Bacon in Pepper Sauce

105   Chicken Livers with Wild Rice and Almonds

106   Vermicelli with Liver and Pine Nuts

107   Turkey El Café

108   Grilled Turkey Breast with Rhubarb Sauce

109   Turkey Cutlets with Horseradish Cream

110   Turkey Kebabs with Fresh Pineapple

111   Gooseberry-glazed Game Hens with Sage Stuffing

112   Raspberry Game Hens

113   Game Hens with Bacon and Beans

114   Game Hens Perugino

Roasted Lemon Chicken

Spring chickens are small and tender, and even the kind labeled as fryers are delectable when roasted by this classic Italian method. This technique, fast and simple, results in moist, tender meat and crackling skin studded with bits of toasty garlic. The more you baste, the moister the skin will be. If you want to get the flavorful basting mixture into the meat while keeping the skin crisp, make a few slits in the skin and use a baster to whoosh some of the juices over the breast. The potatoes are also glazed with the pan drippings; they puff and turn golden brown on the outside and remain soft and marvelously flavored on the inside. Serve with steamed small carrots and wide red pepper strips tossed with butter, chives, and poppy seeds, and a green salad zipped up with mustard greens. A cool Frascati or an Orvieto will soothe frazzled nerves as you dine in style.

---

1 whole chicken, about 3 pounds
1 tablespoon olive oil
1 tablespoon butter
2 large cloves garlic, pressed
1 lemon, juiced, peel reserved
½ teaspoon freshly grated nutmeg
2 potatoes, quartered lengthwise

●Rinse chicken; pat dry. In a heavy iron frying pan, heat oil and butter over medium heat until foamy. Add garlic, lemon juice, a 1- x 2-inch slice of lemon peel, and nutmeg. Add chicken to pan, breast-side up, and brush lavishly with basting mixture. Put in 350 degree oven to bake. As soon as you put chicken in oven, put potatoes into lightly salted water; parboil for 10 minutes. Drain, dip cut sides in chicken's pan juices, then set them around the chicken. Baste chicken again, return pan to oven, and bake for 30 to 40 minutes. Baste both chicken and potatoes again at least once while baking.

Mushroom-stuffed Chicken Breasts

Fat little bundles of chicken burst with sautéed mushrooms and just a bit of cream cheese, then bake in mild, fragrant balsamic vinegar to a savory finish. Though the vinegar aroma is strong, the flavor is mild. A chilled salad of peeled, thinly sliced blood oranges dressed with walnut oil and raspberry vinegar can be made ahead. An artistic stalk or two of steamed broccoli drizzled with lemon butter, and golden brown fans of butter rolls will round out the menu nicely, as will the addition of a dry chardonnay.

---

2 tablespoons butter
1 cup mushrooms, sliced
1 tablespoon cream cheese
½ teaspoon nutmeg
½ teaspoon freshly ground pepper
1 green onion, minced
1 chicken breast, skinned and boned (2 pieces)
¼ cup balsamic vinegar

●In a frying pan, heat 1½ tablespoons butter over medium heat. Add mushrooms and sauté until all liquid is absorbed, about 10 minutes; cool. Mash cream cheese with nutmeg, pepper, and green onion. Flatten chicken breasts, spoon half the mushroom mixture on each piece, put half the cream cheese on top, then loosely fold chicken sides to middle. Place chicken, seam-side down, in a small casserole dish. Pour vinegar over all, dot chicken with remaining butter, and bake, uncovered, in 350 degree oven for 25 to 30 minutes, basting at least once. Serve hot.

Chicken Caribbe

This is a very pretty dish; pink bananas, creamy orange sweet potatoes, and golden chicken are accented with flecks of lime and cilantro and sauced with heavy cream. It is quick to prepare and ineffably aromatic when brought to the table. The red-skinned sweet potatoes called "Jewel" are the sweetest, as are the solid, meaty red bananas, but any kind will be good. All you need to round out the meal is a plain green salad, rice, and warm rolls or thick slices of Anadama bread to sop up the sauce. Have a very dry white wine with this, or a crisp ale.

---

1 tablespoon butter
1 large sweet potato, peeled and sliced into ¼-inch rounds
2 red bananas (or 1 semiripe yellow one), peeled and sliced diagonally into thick pieces
1 whole chicken breast, skinned, boned, and halved
2 teaspoons chopped fresh cilantro
1 to 2 fresh chiles serraños, trimmed, seeded, and finely chopped
1 large lime, juiced (reserve 5 1-inch strips of peel)
4 tablespoons heavy cream

●Rub a 1½-quart casserole with 1 teaspoon butter; layer in sweet potatoes and top with bananas. Tuck chicken breasts in and sprinkle with cilantro and chiles. Pour lime juice over chicken and add peel. Dot with remaining butter. Bake, covered, in 350 degree oven for 35 to 40 minutes, until edges of sweet potatoes are golden and caramelized. Add cream, heat for additional 10 minutes, then serve very hot.

Tomatillo Chicken

Tomatillos give the sauce its distinctive flavor. They are a common ingredient in South American cookery and are often found in American supermarkets as well. They look like tiny green tomatoes wrapped in papery husks—gardeners will recognize their close relationship with the lantern flower (*Physalis franchetii*). Choose firm, unblemished fruit, for soft or blackish spots bode ill for the future meal. To use tomatillos, pull off the husks and rinse any stickiness away. The fruits can be used in hot sauces or fresh salsas, especially salsa verde, in which they are fragrant, tart, and indispensable. If you can't find tomatillos, you could substitute two thirds of a cup of green chile sauce or a commercial green salsa. Warm blue corn or whole wheat tortillas, a green salad, chunky with marinated baby zucchini, a dark beer, and a platter of fresh pineapple will round out the meal wonderfully.

---

1 whole chicken breast, split in half
1 lime
1 teaspoon sesame oil
2 tablespoons chopped fresh cilantro
1 tablespoon chopped fresh mint
8 tomatillos, husked, well rinsed, and quartered
¼ cup fresh salsa

●Start coals in grill. Rinse chicken, pat dry. Juice half the lime, grate peel. Cut other half in 2; spritz and rub each piece of chicken with 1 piece of lime. Brush each piece of chicken with sesame oil. Mix cilantro and mint. Sprinkle ¼ teaspoon peel and 1 teaspoon herbs on skin side of each, patting them on lightly. Let sit for 5 minutes. Grill over medium-hot coals for 12 to 14 minutes per side (rub all over with squeezed lime pieces before turning), or bake in 350 degree oven for 35 to 40 minutes, or until juices run nearly clear when chicken is pierced with a fork. Make sauce while chicken is cooking. In a saucepan, combine tomatillos, salsa, lime juice and ½ teaspoon peel, and remaining cilantro and mint over medium heat. Partially cover and simmer for 12 to 15 minutes, until tomatillos are soft. To serve, spoon sauce in a broad ribbon over each piece of cooked chicken, pass remaining sauce in a bowl.

Thai Banana Chicken

Several very ordinary ingredients are totally transformed by the addition of a few less familiar ones, like firm, red bananas, big ti leaves for wrapping (you can substitute spinach or cabbage leaves, or simply use foil), and the blazing hot Thai chiles—use a combination of milder fresh chiles if these leave you tongue-Thaied. Serve with plenty of rice, perhaps cooked with a cardamom pod or two, a salad of spinach, romaine, and green onions in a peanut-garlic dressing, and a cold ale.

1 chicken breast, skinned and boned (2 pieces)
1 tablespoon butter
½ cup chicken stock *or* chicken bouillon
½ teaspoon nutmeg
2 red bananas, halved lengthwise
1 to 3 fresh Thai chiles *or* jalapeños, seeded and chopped
4 ti leaves *or*
  1 bunch spinach

●In a frying pan, melt 2 teaspoons butter over medium-high heat. Add chicken and brown on all sides. Add stock and nutmeg and simmer, covered, for 10 minutes. Line individual casseroles with 2 ti leaves in each, criss-crossed, or with overlapping spinach leaves. Add 1 piece of chicken to each casserole and spoon 2 tablespoons of stock into each. Scatter half the chopped chiles over each. Briefly sauté bananas in remaining butter. Criss-cross bananas over chicken, fold leaves tightly over all, and bake in a 350 degree oven for 30 minutes.

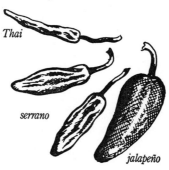

Thai

serrano

jalapeño

chiles

Chicken in White Burgundy

A whole chicken simmers in white Burgundy with bacon, tarragon, garlic, and peppers. Even a tiny chicken will feed two handily with enough left over for sandwiches. Add a handful of meat scraps and rice or noodles to the broth to make an excellent soup. The first time around, serve slices of chicken with the pepper and bacon sauce spooned over it, long grain rice or potato chunks with parsley butter, a quick sauté of turnips and carrots, and the rest of the Burgundy.

---

1 whole chicken (reserve inner bag)
4 strips bacon, cut crosswise into small strips
2 cloves garlic, mashed
1 medium onion, cut into 8 pieces
2 carrots, cut into chunks
1 teaspoon dried tarragon
1 teaspoon black peppercorns, cracked
⅔ cup white Burgundy

●Rinse chicken inside and out, pat dry. Remove livers from inner bags (discard the rest or give it to the cat). In a heavy pot or Dutch oven, cook bacon over medium-low heat for 5 to 6 minutes; increase heat to medium high. Add garlic. Add chicken and brown quickly on all sides; reduce heat to medium. Remove and discard garlic. Add onions, carrots, tarragon, and peppercorns. Dice livers into small bits and add to pot; stir and cook for 3 to 4 minutes. Pour in wine; cover and reduce heat to medium low. Simmer, covered, for 45 to 60 minutes. Serve cut up or sliced with a spoonful of sauce over each portion.

Spicy Cardamom Chicken

Thai dishes can be overwhelmingly hot, but this one is only moderately blazing. For more heat, up the number of chiles; total heat cowards can omit them altogether. Look for boxed coconut cream in the freezer section of your supermarket. It's a fascinating ingredient to experiment with; grainy yet smooth in flavor, sweet, rich, and exotic, it is often called for in Indian and Thai recipes. Frozen or canned, condensed coconut milk or cream can be substituted. Serve with shredded cabbage and carrots with a sweet-and-sour dressing and basmati or long grain rice for a quick but memorable meal. Ale or Soave Classico go well with this.

---

1 whole chicken breast, skinned, boned, and halved
1 to 2 teaspoons hot chili oil *or* peanut oil
2 cloves garlic, thinly sliced
6 cardamom pods
1 teaspoon coriander
1 to 4 fresh chiles, seeded and finely chopped
2 tablespoons coconut cream (or see above)
2 tablespoons roasted salted peanuts

● Rinse chicken, pat dry. In a large skillet, heat oil over medium heat. Add garlic, cardamom and coriander; cook for 3 to 4 minutes. Add chicken and brown lightly on all sides. Add chiles and stir-fry for 2 to 3 minutes. Add up to ½ cup water and simmer for 12 to 15 minutes. Stir in coconut cream (if you use stiff paste-forms, or if you use hard blocks, cut into chunks first, then add and stir until melted). Add up to ½ cup more water as needed to thin sauce to the consistency of cream (this will depend on the form of coconut cream used). Heat through, remove cardamom pods, and serve hot with peanuts scattered on top.

Chicken with Plums and Ginger

When tiny Damson plums hit the market late in summer, this is a splendid way to enjoy them—warmed until their juices run, but still plump and firm. Greengages or Italian prune plums have a similar tart-sweet flavor. Fresh ginger and garlic bring heat and depth to modify the intense flavor of the plums in a sauce reminiscent of unsweetened Scandinavian fruit soups. Crème fraîche lightens the sauce to a vivid pink, making it as beautiful as it is flavorful. Dark green spinach and romaine salad brightened with a red sweet pepper confetti vinaigrette, nut-scented basmati rice, and a dry blush wine round out this elegant meal.

---

1 whole chicken breast, skinned and split in half
1 tablespoon butter
2 cloves garlic, pressed
1½ inches gingerroot, peeled and minced
1 cup plums, halved and stoned
¼ cup crème fraîche *or* sour cream

●Rinse chicken, pat dry. In a frying pan, heat butter over medium heat. Add chicken and brown lightly. Add garlic and ginger and sizzle for 5 minutes, then roll chicken to cover with bits of ginger. Add ½ cup water and bring to a boil; reduce heat, cover pan, and simmer for 15 to 20 minutes, until chicken is fork-tender. Add plums and heat through for 2 to 3 minutes. Stir in crème fraîche and serve at once, spooning sauce over each portion.

Chicken in Cherry Ale

This is a pretty dish to set amid flowers on a summery table. The key ingredient is the ale; it is brewed in Belgium, first as a traditional lambic beer, using barley and wheat, and selected wild or natural yeasts. The ale is aged in oak barrels. The introduction of ripe cherries initiates a second fermentation. The result is silky, subtle, and dry, more like a fine champagne than a beer. Once you find the ale, the rest is easy, especially if you have a cherry stoner (use one if you can, and keep the cherries whole). A dry white wine can be substituted for the ale in a pinch. Serve a salad of youthful spinach, oakleaf and buttercrunch lettuces, dressed with mustard vinaigrette; basmati rice to sop up the sauce; and, of course, more cherry ale.

---

1 tablespoon butter
¼ cup hazelnuts, chopped
1 whole chicken breast, skinned, boned, and halved
6 ounces lambic cherry ale
8 ounces cherries, rinsed and stoned (reserve a few whole pairs on stems)
½ teaspoon fresh minced thyme *or*
  ¼ teaspoon dried
¼ cup crème fraîche *or* sour cream

●In a saucepan, melt butter over medium heat until foamy. Stir in nuts; sauté until golden, about 5 minutes. Add chicken and brown quickly on all sides. Pour in ale; cover and simmer for 10 minutes. Add cherries and thyme to chicken; uncover and cook an additional 3 to 5 minutes, until cherries are hot through. Remove chicken with tongs and arrange on 2 plates. Fish out cherries with a slotted spoon and tuck half to one side of each chicken piece. Keep plates warm in heated oven while you finish sauce. To pan juices, add crème fraîche; stir over medium heat, until sauce is bubbling and cream is melted. Pour onto plate beside chicken and garnish with fresh cherries.

Chicken Orangerie

Skin the chicken breasts so that the silky combination of orange juice, tarragon, wine, and cream penetrates the meat. Big eaters may want to double the recipe using a whole, cut-up chicken. If you prefer, use black pepper rather than white for a more pronounced bite. Fingerling carrots glazed with ginger and honey are nice with this. For a tart contrast, try a lemon-sesame dressing on spinach greens with a handful of toasted sesame seeds for extra crunch. Start with oysters or steamer clams and a Pouilly-Fuissé. To serve with the meal, consider a California chardonnay or white Côtes du Rhône.

---

1 tablespoon butter
1 whole chicken breast, skinned, boned, and split in half
½ teaspoon dry tarragon
2 tablespoons orange juice concentrate
½ teaspoon white pepper
½ cup white wine
½ cup heavy cream

●In a heavy frying pan, heat butter over medium-high heat. Add chicken and brown quickly on all sides. Add tarragon and cook for 3 to 5 minutes. Add orange juice, pepper, and wine. Partially cover and simmer for 15 to 20 minutes until chicken is tender. Remove meat to warm plates. Heat pan juices until bubbling; stir and cook, until sauce is reduced by half. Add cream and heat through. Pour sauce around chicken, ribboning a spoonful over each piece.

Chile Cream Chicken

Creamy shredded chicken and cheese are lit up by searing, hot chiles—fiery árbol, milder anchos, or gentle Anaheims—in this version of a traditional Southwestern sopa. Blue corn tortillas are softly chewy, with a deep, distinctive corn flavor; use them, warm from the oven, to sop up the rich soupy sauce. Make a couple of quesadillas for each person as well (warm tortillas quickly in olive oil, top half with grated cheese, fold over and keep in warm oven). Add a bowl of fresh salsa and warm chips, a simple salad of mixed greens and scallions in a sharp vinaigrette, and chilled light or dark Mexican beer for a meal to remember.

---

1 package medium blue corn tortillas
1 whole chicken breast, split in half
2 teaspoons olive oil
1 red dried chile
1 7-ounce can roasted, chopped green chiles, drained
⅔ cup heavy cream
1 cup coarsely grated jack cheese
1 cup romaine *or* Napa cabbage, shredded

●Loosely wrap in foil as many tortillas as you think you will eat, keep in warm oven. Put chicken in pot with lightly salted water to cover. Bring water to a boil, reduce heat, cover and simmer for 20 minutes. Cool, then skin, bone, and shred chicken; set aside. In a heavy pan, heat olive oil over medium heat. Add dried chile and brown lightly on all sides; remove and discard chile. Add green chiles and shredded chicken; stir and cook for 2 to 3 minutes. Pour in cream and heat gently until warm through. Stir in ½ cup cheese and heat, until cheese is melted. To serve, put shredded greens in warm tortillas, spoon chicken mixture over greens, and sprinkle with remaining cheese.

Napa cabbage

Coconut Chicken with Two Corianders

Many supermarkets stock canned coconut milk or cream in the wine section, evidently because it is mostly used for mixing exotic drinks. We will put it to better use in this biting, velvety entrée in which pan-browned chicken swims in a sauce sparked with hot chiles, smooth with coconut cream, and bright with two corianders. (Cilantro leaves and coriander seeds come from the same plant.) Rice, plain or pilaf, is a natural with this one, with either a simple stir-fry of zucchini, tomatoes, and tomatillos, or tossed greens with a citrusy vinaigrette. A glass of crisp ale or a fruity sauvignon blanc rounds things out satisfyingly.

---

2 to 4 pieces chicken
2 teaspoons oil
1½ inches gingerroot, peeled and minced
2 cloves garlic, minced
1 to 3 green chiles, trimmed, seeded, and finely chopped
1½ teaspoons powdered coriander
1 tablespoon minced fresh cilantro leaves (reserving sprigs
   for garnish)
½ cup coconut cream *or*
   1 cup coconut milk

●Rinse chicken, pat dry. In a frying pan, heat oil over medium-high heat. Add chicken and brown quickly on all sides. Reduce heat and add garlic, gingerroot, and chiles; stir and simmer for 5 minutes. Add coriander; stir and cook for another 5 minutes. Pour in ½ cup water (or coconut milk); partially cover and simmer for 20 minutes. Add coconut cream and cilantro; stir and cook for 10 minutes. To serve, pour sauce on plates, set chicken on top, and garnish with a few sprigs of cilantro.

Jícama and Chicken Soup

This New Mexican soup pairs shredded chicken with grated jícama, tart tomatillos, and ripe tomatoes. These same ingredients are combined in hundreds of Southwestern entrées, always to different effect. Here, they are plumped out with fresh salsa, pungent cumin, and cheese, which combine to happy effect. If fresh salsa is hard to come by, it is quite easy to make your own. Simply cut up an onion or two, as many chiles—of all heats, colors, and sizes—as you think you can handle (seed them first), a dozen tomatillos, husked and rinsed, and some ripe tomatoes. Add up to a bunch of cilantro, several cloves of garlic, and the juice and some grated rind of an orange. Toss it all in the blender, along with a quarter cup of cider vinegar, and buzz away. Vary the amounts of everything until you achieve personal culinary bliss. This soup is perfect beach cottage fare, especially when accompanied by quesadillas of blue corn tortillas and mellow jack cheese, a quickly tossed salad with pine nut dressing, and cold Mexican beer.

---

1 whole chicken breast, split in half
4 cloves garlic
1½ teaspoons cumin
8 tomatillos, husked, well rinsed, and quartered
5 tomatoes, 2 diced (reserve juice), 3 cut into wedges
6 ounces jícama, peeled and coarsely grated
¼ cup fresh salsa
2 ounces string cheese *or* mozzarella cheese, coarsely chopped

●Using a 2-quart saucepan, bring 5 to 6 cups salted water to a boil. Rinse chicken, place in boiling water. Add 2 cloves garlic and 1 teaspoon cumin. Return to boil, then reduce heat; cover and simmer for 20 minutes or until cooked through. Strain broth through a sieve; reserve. Set chicken aside to cool. When cooled, skin, bone, and shred chicken into small pieces. Heat 1 cup strained broth with tomatillos, tomato wedges, the remaining cumin, and the remaining garlic. Simmer briskly for 6 to 8 minutes until tender. Pour into blender or food processor and liquify. Return to pan with another 2 to 3 cups broth, jícama, chicken, diced tomatoes, and salsa; heat. Divide cheese between 2 large soup bowls, ladle hot soup over each, and serve.

Liver, Shrimp, and Bacon in Pepper Sauce

This may seem like an offbeat combination, but it has been a
West Coast favorite for many years. Variations of this recipe
may be found from California to British Columbia. In this one,
the three main ingredients are bathed in a sauce of red sweet
pepper that is enlivened with the subtle touch of fiery dried
peperoncini and the mild tang of balsamic vinegar. Offer a
salad of raw vegetables with a citrus dressing, rice or hot herb
rolls, and a glass of ale or velvety stout.

---

4 strips bacon
1 to 2 dried peperoncini
1 onion, sliced into rings
1 red sweet pepper, sliced lengthwise
8 ounces chicken livers, halved
8 ounces shrimp
1 to 2 tablespoons balsamic or raspberry vinegar

●In a heavy frying pan, cook bacon over medium heat until
crisp but still flexible; remove and drain on paper towel. Pour
off all but 2 teaspoons of drippings; add whole peperoncini
and cook over medium heat. Add vegetables to pan; stir and
cook for 3 to 5 minutes. Add livers; stir and cook for 6 to 8
minutes, until juices stop running. Add shrimp and vinegar;
stir and cook for 3 to 5 minutes more until hot through.
Remove and discard peperoncini. Sprinkle crumbled bacon
on top and serve.

Chicken Livers with Wild Rice and Almonds

Wild rice has a wonderful grainy texture and nutlike flavor,
which makes it an especially good partner for dense, tender
chicken liver. The livers are cooked with butter and ripe
tomatoes, then steeped in a subtle sauce of shallots, almonds,
and cream. Start the rice and pour yourself a glass of merlot.
The sauce can be put together leisurely. Assemble a salad of
romaine, ornamental cabbage, carrots, and more almonds, and
toss with a green onion and red wine vinegar dressing. Serve
merlot with your meal.

½ cup uncooked wild rice
2 tablespoons butter
2 to 3 shallots, peeled and thinly sliced
8 ounces chicken livers, trimmed
1 to 2 ripe, medium tomatoes, thickly sliced
½ teaspoon freshly ground pepper
2 tablespoons heavy cream
2 tablespoons sliced almonds, toasted

●Rinse rice, drain in wire mesh colander. In a heavy saucepan,
melt 1 tablespoon butter over medium heat. Stir in rice and
cook for 3 to 4 minutes (add salt if you like). Add 2 cups boiling water to pan; return to boil, cover, and reduce heat to low.
Cook, covered, until rice is fluffy and tender but still chewy,
about 30 to 35 minutes. In a heavy frying pan, heat 1 tablespoon butter over medium heat until foamy. Add shallots and
livers, stir. As soon as liver juices stop running, add tomatoes
and pepper. Simmer for 4 to 5 minutes. Turn livers and
tomatoes and let simmer for another 2 to 3 minutes. Add
cream and heat through. Serve over rice, top with almonds.

Vermicelli with Liver and Pine Nuts

If big chunks of liver leave you cold, this might be the recipe
for you. Small chicken livers are mildly flavorful and have a
delicate texture. When liver is properly cooked—either slowly
and very gently or quickly and not too long—even hardened
liver haters might be converted. Livers ought to be fresh looking with a slight, not unpleasant, odor. Cook them just until
the edges curl (something like oysters) and the red juice stops
running (longer cooking makes liver tough and rubbery unless
slow, moist heat is used). Slice oranges and onions very thin
and drizzle them with rosemary vinegar and a fruity olive oil
for a fresh-tasting winter salad to accompany this dish, with a
glass of merlot or a cabernet sauvignon.

---

2 teaspoons olive oil
2 cloves garlic, peeled and thinly sliced
1 to 2 dried red peperoncini
2 tablespoons pine nuts
8 ounces chicken livers, trimmed and halved
⅓ cup red wine
1 15-ounce can diced tomatoes in sauce
8 ounces fresh vermicelli *or*
  4 ounces dry

●Boil water for pasta. In a heavy frying pan, heat olive oil
over medium heat. Add garlic, peperoncini, and pine nuts;
cook for 4 to 5 minutes until golden. Remove pine nuts and
drain on paper towel. Add livers to oil, turning quickly to coat
with oil. Cook undisturbed for 2 to 3 minutes. Turn and sauté,
until all sides are browned and the edges just crisp. Add wine
and tomatoes and simmer. Meanwhile, cook vermicelli in the
boiling water. When the vermicelli is al dente, divide onto
plates. Remove peperoncini from sauce, then pour sauce over
pasta; sprinkle on the pine nuts and serve.

Turkey El Café

Thanksgiving leftovers will have a whole new meaning after you try this tasty entrée. The original dish, complicated and marvelous, was a popular favorite at Seattle's El Café for many years. This modest version proves that cold turkey can be festive, especially if served with a Yucatan twist. Accompany with a green salad, sharpened with a few shreds of arugula, and tossed with a cilantro and avocado dressing; warm, fresh tortillas or quesadillas; and Mexican beers.

---

1 Danish *or* acorn squash
6 to 8 dried apricots, cut into small strips
1 to 2 tablespoons dry sherry
1 cup cooked turkey, cut into small chunks
¼ cup walnuts, toasted
2 to 3 tablespoons salsa
½ cup sour cream
2 ounces grated cheese (Cheddar *or* jack)

●Trim squash so blossom and stem ends are flat; cut in half sideways, discard seeds and pulp. Steam, cut-side down, until just tender, about 15 minutes. Place turkey and apricots in small bowl with 3 tablespoons hot squash water, cover and let soak until plump, 3 to 5 minutes. Drain and toss with sherry, turkey, and walnuts. Fill squash shells with this mixture. Combine salsa and sour cream to taste. Spoon salsa over filled squash, covering edges of squash; top with cheese. Set squash in a shallow pan with an inch of water (to prevent scorching). Bake in 350 degree oven for 25 to 30 minutes.

Grilled Turkey Breast with Rhubarb Sauce
(Serves 4)

This thick, spunky sauce of the hot sweet-and-sour persuasion is equally delightful when brushed over skewers of pork and fresh apricots, plump salmon steaks, or lamb kebabs. Chutney fans will slather it on burgers with abandon. This is a great way to use the last of the local rhubarb, after you have used the tender early crop for pies. Taste as you stir up the sauce, altering sweetness and firepower to suit your tolerance. White or green cardamom pods are spicy sweet and very fragrant, but the larger black kind have a distinctly bitter undertone, which many people find unpleasant. Leftover sauce will keep in the refrigerator for up to a month, steadily improving in flavor (use a glass jar; plastic containers will never recover). Roast sweet potatoes, ears of corn, and thick slices of onion at the side of the grill. Serve up a plate of sliced tomatoes dressed with a basil vinaigrette, and have lots of iced tea, adding a few cardamom pods to the boiling water when you brew it, or crimson rhubarb wine.

---

4 to 5 stalks rhubarb, cut into 1-inch pieces
½ cup honey
¼ cup cider vinegar
1 to 3 chiles, seeded and diced
4 cloves garlic, chopped
8 whole cardamom pods
1 bunch fresh cilantro, chopped
2 to 3 pounds turkey breast, with skin

●Start coals in grill. In a heavy saucepan, combine rhubarb, honey, vinegar, 1 chile, garlic, and cardamom. Add enough water to barely cover rhubarb. Bring to a boil, cover, and simmer for 10 minutes. Taste, adding more chiles and honey as desired. Add cilantro and simmer, uncovered, for 5 more minutes. Baste turkey lightly with sauce and grill 20 to 30 minutes, turning and basting several times. Or, bake in 350 degree oven for approximately 1 hour.

Turkey Cutlets with Horseradish Cream

Boneless turkey breast is amazingly adaptable; it can be roasted or baked, poached or grilled, and dozens of sauces can play it up to cuisine élevée or way down home. Here, thick slices are dipped in egg and seasoned flour, then pan-fried to a golden, savory crispness. The dreamy diner is jerked wide awake by the spunky sauce of freshly grated horseradish folded into satiny clouds of whipped cream. The contrast is striking, the flavor is sumptuous, and best of all, it's dead easy. Have steamed green beans with orange butter, basmati rice, and a bottle of Vernaccia.

½ cup whipping cream
1 to 2 tablespoons grated horseradish root
2 tablespoons grated Parmesan cheese
3 to 4 tablespoons flour
½ teaspoon freshly ground black pepper
2 teaspoons olive oil
1 pound boneless turkey breast, thickly sliced
1 egg, slightly beaten

●Whip cream until soft peaks form. Fold in horseradish and 1 tablespoon of cheese; refrigerate until needed. Blend together flour, remaining cheese, and pepper, in a cake or other flat, wide pan. In a heavy iron frying pan heat oil over medium heat. Dip turkey slices in egg on both sides, then in flour mixture. Cook 5 to 6 minutes on each side until crisp and golden brown. Transfer each piece to a warm platter in oven while the others cook. To serve, present turkey slices with a small puff of whipped cream, and pass remaining cream in a bowl.

Turkey Kebabs with Fresh Pineapple

Pineapple is often given a salty-spicy treatment with ginger and soy sauce, but this recipe has classical Italian roots. Chunks of fresh pineapple and turkey are bathed in a garlic and lemon marinade, then skewered with red sweet pepper and onion in a sweet-savory combination dripping with juice. Mushrooms hold it all in place, absorbing flavors from everything rewardingly. This is a great way to use leftover turkey, which needs to be grilled only briefly. Serve with a spinach and romaine salad with pesto dressing, long grain rice on which to bed the skewers, and a Soave or a hoppy Italian beer.

2 tablespoons olive oil
½ lemon, juiced
2 cloves garlic, mashed
8 ounces uncooked turkey breast, cut into 1-inch cubes
1 pineapple, trimmed and cut into 1-inch cubes
12 mushrooms, trimmed
1 medium onion, sliced into wedges
1 red sweet pepper, sliced into wide strips

●Combine olive oil and lemon juice with garlic in a zip-lock bag. Add turkey and toss gently to cover, then add pineapple. To assemble kebabs, thread a mushroom on each of 6 skewers, then alternate chunks of onion, turkey, pineapple, and pepper, ending with a second mushroom. Brush vegetables lightly with remaining marinade, then grill or broil for 3 to 5 minutes per side, turning 3 or 4 times. Serve hot.

Gooseberry-glazed Game Hens with Sage Stuffing

It is amazing how few Americans have ever eaten a goose-berry. In Europe, dozens of hybrids are grown, valued for fools, trifles, and the assertive, piquant preserves called for in this recipe. Should you happen to find ripe, fresh gooseberries on the market, stew half a cup of them in a few tablespoons of white wine vinegar until they pop (about ten minutes) and substitute the results for the preserves—it is even more wonderful than the following, which is very good indeed. While the game hens bake, put together a salad and a lightly curried vinaigrette, start some rice, then relax with an aperitif. A full, dry but mellow white wine will do best here, perhaps a buttery chardonnay or an Alsatian riesling.

---

2 game hens (reserve inner bags)
2 teaspoons butter
1 medium onion, chopped
½ teaspoon dried sage
2 slices bread, cut into ½-inch cubes
2 tablespoons gooseberry preserves
1 tablespoon Dijon mustard
1¼ teaspoons green peppercorns in vinegar

●Rinse hens inside and out. Remove livers from inner bags and chop into small bits. Sauté livers in 1 teaspoon butter with onion and sage for 3 to 5 minutes. Toss in bread cubes. Fill hens with stuffing and bake in 375 degree oven for 10 minutes; reduce heat to 350 degrees and bake 45 to 50 minutes longer. For glaze, melt remaining butter in a small saucepan over low heat. Stir in gooseberry preserves, mustard, and peppercorns with their vinegar. Keep glaze warm on back of stove, but do not cook it. Brush some of this glaze over hens two or three times as they bake, beginning after temperature is reduced. Pour remaining glaze over hens at serving time.

Raspberry Game Hens

Strong flavors combine in a sharp, silky sauce of distinction, popular even with those who don't like mustard. All sorts of mustards will work: tarragon, herbes du Provence, Dijon, or whatever you fancy. Removing the skin from the game hens allows the flavors to permeate the meat, while the mustardy mask keeps it from drying out. A salad of fresh spinach, slivers of Napa cabbage, and toasted hazelnuts dressed with a simple vinaigrette of more raspberry vinegar and olive oil makes a nice touch. A mellow, rounded red Côtes du Rhône suits this dish well.

---

2 teaspoons olive oil
2 cloves garlic, pressed
3 slices bacon, chopped
2 game hens, cleaned, breast skin removed
1 medium onion, chopped
2 tablespoons mustard
¼ cup raspberry vinegar

●In a heavy iron pan, heat oil over medium heat. Add garlic and brown lightly. Add bacon and cook for 3 to 5 minutes until soft. Add game hens and quickly brown, then turn them breast up in pan. Add onion; stir and cook for 2 to 3 minutes until barely soft. Cover game hens with mustard. Add raspberry vinegar to pan and bake, covered, in 350 degree oven for 35 to 40 minutes. Serve with a scoop of sauce on each portion, and pass remaining sauce.

Game Hens with Bacon and Beans

These little hens have flavorful skins, thanks to multiple bastings. Runner beans, broad beans, even Kentucky wonders can be used in this savory sauce. The celery acts as a rack to keep the hens from sticking to the pan and as a stuffing to give the meat extra flavor. Serve rice or mashed potatoes topped with the extra gravy, corn or peas with a bit of tarragon, and a dry blush, rosé, or ale.

---

2 game hens (reserve inner bag)
2 onions, 1 quartered, 1 sliced
1 bunch celery, trimmed
4 strips bacon, chopped
4 ounces runner *or* any fresh beans, trimmed and sliced
1 teaspoon chopped fresh savory *or*
  ½ teaspoon dried
1 teaspoon chopped fresh thyme *or*
  ½ teaspoon dried
1 tablespoon flour

●Rinse birds inside and out, pat dry. Remove livers from inner bags. Drop livers in a saucepan with enough salted water to cover; cook, cool, and dice, reserving water for gravy. Put 2 pieces of quartered onion and ½ stalk celery into each bird. In a frying or roasting pan, arrange birds on all but 2 celery stalks. Bake in 350 degree oven, basting three times with pan juices, for 40 to 45 minutes until golden brown. Slice remaining celery. In a medium frying pan, cook bacon over medium heat. Drain off all but 2 to 3 teaspoons drippings; add sliced onion, celery, beans, liver, and herbs. Stir and cook over medium heat for 3 to 5 minutes. Stir in flour and blend well. Add water to reserved liver water to equal 1 cup, add to bacon mixture, and heat until bubbling gently. Continue stirring as gravy mixture thickens, then occasionally. Add more stock as needed to keep sauce the consistency of cream. When hens are done, pass gravy in a bowl.

Game Hens Perugino

My landlady taught me to make this Italian dish back in my student days. I had never seen a bird with all the attachments before and had no idea how to get rid of them. After the anatomy lesson, this is how she baked them—crackling crisp and golden with moist meat and a stuffing of rosemary, oranges, and onions. Bake potatoes with the game hens, toss steamed spinach with cocktail onions in vinegar and a spoonful of yogurt or sour cream, and pour out a foamy amber ale, a rosé, or a fumé blanc.

---

2 game hens
4 carrots, 3 sliced in half, lengthwise, 1 grated
2 oranges, 1 juiced plus grated peel, 1 quartered
2 onions, 1 chopped, 1 quartered
3 teaspoons chopped fresh rosemary (3 sprigs)
4 to 6 ripe tomatoes, diced (reserve juice) *or*
   1 15-ounce can in sauce
2 strips bacon, chopped
1 teaspoon green peppercorns in vinegar

●Rinse hens inside and out, pat dry. Arrange carrot slices in roasting pan; place hens on top. Stuff each hen with 2 pieces of orange and 2 pieces of onion, add 1 teaspoon or sprig of rosemary. Bake in 350 degree oven for 40 to 45 minutes, basting at least twice with pan drippings. In a frying pan, sizzle bacon. Add chopped onion and cook 3 to 5 minutes until just tender. Stir in grated carrot, remaining rosemary, orange juice and peel, tomatoes, and peppercorns. Heat until bubbling, then reduce heat and simmer gently, until hens are done. Serve each bird surrounded by sauce.

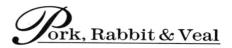

ork, Rabbit & Veal

117   Pork with Pineapple Oranges

118   Pork Roast with Chestnuts

119   Pork with Apples and Yams

120   Pork Chops with Pears and Ginger

121   Chutney Chops

122   Pork with Fresh Mango Chutney

123   Pork Palau

124   Broiled Pork Chops with Potatoes and Sauerkraut

125   Pork with Sunburst Squash

126   Pork Cutlets with Sorrel

127   Pecan Pork

128   Pork Strips with Hot Potato-Avocado Salad

129   Pork Kebabs with Fresh Pineapple

130   Pork Kebabs with Three Peppers

131   Hunter's Rabbit

132   Rabbit with Bacon and Mushrooms

133   Sizzling Walnut Rabbit

134   Rabbit with Sherried Chestnuts

135   Rabbit with Green Peppercorns

136   Rabbit in Balsamic Vinegar

137   Rabbit Piccata

138   Rabbit Grilled over Alderwood

139   Rosemary Rabbit

140   Pueblo Rabbit Stew

141   *Veal with Artichokes*

142   *Veal with Peaches and Almonds*

143   *Veal with Leeks, Bacon, and Tomatoes*

144   *Veal Marsala*

145   *Veal with Capers*

146   *Veal in Buttermilk*

147   *Veal Stew with Cocktail Onions*

Pork with Pineapple Oranges

Pork is often hailed as the new white meat, and for good reason. Lean, boneless, and delicately flavored, pork can be treated like chicken, and many recipes will work well for either one. This entrée is lovely to look at, refreshingly fragrant, and very quickly made with whichever meat you choose. The pineapple orange, like pineapple sage, is named for its allusive scent. The oranges come from Florida and California during most of the year, though summer crops are often from Chile. This recipe is equally good if made with many other citrus varieties that appear in the markets from time to time—honey tangerines, as sweet as you might expect, emerald satsumas, green as grass with golden flesh, or the dark, dramatic blood oranges with ruby-colored juice. With this entrée, cook up some long grain or basmati rice with a few whole cardamom pods and a good pinch of grated orange rind. Sautéed snap beans and oyster mushrooms, a small salad with tarragon pesto dressing, and a Vernaccia or white Côtes du Rhône will round the meal out well.

---

1 tablespoon olive oil
2 boneless pork loin cutlets (6 to 8 ounces total)
1 small red onion, sliced into thin strips
2 pineapple oranges, 1 juiced plus finely grated rind, 1 sliced into thin rounds
8 slim stalks asparagus (about ½ pound), trimmed and cut into 1-inch pieces
1 teaspoon fresh tarragon *or*
  ½ teaspoon dried
½ teaspoon freshly ground white pepper

●In a frying pan, heat oil over medium heat. Add pork and quickly brown on both sides; reduce heat. Add onions; stir to coat with pan juices. Add orange juice and 1 teaspoon grated orange rind to pan; cover and simmer about 10 minutes. Add asparagus, and tarragon. Add pepper and simmer another 8 to 10 minutes. Serve each cutlet with a spoonful of sauce and vegetables. Garnish with orange rounds.

Pork Roast with Chestnuts
(Serves 4 to 6)

Preparation time for this sumptuous, satisfyingly rich holiday entrée is under fifteen minutes. It's a terrific ace in the hole when you don't have time to go all out but want dinner to look (and taste) as if you had. The meaty sweetness of the chestnuts blends with the pan drippings to make a sauce par excellence to spoon over the sliced meat. Serve this roast with tart, fragrant cranberry chutney, tossed greens with avocados, and toasted cashews. Drink a full-bodied Burgundy for an appropriately self-indulgent experience.

---

3 pounds pork loin roast
6 shallots, peeled and thinly sliced
3 carrots, peeled and cut into chunks
2 turnips, peeled and cut into chunks
1 8-ounce jar peeled chestnuts
1 teaspoon lemon thyme
2 teaspoons coriander

●In a heavy cast-iron skillet, heat oil over medium-high heat. Add roast and quickly brown all over. Cover and let simmer for 6 to 8 minutes. Add shallots, carrots, and turnips, coating with pan drippings. Drain chestnuts and tuck them in beside meat. Sprinkle thyme and coriander over all. Bake in 325 degree oven about 1½ hours, or until a meat thermometer registers 160 degrees (interior temperature).

Pork with Apples and Yams

Raw, wet days demand heartening meals like this one, delicious enough for company, yet simple enough for quick assembly. Choose thick-cut pork medallions or use chops, and opt for firm, meaty apples like Rome Beauties, which hold up nicely to cooking. If you can't find small red yams, use the "Garnet" sweet potatoes; both look pretty in wide golden slices rimmed with red skins. Rosemary is evergreen, and a fat sprig can garnish each plate as well as lend its pungent savor to this dish. Serve this with hot, crusty rolls, a salad of butter lettuce, red sweet pepper strips, and toasted almonds with a garlic dressing, and a glass of bold merlot.

---

2 teaspoons olive oil
2 cloves garlic, pressed
1 teaspoon chopped fresh rosemary *or*
  ½ teaspoon dried
2 to 4 thick-cut pork loin medallions *or*
  chops (8 to 12 ounces total)
2 small, unpeeled yams, sliced
2 medium apples, cored and sliced
1 medium onion, sliced
½ cup red wine

●In a heavy Dutch oven or casserole, heat oil over medium heat. Add garlic and rosemary. Add pork and brown quickly on both sides. Remove pork and layer in yams, apples, and onion in alternating slices. Put pork on top, pour on wine and bake, covered, in 350 degree oven for 30 minutes.

Pork Chops with Pears and Ginger

Fall pears are crisp and flavorful even when slightly under-ripe, the condition in which they are generally discovered in modern supermarkets. This recipe takes advantage of the slightly astringent quality of firm, fresh pears, combining them to mutual advantage with pork chops and gingerroot. Potato chunks or warm onion-herb rolls, a salad alive with mustard greens or ribbons of radicchio, and a Chianti or Valpolicella make a friendly, comfortable meal.

---

2 thick-cut pork chops (8 to 12 ounces total)
1 teaspoon butter
1 inch gingerroot, peeled and grated or minced
1 medium white onion, halved and thickly sliced
2 firm pears, peeled, cored, and cut into 4 wedges each
½ cup red wine

●Rinse pork, pat dry. In a heavy frying pan, melt butter over medium heat. Add pork chops and brown quickly on both sides, then place them in a 1½-quart baking dish. Add gingerroot, onions, and pears to frying pan; cook for 5 to 6 minutes until just soft. Layer them over pork chops, pour red wine over all, cover, and bake in 350 degree oven for 45 to 50 minutes.

Chutney Chops

This quick and simple recipe makes a surprisingly complex dish, thanks to the chutney, which bestows both lively fragrance and rich flavor. Try using local chutneys, cranberry or blueberry for preference, and a firm, late apple, perhaps Winesap or Jonathan. This makes a perfect meal for those wintery nights when you want something savory to warm up the evening in a hurry. Have basmati rice, sautéed apple rings or pickled beets with sushi ginger, a spinach and mustard green salad, and a fruity riesling or pinot noir.

---

2 thick-cut pork chops (8 to 12 ounces total)
1 medium white or yellow onion, cut into thick slices
1 medium, unpeeled apple, cored and sliced into thick rings
4 tablespoons chutney

●Rinse pork, pat dry. Arrange 2 large onion slices in a 1½-quart baking dish, put the chops on top, layer on the remaining onion alternating with the apple rings. Spoon the chutney over all; cover and bake in 350 degree oven for 45 to 50 minutes.

Pork with Fresh Mango Chutney

A mélange of mango and mint, garlic and green chiles makes the fresh chutney in this spicy yet refreshing entrée. Such fresh chutneys (usually far more complex) are made daily in many Indian households, varying to suit the dish, the day, and the cook, just as we might stir up a batch of muffins. Since commercial chutneys can be expensive, it's worth learning how to make your own: pear and pepper, apple and green tomato, peach and ginger, are a few of the possibilities. Have this one with rice or warm chapatis (frozen ones reheated in foil), mixed green salad dressed with curried vinaigrette, and a glass of dry gewürtztraminer or zinfandel, or an ale.

8 ounces lean, boneless pork steaks
1 to 2 teaspoons oil
2 cloves garlic, pressed
1 medium onion, halved and thinly sliced
1 to 3 fresh chiles, seeded and finely chopped
1 mango, peeled, seeded, and chopped into chunks
¼ chopped fresh mint
1 tablespoon golden raisins

●Rinse pork, pat dry, and cut in ½-inch cubes. In a heavy pan, heat oil over medium-high heat. Add pork and sear quickly on all sides. Reduce heat to medium low and add garlic. Add onion and chiles, stir and cook for 2 to 3 minutes. Add mango, mint, and raisins; stir and cook for 2 to 3 minutes. Add ½ cup water, partially cover, and simmer for 15 to 20 minutes, until pork is tender. Serve hot.

Pork Palau

A friend, who spent many years on the island of Palau, near Guam, taught us to make this traditional dish. Strips of pork, stir-fried with hot wax peppers, tumble with juicy chunks of ripe papaya in a sauce bright with fresh lime juice. Hungarian peppers are only medium hot, so add some or all of the seeds to increase the heat. Toasted peanuts top this zesty, piquant mélange. With rice and a leafy salad of mixed greens, this entrée will perk appetites, even in the hottest weather. Choose a hoppy ale with this, and end the meal with a fresh fruit sorbet.

---

8 to 12 ounces boneless pork tenderloin, sliced into thin strips
1 ripe papaya, peeled, seeded, and chopped
1 large lime, juiced
1 tablespoon peanut oil *or* vegetable oil
1 medium onion, halved and thinly sliced
1 to 3 yellow hot peppers (Hungarian hot wax), seeded
   and chopped
¼ cup peanuts, toasted

● Arrange sliced pork and papaya chunks in separate small bowls; pour half the lime juice over each. Let marinate a few minutes. In a heavy frying pan, heat oil over medium-high heat. Drain pork strips, then quickly sear in oil, cooking for 1 to 2 minutes on each side. Add onion slices and pepper; stir to coat with oil, then cover pan, reduce heat to medium, and cook for 5 to 7 minutes, until vegetables are tender-crisp. Add papaya chunks with lime juice marinade, heat until warm through, and serve at once, topping each portion with toasted peanuts.

Broiled Pork Chops with Potatoes and Sauerkraut

Thick-cut chops need a few extra minutes under the heat, so position the rack a bit lower than usual to prevent overcooking them. If the chops are less than an inch thick, ten to twelve minutes on each side will probably do it. This recipe makes the better part of a meal; you need only steamed broccoli or spinach with lemon butter, and a glass of dark beer to complete it.

---

2 thick-cut pork chops (8 to 12 ounces total)
4 teaspoons wine mustard
1 tablespoon vegetable oil
2 potatoes, cut into 1-inch cubes
1 medium onion, chopped
1 medium, firm apple, cored and chopped
2 tablespoons dried currants
1 cup sauerkraut

●Rinse pork, pat dry. Mix 1 teaspoon mustard with ½ teaspoon oil; brush over chops. Preheat broiler, lowering rack a notch from your usual broiler position. Put chops on rack, broil for 14 to 16 minutes on each side. While chops are cooking, cook potatoes in boiling salted water for about 12 minutes until tender; drain. In a heavy skillet, heat 2 to 3 teaspoons oil over medium heat. Add onion and apple; stir and cook for 3 to 4 minutes. Add 3 teaspoons mustard and currants; stir and cook for 5 to 6 minutes. Add potatoes. Drain sauerkraut (rinse if too salty), stir in gently, and heat through. To serve, drain potato mixture with slotted spoon (keeping liquid in pan), heap next to chops, and pour pan juices over chops.

Pork with Sunburst Squash

Gold and green, this dish displays the ripe vegetables of high summer most attractively. The squash are nicest when still under five inches across, the beans when pencil slim. The bite of green peppercorns and ginger balances with Mediterranean herbs in a piquant but understated sauce. If you don't have a Mediterranean herb blend, you can make some quickly by combining equal amounts of rosemary, oregano, marjoram, thyme, and, if you like, a little nutmeg. Try this combination in salad dressings, herb butter, or simple summer sauces like this one. If the herbs are fresh, so much the better, but dried ones will do fine.

---

8 ounces lean pork
1 teaspoon walnut oil *or* olive oil
1 onion, quartered and sliced into ¼-inch pieces
1 inch gingerroot, julienned
1 teaspoon dried herbes du Provence
1 small sunburst squash (yellow pattypan), quartered
  and sliced
12 runner *or* broad beans, cut on diagonal into ¼-inch pieces
1 teaspoon green peppercorns in vinegar

●Rinse pork, pat dry. Slice pork into thin strips 2 or 3 inches long. In a large frying pan, heat oil over medium heat until sizzling. Add pork strips and quickly brown on both sides. Add onion and gingerroot, cook for 3 to 4 minutes, until onion is lightly browned. Add herbs and vegetables, green peppercorns with their vinegar, and 3 to 4 tablespoons water. Partially cover, reduce heat, and simmer for 6 to 8 minutes, until vegetables are tender but still brightly colored. Serve hot.

Pork Cutlets with Sorrel

This smooth, frothy sauce of sorrel and mint deepened with white wine is equally delightful with chicken or even fish, but can be made only with fresh herbs. Since sorrel has two seasons, spring and fall, this entrée can be served as a light spring meal—with a small salad of fresh greens in a citrus vinaigrette, warm rolls, and a crisp dry white wine—or a hearty autumn one—with baked potatoes, steamed broccoli in a walnut-mustard sauce, and a dark bock beer.

---

2 to 4 pork cutlets (8 to 12 ounces total)
2 teaspoons butter
2 shallots, thinly sliced
2 tablespoons minced fresh mint
1 bunch fresh sorrel, chopped
¼ cup dry white wine

•Put plates in warm oven. Rinse pork, pat dry. In a frying pan, heat butter over medium heat. Add pork and shallots and brown, cooking for 8 to 10 minutes on the first side. Turn and cook for another 8 to 10 minutes until tender; remove to warm plates in oven. To pan drippings, add mint and sorrel; stir and cook for 3 to 5 minutes until softened and limp. Add wine, scraping pan to loosen bits of meat. Stir and cook for 4 to 5 minutes. Pour sauce into blender or food processor; buzz until smooth, adding 1 to 2 tablespoons water if needed. Return sauce to pan, heat quickly, and pour around cutlets.

Pecan Pork

Subtle but flavorful, this understated dish expands upon the palate as you enjoy your meal, and lingers, tantalizing in the memory. Toast the pecans for extra buttery flavor; use slim spears of new asparagus, and teeny zucchini—if they still have their flowers attached, so much the better, for the blossoms have a fine, peppery flavor. Rice vinegar is mild, slightly sweet, and most complementary to the delicate flavors of young vegetables. Have Chinese noodles or rice to soak up the sauce, and a side dish of infant corn on the cob tossed with mirin (sweet rice sake) and shoyu (Japanese soy sauce). A frosty pale or bitter ale does great things for such a meal.

---

8 ounces boneless pork, cut into thin strips
1 teaspoon sesame oil
12 spears asparagus, trimmed at base
6 3-inch-long zucchini, quartered lengthwise
6 green onions, sliced into long diagonals
2 tablespoons rice vinegar
2 teaspoons shoyu (Japanese soy sauce)
3 tablespoons pecans, toasted

●In a frying pan, heat oil over medium-high heat. Add pork and quickly brown on both sides. Add vegetables; stir and cook for 1 minute. Cover pan, reduce heat, and steam in their juices for 3 to 5 minutes until barely tender. Add vinegar, shoyu, and pecans; stir and cook over medium-high heat for 2 minutes. Serve very hot.

green onion brooms, slivers, diagonals

Pork Strips with Hot Potato–Avocado Salad

Lean pork strips sear quickly in garlicky olive oil with fresh
sage and potatoes, then simmer in red wine vinegar broth.
Sliced avocados and swirls of thick clotted cream or crème
fraîche finish this up in style. A leafy salad of mixed greens
with a walnut and mustard dressing, a plate of pears, apples,
and Stilton cheese, and a bottle of fine ale make it a princely
meal.

---

10 ounces lean boneless pork, cut into strips
2 teaspoons olive oil
2 cloves garlic, mashed
1 tablespoon minced fresh sage *or*
  1 teaspoon dried
2 medium potatoes, diced
3 tablespoons red wine vinegar
1 avocado, in wedges
2 tablespoons clotted cream, crème fraîche *or*
  sour cream

●In a frying pan, heat oil over medium heat. Add pork and
garlic and brown. Reduce heat and add sage and potatoes. Stir
to coat with oil; cover and cook for 5 minutes. Add vinegar
and ½ cup water; bring to a boil, reduce heat, partially cover,
and simmer for 12 to 15 minutes, until potatoes are tender.
Add avocado wedges, heat for 2 to 3 minutes and serve, topping each portion with a swirl of clotted cream.

Pork Kebabs with Fresh Pineapple

Fresh pineapple marinates with lean pork in gingery shoyu and sake, resulting in a savory, sizzling entrée. The predominant flavors are tart and tangy rather than the usual sweet and salty. Have rice, of course, and a green salad punctuated with green onions, sesame seeds, and a citrus dressing. A full-bodied pale ale will suit this meal nicely.

---

12 ounces lean, boneless pork
2 cloves garlic, minced
1½ inches gingerroot, peeled and minced
1 tablespoon shoyu (Japanese soy sauce)
1 tablespoon sake *or* rice vinegar
½ pineapple, trimmed and cut into 1-inch cubes
1 medium onion, cut into ⅛-inch pieces

●Put garlic, ginger, shoyu, and sake into zip-lock bag; shake well. Drop in pork and pineapple and shake again. Start the coals. To cook, thread chunks of pork, then pineapple, then a piece of onion onto skewers, alternating items until each skewer has 3 or 4 pieces of meat. Grill over medium-hot coals for 3 to 4 minutes on each side, turning several times. Serve very hot.

Pork Kebabs with Three Peppers

Plump cubes of lean pork mingle with wide strips of red and yellow sweet peppers and pretty, golden fans of mandarin oranges or satsumas, then take a bath in fiery chili oil (the third pepper), shoyu, and garlic before grilling. Chili oil is very hot, so start with the lesser amount and taste before going all out. Have big balls of sticky rice, a salad of shredded Napa cabbage, green onion strips, and threadlike enoki mushrooms dressed with mirin (sweet sake), rice vinegar, and shoyu (the less salty Japanese soy sauce), and a crisp ale or hot tea.

---

10 ounces lean boneless pork, cubed
1 red sweet pepper, cut into strips
1 yellow sweet pepper, cut into strips
2 mandarin oranges, satsumas, *or* tangerines, peeled and
    cut into fans
1 tablespoon peanut oil
1 to 2 teaspoons chili oil
2 teaspoons shoyu (Japanese soy sauce)

●Thread chunks of pork, peppers, and orange fans on skewers. Blend peanut oil, chili oil, and shoyu and brush generously over skewers. Grill or broil for 5 to 6 minutes on a side, turning several times. Serve hot.

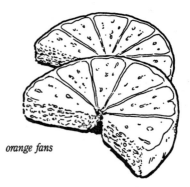

orange fans

Hunter's Rabbit

Rabbit has a stronger flavor than chicken, though not by much, and farm raised animals have none of the gamier overtones often found in wild rabbits. You can use nearly any chicken recipe with rabbit, allowing a bit more cooking time, and conversely, any of these rabbit recipes can be made with chicken or game hens. This one uses the herbs of the Mediterranean fields in a combination favored by hunters, who might gather the herbs as they wandered home, rabbit in the bag. Sometimes garlic tips are sold in the markets along with Chinese mustard greens. If you garden at home, you can snip the shoots of the emerging garlic without hurting the plants one bit. Garlic chives or a clove or two of garlic make a very acceptable substitute. Sweet potatoes and parsnips may be parboiled and grilled along with the rabbit, or serve up new potatoes, infant peas, and tiny fingerling beans in dill and chive butter. Warm rolls for sopping up the satiny sauce will be welcome, as will a glass of sprightly weissbier or a dry blush wine.

---

1 rabbit, cut up by butcher
2 tablespoons olive oil
½ lemon, juiced
2 teaspoons chopped fresh sage
½ teaspoon black peppercorns, cracked
1 bulb Florence fennel with leaves, thinly sliced
1 bunch garlic tips, chopped (2 to 3 tablespoons)
2 tablespoons balsamic vinegar

●Rinse rabbit, pat dry. In a frying pan, blend oil, lemon juice, sage, peppercorns, and 1 tablespoon fennel leaves over medium heat. Warm combination for 3 to 5 minutes, then lightly brush it on rabbit pieces. Grill rabbit for 10 to 12 minutes on a side, turning several times. Add fennel, garlic tips, and vinegar to remaining oil mixture and simmer for 5 to 7 minutes over medium heat, until fennel is tender-crisp. Serve each portion of rabbit with several spoonfuls of sauce.

Rabbit with Bacon and Mushrooms

Tender, lean rabbit is browned with bacon, then stewed with wine and mushrooms in this savory hunter's pot dish. In Italy, it would be served in shallow soup plates, the salad and vegetable courses preceding it. Florence fennel bulbs, braised in a peppery wine sauce, make a fine accompaniment, followed perhaps by a savory—Roquefort or Stilton, walnuts, and cheese shortbreads. Drink whatever you cook with: Chianti Classico, zinfandel, or pinot noir would be good choices.

---

1 small rabbit, cut up by butcher
½ teaspoon black peppercorns, cracked
¼ cup flour (whole wheat or white)
1 teaspoon dried dill *or* marjoram
4 strips lean bacon, cut into small, widthwise strips
1 onion, chopped
½ cup red wine
4 ounces mushrooms, sliced

●Rinse rabbit, pat dry. Put peppercorns, flour, and dill into zip-lock bag, shake to blend. Drop in rabbit pieces and shake to coat. In a heavy saucepan, cook bacon until crisp but still flexible. Pour off all but 2 to 3 teaspoons drippings. Add rabbit, browning quickly on all sides. Add onion; stir and cook for 3 to 5 minutes until just soft. Stir in any extra flour-pepper mixture, then add wine, stirring all the while. First you will make a smooth paste (except for bacon and onions), then slowly add 1 cup water to thin to a soupy sauce. Bring it to boil, then reduce heat. Add mushrooms, partially cover pan, and simmer for 35 to 40 minutes, until rabbit is fork-tender.

Sizzling Walnut Rabbit

Rabbit takes wonderfully to this singing, fiery treatment, with walnuts, chiles, and sweet potatoes combining in a sweet-hot chorus. Temper the full firepower by using less potent chiles (árbol, Anaheim, and/or jalapeños) or fewer of them. Even at its hottest, this entrée remains flavorful, with a nice interplay of texture and fragrances. Serve with rice—a lot of rice—and cold beer, with a cooling salad of cucumber and mild greens in a citrusy vinaigrette on the side.

---

1 rabbit, cut up by butcher
1 tablespoon peanut oil
1 to 4 chiles, seeded and chopped
3 cloves garlic, mashed
1 orange, juiced plus grated peel
2 teaspoons shoyu (Japanese soy sauce)
2 small sweet potatoes, sliced
¼ cup walnuts, toasted

●Rinse rabbit, pat dry. In a frying pan, heat oil over medium-high heat. Add rabbit and brown on all sides. Reduce heat and add chiles, garlic, juice, and 2 teaspoons grated peel; stir and cook for 3 to 5 minutes over medium heat. Add shoyu, potatoes, and 1 cup water; cover and simmer for 25 to 30 minutes, until rabbit is tender. Remove and discard garlic. Serve, spooning sauce and potatoes generously on each portion. Top with walnuts.

Rabbit with Sherried Chestnuts

This is the sort of savory, meltingly rich and delicious food that one craves after a long day battling wind and weather on the ski slopes. It is quick to assemble, and you can thaw by the fireplace, sipping mulled wine, while it cooks. If you have a microwave oven, it takes no time at all to shell fresh chestnuts. Pierce the hulls, put them in the microwave for a minute or two, and peel. Serve with long grain or basmati rice tossed with butter and chopped chives, steamed carrots and broccoli drizzled with balsamic vinegar and fruity olive oil, and a bottle of stout or Bordeaux.

---

1 8-ounce jar chestnuts, drained
⅓ cup dry oloroso sherry
1 rabbit, cut up by butcher
1 tablespoon olive oil
1 medium onion, sliced
2 shallots, chopped
1 teaspoon freshly ground black pepper
2 teaspoons minced fresh sage *or* thyme *or*
   1 teaspoon dried

●Combine chestnuts with sherry (sherry should cover chestnuts); set aside. Rinse rabbit, pat dry. In a frying pan, heat oil over medium-high heat. Add rabbit and brown quickly on all sides. Add onion, shallots, pepper, and sage; stir and cook for 3 to 5 minutes. Add 1 cup water; bring to a boil, reduce heat, cover pan, and simmer for 20 to 30 minutes, until rabbit is tender. Add sherried chestnuts (including sherry); uncover pan and simmer briskly for 10 minutes, until chestnuts are hot through. Serve at once, passing extra sauce and chestnuts in a small bowl.

Rabbit with Green Peppercorns

Steaming bowls of this savory, fragrant, and stylish dish elevate an ordinary meal to a midwinter celebration. Although served in bowls, the rabbit is eaten with forks. You can haul out the silver, the Spode, and the crystal, and set a beautiful table while it cooks. Serve Roquefort, Gorgonzola, or a sharp Cheddar with sesame crisps for an appetizer. Toss romaine with green onion slivers and grated black radishes in a garlic vinaigrette, tuck warm onion rolls into a napkined basket, and bring the Chianti to room temperature. *Salute!*

---

1 small rabbit, cut up by butcher
2 teaspoons walnut oil *or* olive oil
1 fat clove garlic, mashed
2 tablespoons chopped fresh mint *or*
  2 teaspoons dried
1 teaspoon green peppercorns
¼ cup wine vinegar
¼ cup oatmeal
2 tablespoons sour cream

●Rinse rabbit, pat dry. In a heavy pan or Dutch oven, heat oil over medium-high heat. Add garlic to oil with rabbit; brown both all over. Add mint, green peppercorns, and vinegar. Pour in enough water to cover rabbit halfway. Bring to a boil; reduce heat to medium low, cover, and simmer for 30 to 35 minutes, until rabbit is tender. Grind up oatmeal in blender or food processor to make coarse flour. Put into small bowl, stir in ½ cup hot rabbit broth to make a smooth paste. Stir paste into the pot of broth, mixing well. Simmer, stirring occasionally, for 10 to 12 minutes as broth thickens. To serve, arrange pieces of rabbit in soup plates or bowls, ladle in broth, and swirl a dollop of sour cream into each bowl.

Rabbit in Balsamic Vinegar

This cooking method renders rabbit exceedingly tender and flavorful. Aromatic balsamic vinegar is etherealized to a fragrant suggestion of its usual self. True balsamic vinegar is made from the concentrated essence of Trebbiano grapeskins, originally the leftovers from that region's famous white wines. The stuff is aged for at least ten years in an esoteric process involving periodic removal to barrels of various woods, notably oak and juniper. It is obvious that what is widely sold in the supermarkets is far from authentic, especially if not actually made in Italy, where production is guided by legal restrictions to keep it consistent. Even so, some brands are not bad, and several are reasonable reproductions of the real thing. The best balsamic vinegars are fabulously expensive, but worth it, for the genuine article has a heady aroma and an unforgettable flavor. A little goes a long way, making the cost slightly less outrageous.

---

1 rabbit, cut up by butcher
1 teaspoon black peppercorns, cracked
1 tablespoon olive oil
¼ cup balsamic vinegar
1 anchovy, mashed
1 tablespoon minced fresh sage *or*
    1 teaspoon dried
6 whole cloves
1 medium onion

●Rinse rabbit, pat dry, and roll in cracked peppercorns. In a heavy skillet, heat oil over medium-high heat. Add rabbit and brown quickly on all sides. Add vinegar, anchovy, sage, and 1 cup water. Bring mixture to boil. Reduce heat, cover, and simmer for 10 minutes. Push stems of cloves into onion and add it to pot. Simmer, partially covered, for 20 to 30 minutes, until rabbit is tender. Serve hot.

Rabbit Piccata

This classic lemon and wine sauce is generally used with veal, but its mellow bite serves to set off the mild richness of rabbit. Sound contradictory? A taste or two will make it clear, for the sauce is both smooth and sharp, the meat is both delicate and savory, and the combination is complex and satisfying. Traditionally, this is a fairly salty sauce, so you may want to add a shake to the flour mixture. Lemon should predominate, with the sparkly tang that only comes from fresh juice; start with half the lemon and add more until there is a distinct but not overwhelming tingle of lemon. Wild rice mixed with long grain white rice, chopped almonds, and mushrooms complements this entrée. In addition, serve steamed broccoli in basil butter, or brussels sprouts in garlic butter, and a glass of Chianti or a golden, crisp Bartlett pear wine.

---

1 rabbit, cut up by butcher
¼ cup flour
½ teaspoon freshly ground black pepper
1 tablespoon olive oil
1 tablespoon butter
1 cup dry white wine
1 lemon, juiced
1 teaspoon capers

●Rinse rabbit, pat dry. Blend flour, (salt), and pepper. Add rabbit pieces and dredge lightly in flour. In a heavy saucepan or Dutch oven, heat oil and butter over medium-high heat. Add rabbit and brown quickly on all sides. Reduce heat and add wine. Cover pan and simmer for 20 to 25 minutes, until rabbit is tender. Or bake in 350 degree oven for 35 to 40 minutes. Add lemon juice to taste, stir in capers, and serve hot.

Rabbit Grilled over Alderwood
(Serves 4)

My brother-in-law brings us Southwestern specialties when he visits from Nevada. He used to bring mesquite, but this time he explained that, once ubiquitous, mesquite is now an endangered species. Even smallish plants can take a hundred years to mature; once these are gone to feed the barbecues of the world, they are simply not replaceable. Luckily, Northwestern alderwood or Eastern maple, Southern hickory, or any kind of fruitwood make splendid substitutes. Aromatic juniper berries lend their pungent, distinctive flavor to this dish as they do to gin. The rabbit can be refrigerated to marinate overnight, or as long as it takes to fire up the alderwood. Warm tortillas or quesadillas, fresh raw vegetables, and corn on the cob go wonderfully with this meal, as will cold beer or a Beaujolais.

---

1 3- to 4-pound rabbit, cut up by butcher
¼ cup olive oil
¼ cup red wine vinegar
1 lemon, juiced plus 2- x 2-inch strips peel
6 juniper berries, lightly crushed
6 black peppercorns, lightly crushed
1 teaspoon fresh sage *or*
  ½ teaspoon dried
1 teaspoon fresh thyme *or*
  ½ teaspoon dried

●Rinse rabbit and pat dry. In a large plastic zip-lock bag, mix olive oil, vinegar, lemon juice, and peel (set the bag in a bowl while you work). Then add juniper berries, peppercorns, sage, and thyme; shake. Add rabbit, press out air, and tightly seal bag. Start coals in grill. Carefully remove rabbit from bag, reserving marinade, place on grill, and cook 10 to 15 minutes on each side, brushing several times with marinade.

Rosemary Rabbit

This may sound like a kids' book or a horror movie, but the results are neither childish nor hare-raising, just delicious. The rosemary pasta adds panache to this Northern Italian dish; if it is not locally available, add several sprigs of fresh rosemary (or a teaspoon of the dried herb) to the pasta water and garnish the plates with more. Ivory green with a rippled, scalloped edge, pattypan squash have the finest texture and flavor when used quite young, about the size of an apple. Sunburst is a golden pattypan variety for which you can always substitute golden summer squash. Bake cornbread in a heavy iron frying pan (to get the crispest of crusts), toss a salad with pesto vinaigrette, and pass around a bottle of Soave Classico or a full-bodied microbrewed ale.

---

1 small rabbit, cut up by butcher
2 to 3 teaspoons olive oil
1 8- to 10-ounce jar cocktail onions in vinegar
1 bunch fingerling carrots
2 pattypan or sunburst squash, trimmed, *or*
  2 to 4 small zucchini, trimmed
1 bunch fresh basil, coarsely chopped
8 ounces fresh rosemary pasta *or*
  4 ounces dry
¼ cup crème fraîche *or* sour cream

●Rinse rabbit, pat dry. In a heavy pan or Dutch oven, heat olive oil over medium-high heat. Add rabbit, brown quickly on all sides. Pour in onions and their vinegar. Add lightly salted water as needed to cover rabbit halfway. Cover pan and simmer for 8 to 10 minutes over medium-low heat. Add whole carrots and squash to rabbit pan. Simmer, partially covered, for 25 to 30 minutes, until both rabbit and vegetables are tender. Add basil and pasta to rabbit. Cook until pasta is al dente, swirl in crème fraîche, and heat through. Serve hot in soup plates or pasta bowls.

Pueblo Rabbit Stew

New Mexican cooking combines the wild and cultivated foods available on the reservation with simple cooking techniques to produce timeless, wonderful food. This one is quickly assembled, and you can make some cornbread or relax with a rousing crossword puzzle while it cooks, filling the kitchen with good smells. Traditionally, the stew is thickened with blue cornmeal or haranilla, but you can use white or yellow masa harina, the special, widely available cornmeal for making tortillas. Another traditional thickener is pumpkin seed flour, which can be made by toasting the seeds, then grinding them in a blender, food processor, or even a coffee grinder. Round out the meal with steamed greens with vinegar and chopped nuts, and a cold beer or dry, hard cider.

---

2 pounds rabbit, cut up by butcher
2 teaspoons oil
1 medium onion, chopped
2 mild green chiles, seeded and chopped
4 black peppercorns
4 juniper berries
1 pound pumpkin *or* winter squash, peeled and cut
    into chunks
3 tablespoons blue cornmeal, masa harina *or*
    ⅓ cup pumpkin seeds

●Rinse rabbit, pat dry. In a large pan, heat oil over medium-high heat. Add rabbit and brown quickly. Add onions and chiles. Mix peppercorns and juniper berries, and crush them with the back of a heavy knife. Stir in with rabbit. Add water to barely cover meat, bring to a boil, then reduce heat, partially cover, add pumpkin to stew, and simmer 25 to 30 minutes. If you are using pumpkin seeds, buzz them to a coarse meal in blender or food processor. When meat and pumpkin are tender, blend the meal with 2 tablespoons hot stew water, then stir it quickly into stew (to avoid lumps). Simmer over low heat for another 10 minutes, until sauce is thick. Serve in soup plates or bowls.

Veal with Artichokes

Double this quick yet elegant entrée when company comes on short notice; it is almost effortless, yet good looking and tasty. When baby cocktail artichokes aren't available, use your favorite kind of marinated or canned artichoke hearts instead— either kind work fine, though they taste quite different. A blend of wild and long grain rice, a salad of Napa cabbage and bok choy dressed with bacon and garlic, and a flowery glass of Fleurie Beaujolais make the whole meal worth a toast.

---

8 to 12 ounces veal shoulder steak
4 cocktail *or* baby artichokes *or*
  1 5- to 7-ounce jar marinated *or*
  ¾ cup canned, drained and sliced
1 teaspoon minced fresh thyme *or*
  ½ teaspoon dried
1 teaspoon olive oil
1 teaspoon butter
1 medium onion, halved lengthwise and sliced
3 tablespoons dry sherry
1 ounce shredded Parmesan cheese

●Rinse veal, pat dry. Trim outer leaves, stems, and tips from artichokes; cut in half, removing chokes from bigger ones. Cut each half into quarters; set aside. In frying pan, heat oil and butter over medium-high heat until foamy. Add veal and thyme; cook about 6 minutes until golden. Turn veal, add onion to pan, stirring to coat. Reduce heat, add artichokes and sherry; cook, covered, for 12 to 15 minutes, until artichokes are tender. Uncover and cook briskly, until sauce is reduced by half, perhaps 3 minutes. Sprinkle with cheese; cover and cook for another 2 to 3 minutes, until cheese is soft and barely melted. Serve at once.

Veal with Peaches and Almonds

This recipe emphasizes the almond undertones in ripe peaches. The sauce is light and subtle enough that the delicate veal is not overwhelmed. Basmati rice cooked with cardamom pods and lemon peel is a fragrant companion dish, as are steamed, gingery green and gold wax beans or romanesco broccoli drenched in peach or raspberry vinegar while very hot. Drink a soft, fruity riesling, a Frascati, or minted fruit vinegar spritzers.

---

8 ounces boneless veal *or*
  1 pound veal steak (shoulder)
1 teaspoon almond oil *or* butter
2 cloves garlic, mashed
6 white *or* green cardamom pods
⅓ cup white wine
2 ripe peaches, peeled, stoned, and quartered
2 tablespoons whole almonds, toasted and coarsely chopped

● Rinse veal, pat dry. In a heavy sauté pan, warm oil over medium-high heat. Add garlic and cardamom pods. Add veal; cook for 4 to 6 minutes, turn and brown quickly. Add wine; reduce heat to medium low and simmer for about 15 minutes until tender. Slide peaches into wine sauce, spooning it over each piece. Simmer for 2 to 3 minutes until hot through. Remove and discard garlic and cardamom. Pour sauce on 2 plates. Divide veal, setting half on each plate, surround with peaches, sprinkle nuts over veal, and serve.

Veal with Leeks, Bacon, and Tomatoes

Use the leanest bacon you can find, thick cut and alder or hickory smoked. It is very easy to slice slippery bacon if it is partially frozen, so put what you need in a plastic bag in the freezer to chill while you assemble ingredients and utensils. By the time you need it, it will be firm enough to slice readily. In the summer, ripe tomatoes and fresh basil make the sauce tangy and sweet scented, but dried herbs and canned tomatoes in sauce do just fine the rest of the year. Serve pasta, new potatoes, or long grain rice with this savory sauce, or just sop up the tasty juices with chunks of French bread. Salad with a citrus dressing makes a zippy accompaniment, and a chenin noir, or clean, dry Orvieto white will, too.

---

8 to 12 ounces veal
4 strips bacon, cut into small strips
2 leeks, trimmed and cut into 1-inch chunks
2 ripe tomatoes, cut into chunks (reserve juice)
4 leaves fresh basil, minced
Freshly ground black pepper
2 tablespoons heavy cream

●Rinse veal, pat dry. Cut into 1-inch chunks as for stroganoff. In a frying pan, sizzle bacon until crisp but not dry; remove and drain on a paper towel. Pour off all but about 2 teaspoons drippings; add veal chunks and stir to coat. Quickly brown veal on both sides. Add leeks, stirring to coat, and cook for 12 to 15 minutes, until veal is tender. Add tomatoes with their juice, basil, and lots of freshly ground black pepper. Heat until bubbling. Add cream, heat through, and serve.

Veal Marsala

Marsala might be considered the Sicilian version of sherry. There are sweet and dry types—some best used as dessert wines, others best with savory appetizers—both are marvelous cooking wines. They warm and color a sauce without overwhelming gentler flavors. Fresh fettuccine or Parmesan rice, steamed broccoli and orange sections drenched with balsamic vinegar, and a Tuscan red or a young Valpolicella will make excellent additions to this meal.

---

2 veal cutlets
2 to 3 teaspoons butter
2 cloves garlic, mashed
1 tablespoon golden raisins
2 tablespoons dry Marsala
2 to 3 tablespoons heavy cream
2 tablespoons pine nuts, toasted

●Put plates in oven to warm. Rinse veal, pat dry. Thump cutlets gently with back of heavy knife to flatten. In a heavy skillet, heat butter over medium heat until foamy. Add garlic and veal. Cook veal for 4 to 6 minutes. Turn, reduce heat to medium low, add raisins, and cook for 3 to 5 minutes more, until juices stop running and veal is pale golden brown. Transfer veal to warm plates. Remove and discard garlic cloves. Add Marsala to pan juices and cook briskly over medium-high heat for 2 to 3 minutes, stirring often as sauce reduces. Add cream, heat through, and pour around veal, adding a thin ribbon of sauce across each cutlet. Scatter with pine nuts, serve.

Veal with Capers

Pickled capers, tangy and slightly bitter, are used extensively throughout the Mediterranean, North Africa, and well into India. Americans tend to use them in Italian food, if at all, but they are worth experimenting with, for their mild, piquant bite gives an edge to buttery sauces, or plays up sharp ones nicely. Here, capers and mustard spark a simple reduction of the veal's pan juices, blended with wine, shallots, and butter. Serve steamed spinach tossed with chopped onion and sour cream, and rice to soak up the extra sauce. A glass of a crisp Tuscan white will go well.

½ teaspoon freshly ground black pepper
10 ounces boneless veal cutlet, in 2 pieces
1 tablespoon butter
1 shallot, chopped
2 tablespoons dry white wine
½ teaspoon capers
2 teaspoons whole-seed mustard

● Warm serving plate in oven. Pat pepper onto both sides of veal. In a frying pan, heat butter over medium heat until foamy. Add veal and shallot and cook for 4 to 6 minutes on each side, depending on thickness. Remove veal to warm serving plate and hold in warm oven. Stir wine into pan juices, scraping to loosen all bits of meat. Boil briskly for 2 to 3 minutes, until sauce is reduced by nearly half. Stir in capers and mustard, cook for 1 minute. To serve, pour sauce over meat.

Veal in Buttermilk

There is more to sage than turkey stuffing. In this silky, complex-tasting Italian entrée, it provides a subtle, woodsy background that emphasizes the flavor of veal. Fresh tomatoes can be used in season, though the flavor of well-cured sun-dried tomatoes is more similar to that of home-dried apricots. Have hot garlic rolls or fresh fettuccine, carrots and turnips glazed with orange juice, a green salad, and a Chianti or nebbiolo.

---

2 veal cutlets (12 ounces total)
1 tablespoon flour
½ teaspoon freshly ground black pepper
2 teaspoons butter
1 clove garlic, pressed
½ teaspoon dried sage
5 to 6 sun-dried tomatoes, snipped into pieces
⅔ cup buttermilk

● Rinse veal, then lightly pound with back of heavy knife to flatten. Blend flour with pepper, pat it all over meat, pressing gently to make it stick. In a frying pan, heat butter over medium-high heat until foamy. Add garlic, crumble in sage. Slide in veal, add tomatoes, and cook for 4 to 5 minutes until first side is pale golden. Flip cutlets; cook for 2 to 3 minutes. Add buttermilk, cover, and simmer over medium-low heat for 10 minutes. Serve hot, with extra sauce spooned over meat.

Veal Stew with Cocktail Onions

Cocktail onions are designed to be put into nasty drinks, but they are much nicer in this veal stew, where they mingle happily with a peperoncino and thyme. The sauce is snappy, but the veal and leeks preserve their own milder flavors stoutly. This stew is the French sort, made to be served on a big, lipped plate, all by itself. Small dishes of au gratin potatoes or Florence fennel are in order, with a salad arriving as a first course, accompanied by a dry blush wine.

---

8 ounces veal shoulder
1 tablespoon whole wheat pastry flour
½ teaspoon dried thyme
2 leeks, trimmed and cut into 1-inch slices
2 teaspoons olive oil *or* walnut oil
1 red peperoncino
½ cup cocktail onions in wine vinegar
2 tablespoons sour cream

●Rinse veal, pat dry, and cut in 1-inch cubes. Mix flour with thyme in a plastic bag, add veal, and toss until dusted. In a large pan, heat oil over medium heat. Add peperoncino, turning it until browned all over, then discard. Quickly brown veal chunks on all sides. Add onions and their vinegar; cover, reduce heat, and simmer until tender, about 20 minutes. Add sour cream, heat through, and serve at once.

$\mathcal{B}$eef & Lamb

151   *Beef in Merlot*

152   *Sirloin Tip with Pan-fried Tomatoes*

153   *Pepper Steak*

154   *Broiled Steak with Tomato Coulis*

155   *Beef Do Pyaza*

156   *Burgers in Bitter Beer*

157   *Summery Beef Sauté*

158   *Squash Blossom Stew*

159   *Fajitas with Avocado Sauce*

160   *Lamb Chops with Baked Garlic*

161   *Lamb and Cucumber Sauté*

162   *Lamb with Mint Raita*

163   *Lamb and Beans*

164   *Lamb with Emerald Satsumas and Kumquats*

165   *Lamb Medallions in Pumpkin Sauce*

166   *Zuñi Lamb Stew*

Beef in Merlot

Slow cooking with lots of bacon makes this a very tender dish. It takes a couple of hours, but requires almost no attention—great for busy evenings when you plan to dine late. The sauce makes itself; lemon thyme, garlic, onions, and merlot simmer with bacon and peppercorns. Spoon it generously over thick slices of beef and ladle it over rice or boiled potatoes. The extra sauce tastes even better the next day. Serve a dish of peas with a bit of mint snipped in or steamed beets with horseradish, and more merlot.

---

2 to 3 pounds lean beef, top clod, or any boneless roast
5 strips lean bacon
3 cloves garlic, crushed
1 medium onion, thickly sliced, then quartered
1½ teaspoons dried lemon thyme
2 dried peperoncini
1 teaspoon whole black peppercorns
1 cup merlot *or* dry red wine

●Rinse beef, pat dry. Stack 4 slices bacon and put in freezer in a plastic bag. Cut remaining strip into a large heavy pan or Dutch oven and cook slowly over low heat. Add garlic to bacon and cook over medium heat until golden. Add beef, brown quickly, giving it a couple of minutes on each side; reduce heat to low. Put onions over and around beef, scatter in thyme, peperoncini, and whole peppercorns. Slice cold bacon widthwise into thin strips ¼- x 1-inch, strew over beef and onions. Cover and cook over low heat for 1 hour. Turn beef, add merlot, pouring it over beef and scooping some bacon and onions over as well. Cover and cook for another hour, or several hours, until you are ready to eat. To serve, slice meat thickly, top with sauce.

Sirloin Tip with Pan-fried Tomatoes

Red meat has been unfashionable for some time, but that never stopped people from buying it. It did, however, prompt meat department managers to stock leaner cuts, in smaller portions, and both of these moves have been well received. A good steak needs very little help, but it must be acknowledged that leaner cuts, though nutritiously sounder, are less flavorful than well-marbled ones, for the fat carries much of the flavor. Slimmed-down cuts call for more exciting treatments—rich, spicy, or savory ones that emphasize rather than mask the flavor of the meat. Add a spinach, snow pea, and walnut salad, toss it with a mustardy vinaigrette, and pass around a bottle of Chianti Classico.

---

12 ounces thick-cut sirloin tip steak
½ teaspoon freshly ground black pepper
1 tablespoon butter
2 tomatoes, halved
1 tablespoon minced fresh basil
1 tablespoon minced fresh chives
¼ cup crème fraîche *or* sour cream

●Start coals or preheat broiler. Rinse steak, pat dry. Pat pepper onto both sides of steak. In a heavy frying pan, melt butter over medium heat until foamy. Add tomatoes, cut-side down, and herbs. Pierce tomatoes several times with a knife tip. Cook tomatoes slowly for 10 minutes, turn and cook for another 10 minutes. Start cooking steak, allowing 6 to 8 minutes per side. When steak is turned to second side, swirl crème fraîche into sauce, but do not break up tomatoes. To serve, cut steak in 2 portions, set each on a plate with 2 tomato halves, and pour sauce around each serving. Garnish with a few herb leaves.

Pepper Steak

Whether you splurge on plump, fork-tender filets mignons, or use bargain-priced sirloin tip or strip steak, this classic method always yields results fit for your favorite guest, and in very short order. The salt helps sear the meat quickly, sealing in the juices and preventing the meat from sticking to the pan. The sauce is smooth, glossy, and lively with lemon; start with the lesser amount and add more to taste. Serve with chunked, boiled potatoes tossed with butter and flat Italian parsley, a plain salad with freshly made vinaigrette, and a full-bodied Bordeaux.

---

2 filets mignons *or*
  8 ounces sirloin steak
2 teaspoons black peppercorns, cracked
Salt
1 tablespoon butter
1 lemon, juiced
Worcestershire sauce

●Rinse steak, pat dry. Trim off extra fat, and score or slash edges to keep meat from curling as it cooks. Preheat oven to warm. Press peppercorns into both sides of steaks with palm of hand. Scatter ⅛ teaspoon salt into a heavy frying pan over high heat, cook until salt begins to brown. Add steaks, browning quickly on the first side for 3 to 5 minutes. Flip steaks, reduce heat to medium and cook for another 5 to 8 minutes, depending on how rare you like your meat. Remove meat to a warm plate in oven. Add butter to pan juices, and when it melts, pour in 1 to 3 tablespoons lemon juice to taste and ½ to 1 teaspoon Worcestershire sauce to taste. Sizzle sauce for a few seconds, pour over meat, and serve at once.

Broiled Steak with Tomato Coulis

For the French, *coulis* can have several meanings—the running
juices of cooked meat, purees of seafood or shellfish, or various kinds of stock. But for most modern cooks, it refers to a
thick, pureed vegetable sauce like this one—a favorite from
Aix-en-Provence. The coulis can be served with emphatically
flavored fish, such as mackerel, with roast pork or lamb, or
tossed with hot pasta and cheese. Here, it is a tasty accompaniment to broiled steak (as rare as you can stand it), tender
and flavorful on its own, but double good with this lively sauce.
Steamed spinach with lemon butter, a green salad with a
citrus dressing, warm garlic bread or noodles with poppy seeds
make a hearty and attractive meal. Have a cabernet sauvignon
or a full-bodied ale on the side.

---

1 tablespoon olive oil
1 to 2 cloves garlic, mashed
1 medium onion, chopped
1 carrot, coarsely grated
1 15-ounce can diced tomatoes in sauce
1 teaspoon dried basil
8 ounces top round steak
1 tablespoon sharp Dijon mustard

●Preheat the broiler. In a heavy pan, heat oil over medium-
high heat. Add garlic and brown lightly. Add onion and carrot,
stir and cook for 3 to 4 minutes. Add tomatoes and their sauce
and simmer briskly, until sauce is reduced by half, about 10
minutes. Stir in basil; simmer over low heat. Put steak under
broiler for 3 to 5 minutes on each side. When you turn steak,
put sauce in blender with mustard; buzz to liquify, return to
pan, and reheat. Slice steak into thin strips with the grain.
Pour sauce on plates, rearrange steak strips like fallen dominoes on top, and pour a thin ribbon of sauce over each
serving.

Beef and Lamb

Beef do Pyaza

In India, anything cooked *do pyaza* has a lot of onions in it.
This beef dish is lightly seasoned, using a blend of spices called
garam masala, which can be found at specialty stores. If curry
powder from the supermarket has been your standby, this and
other Indian spice blends will be a revelation—there are
dozens of them. Indian women make their own, roasting and
grinding the spices in small quantities. It certainly makes the
house smell great, but it's easier to buy a few kinds to
experiment with. Serve mildly gingered green beans, basmati
rice or new potatoes in yogurt, and have a brisk ale along
with it.

---

8 ounces lean beef
2 teaspoons oil
2 large onions, chopped
2 tablespoons golden raisins
1 to 3 teaspoons garam masala *or*
    1 to 3 teaspoons curry powder
1 inch gingerroot, peeled and thickly sliced
2 tablespoons chopped fresh mint (4 to 6 sprigs)
¼ cup sour cream

●Rinse beef, pat dry. Slice into thin strips. In a large frying
pan, heat oil over medium heat. Brown beef quickly on both
sides. Add onions to beef along with raisins and garam masala.
Put gingerroot in blender or food processor with ¼ cup water
and mint; buzz to blend, then pour over meat. Stir and cook
over high heat for 5 to 6 minutes, until beef is chewy but tender, and sauce is fairly thick. Stir in sour cream, heat for a
minute, and serve.

Beef and Lamb

Burgers in Bitter Beer

When you feel like eating hamburgers, but it's raining too
hard to barbecue, these burgers will lift winter spirits. Outstanding microbreweries are popping up all over the country,
and this recipe was designed for a microbrew with a bitter
character. Such beers lend their distinctive hoppy tang to lean
beef with very pleasant results. When the last of our stored
garlic sprouts, ready for spring, we use the green tips—chopped
in at the last minute—for an extra bite. If you can't find
sprouted garlic cloves or tips in the supermarket, substitute
garlic chives or ordinary chives. Heap the vegetables on the
buns or patties, or if you prefer the patties plain, serve rice,
assorted chutneys, broad beans with a touch of savory and
sour cream. To drink? More beer, of course.

8 ounces lean ground beef
1 large clove garlic, pressed
1 carrot, coarsely grated
1 teaspoon freshly ground black pepper
2 teaspoons butter
1 small yellow onion, thickly sliced into rings
4 ounces mushrooms, thickly sliced
1 10- to 12-ounce bottle bitter beer

•In a mixing bowl, break up ground beef. Add garlic, reserving tips, if any, carrot, and pepper; mix well, but with a light
hand, and form into 2 or 3 patties. In a heavy iron frying pan,
melt butter over high heat until foamy. Add patties and sear
the first side quickly, cooking only 2 to 3 minutes. When well
browned, flip patties and reduce heat to medium high. Add
onions and mushrooms; stir to coat slightly with pan juices.
Cook for 2 to 3 minutes, then pour in 5 to 6 ounces of beer,
drinking the rest, of course. Boil gently for 4 to 5 minutes,
shaking pan now and then to keep things from sticking. When
liquid is reduced by half, toss in garlic tips and serve patties.

Summery Beef Sauté

When the garden is bursting with fresh vegetables, this quick sauté takes advantage of the wealth. Purple beans, golden squash, red tomatoes, and green basil mingle with garlic and capers in an understated but flavorful sauce to top pasta or rice. A green salad with artichoke hearts, warm, crusty bread, and a Bordeaux or Côtes du Rhône make it a simple and delicious meal.

---

8 ounces lean beef
2 teaspoons olive oil
1 clove garlic
2 tablespoons coarsely chopped fresh basil
1 pattypan squash, cut into small chunks
4 ounces purple beans, sliced into 1-inch diagonals
2 tomatoes, cut into wedges
1 teaspoon capers

●Rinse beef, pat dry, and slice into thin strips. In a heavy pan, heat oil over medium-high heat. Add garlic and brown on all sides. Add beef, brown quickly. Add basil, squash, beans, tomatoes, and capers; sauté for 6 to 8 minutes, until vegetables are just tender. Remove and discard garlic. Serve over rice or pasta.

Squash Blossom Stew

Green tomatoes are the bane of gardeners throughout the country. The Hopi Indians of the Southwest use them to transform this stew. Delicious, tart bits of green tomato mingle with chiles and lean beef, cilantro and mint. The addition of tiny baby squash, still bearing blossoms and cooked only until warm, makes this summery dish especially pretty. If your garden (or the neighbor's) is burdened with zucchini, go ahead and use them, since the taste of both flower and vegetable is similar. This meal seems to taste better when eaten out-of-doors. Serve fresh tortillas with a bowl of salsa and several bottles of Mexican beer.

---

8 ounces lean beef
2 teaspoons oil
2 green tomatoes, chopped into chunks
1 fresh red chile, seeded (to taste) and chopped into rings
1 medium onion, thickly sliced
2 tablespoons chopped fresh cilantro
2 tablespoons chopped fresh mint
4 small summer squash with blossoms

●Rinse beef, pat dry. Cut into small cubes. In a heavy pan, heat oil over medium-high heat. Add beef and brown quickly on all sides. Add tomatoes, chile, and onion, stirring to coat with pan juices. Add cilantro and mint to beef along with ¼ cup water. Bring to a boil, reduce heat until bubbling gently, and cook for 15 minutes. Add the whole squash, heat through (it takes 3 to 5 minutes), and serve.

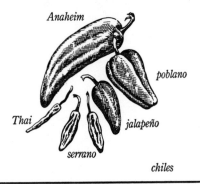

Anaheim

poblano

Thai

jalapeño

serrano

chiles

Fajitas with Avocado Sauce

Whole wheat tacos make an especially chewy wrap-up for the steak and onion filling of this quick and hearty dish. Flour or corn, blue, yellow, or white, will also do—or use several kinds for an uncommonly attractive presentation. The steak is briefly marinated in lime juice and garlic, then quickly broiled or grilled, cut into thin strips, and piled in warm tortillas with slices of red onion, avocado, and a silky, hot sauce. Mixed greens with a Cheddar and salsa dressing and some great beer support the main event.

---

1 package medium flour tortillas
8 ounces top round steak
1 lime, juiced plus grated peel
2 fat cloves garlic, pressed
½ cup sour cream *or* yogurt
2 to 4 tablespoons green or red salsa
1 avocado, ½ mashed, ½ thinly sliced
1 red onion, halved and thinly sliced

●Loosely wrap in foil as many tortillas as you think you can eat; place in warm oven. Rinse steak, pat dry. Place steak on piece of foil. Put 1 teaspoon lime juice in a bowl, the rest over steak. Add half the garlic to bowl, put other half over steak. Marinate steak, turning several times, so both sides have juice and garlic on them. Add sour cream to lime juice in bowl, stir in peel, mashed avocado, and salsa; set aside. Grill or broil steak, 3 to 5 minutes per side. Cut in thin strips with the grain. Put a few pieces of steak, onion, and avocado slices in each tortilla, add sauce, fold, and serve.

Lamb Chops with Baked Garlic

Lamb is especially succulent in partnership with garlic, as
this recipe exuberantly proves. Even stalwart garlic fans may
flinch at the amount, but it isn't all that extreme. Garlic mellows when baked, turning golden and creamily mild. Pop the
little cloves out of the skins one by one to savor their silki-
ness; the next time you make this, you might want to allow a
head of garlic per person. Big eaters may want several chops,
so buy accordingly, and make more sauce. Serve with new
potatoes or onion rolls, a green salad with a sharp, mustard
vinaigrette, and bold nebbiolo or zinfandel.

---

2 thick-cut lamb chops (8 to 12 ounces total)
2 teaspoons olive oil
1 head garlic, whole plus 2 fat cloves, pressed
½ cup artichoke hearts *or*
   1 6-ounce jar (marinated work well)
½ cup red wine
½ to 1 teaspoon dried oregano
1 to 2 dried peperoncini

●Rinse lamb, pat dry, brush lightly with oil. Spread a pressed
garlic clove over each. Brush a 1½-quart baking dish with oil,
arrange chops in single layer. Slice whole, unpeeled garlic
head in half crosswise. Rub cut sides in oil, then bake with
chops in 350 degree oven for 40 to 50 minutes. To make sauce,
combine artichoke hearts, wine, oregano, and peperoncini in a
small saucepan over medium heat; simmer. To serve, put a
chop and half a head of garlic on each plate. Remove and discard peperoncini; spoon sauce over chops and pass any extra
in a bowl.

Lamb and Cucumber Sauté

Most American lamb is raised on intermountain ranches in California and Texas. Spring-born lambs fatten up through the summer, arriving in supermarkets during the fall and winter. What we eat in spring is New Zealand lamb, which can't legally be treated with hormones, tranquilizers, or chemical alterants, so frozen can be better than fresh. Lamb is naturally leaner than beef, and the smaller new cuts, many boneless, are ideal for the quick cooking that best develops its true flavor. Prolonged cooking emphasizes the harsher, stronger subflavors, so if lamb hasn't been a favorite in the past, try a recipe calling for small medallions, quickly broiled, or lean strips of boneless lamb, as in this piquant Indian entrée. Lemon rice or pilaf, mixed greens tossed with lemon-sesame dressing, and a tangy ale accompany this dish well.

---

8 ounces lean, boneless lamb
1 cup yogurt
1½ tablespoons finely chopped fresh cilantro
1½ tablespoons finely chopped fresh mint
3 cloves garlic
1 to 2 teaspoons olive oil
1 to 3 fresh chiles, seeded and thinly sliced
1 cucumber, peeled and cut lengthwise into 8 pieces

●Rinse lamb, pat dry, and slice into thin strips. Blend yogurt with 2 teaspoons each of cilantro and mint. Press in 1 garlic clove; set aside. In a frying pan, heat oil over medium-high heat. Add lamb and brown quickly on all sides. Reduce heat and add chiles, 2 mashed garlic cloves, and remaining herbs; stir and cook for 2 to 3 minutes. Add ½ cup water and cook vigorously, stirring often, for 8 to 10 minutes, or until liquid is nearly gone. To serve, spoon meat mixture onto plates, arrange cucumber spears along the side, and add a dollop of yogurt sauce to each portion.

Lamb with Mint Raita

Raitas, cooling mixtures of yogurt, herbs, and spices, provide soothing contrast to pungent, fiery curry dishes. Here, the sauce is served cold with a speedy, hot lamb curry, which can be mild or explosive, depending on your preference. Raitas make perfect summer salads—add more vegetables, raw or marinated, bits of chicken, shrimp, or fish—or may be thinned with additional yogurt and buttermilk and served as soothing hot-weather soups. Traditional seasonings include cumin, coriander, cilantro, mint, garlic, and nutmeg. Make long grain or basmati rice, spinach salad tossed with nuts and dried apricots and splashed with a fruit dressing, and serve cold ale or a fruity, slightly chilled Beaujolais.

---

8 ounces lean, boneless lamb
1 teaspoon vegetable oil
4 cloves garlic, pressed or mashed
1 large onion, chopped
1 to 2 teaspoons garam masala *or* curry powder
1 cup yogurt
2 tablespoons chopped fresh mint
1 cucumber, peeled, seeded, and chopped into small pieces

●Rinse lamb, pat dry; cut into ½-inch cubes. In a medium frying pan, heat oil over medium-high heat. Add 2 cloves garlic, brown lightly. Add lamb, brown quickly all over; reduce heat. Add all but ¼ cup onion; stir and cook for 5 to 6 minutes. Stir in garam masala or curry powder. Add ½ cup water; stir, reduce heat, cover, and simmer for 20 to 25 minutes, until lamb is tender. Add more water as needed if pan becomes dry. To make raita, press remaining 2 cloves garlic into yogurt. Stir in mint, reserving 2 teaspoons for garnish. Add cucumber to yogurt with remaining onion. To serve, spoon lamb mixture onto center of plates, pour raita in a circle around it. Sprinkle with reserved mint.

Lamb and Beans

Thick lamb medallions broil, grill, or pan-sauté in minutes and need very little help to make them delectable (any of these cooking techniques may be used with the following sauce). Properly cooked lamb, by any method, is fork-tender, pink, and generously juicy when sliced. Overcooked lamb is gray, tough, and nasty; no sauce can really help, so keep your eye on the cooking time. Fresh herbs make a big difference here, especially the savory, though it retains flavor fairly well when dried. Summer savory is the classic companion for fresh beans, just as winter savory (or dried summer savory) goes into the winter bean pot. This entrée invites a simple rice and cilantro pilaf, a cucumber, orange, and onion salad with an herbed vinaigrette, and a glass of chiaretto or a sturdy ale.

---

2 to 4 lamb medallions (8 to 12 ounces total)
2 teaspoons butter
½ teaspoon black peppercorns, cracked
1 onion, cut into thin half-moon slices
4 ounces snap beans, thinly sliced on the diagonal
3 tomatoes, cut into wedges
1 teaspoon chopped fresh lemon thyme
1 teaspoon chopped fresh savory (reserve a few leaves
  for garnish)

●Rinse lamb, pat dry. Rub lightly with butter, pat on cracked peppercorns. Preheat broiler. In a frying pan, heat remaining butter over medium heat. Add onion, beans, tomatoes, and herbs; stir to coat and cook for 5 minutes. Mash tomatoes with a fork, and reduce heat to warm. While vegetables are cooking, broil lamb for 4 to 6 minutes per side. To serve, spoon sauce onto plates, set lamb medallions on top, and garnish with a sprig or 2 of savory.

Lamb with Emerald Satsumas and Kumquats

Emerald satsumas are a green-skinned variety of the sweet-tart Japanese fruit that floods West Coast markets at Christmas time. Mandarin oranges or tangerines will bring a similar flavor, but nothing is so pretty as the twisting, translucent melon-colored fans of fruit, each edged in deepest green. Kumquats, a tiny relative of the satsuma, bring bright color and tangy bursts of flavor to balance the richness of the garlicky lamb. If you haven't enjoyed kumquats before, this might be the recipe to win you over. Serve with basmati rice, a salad of spinach, watercress, and green onions with a walnut and mustard vinaigrette, and a syrah from the Rhône or an Australian shiraz.

---

2 teaspoons olive oil
2 to 4 lamb medallions (8 to 12 ounces total)
2 cloves garlic, sliced
1 medium onion, sliced into thin half moons
2 tablespoons raspberry vinegar
1 bunch fresh cilantro, chopped
12 kumquats
2 emerald satsumas, 1 sliced thinly, 1 juiced

●In a frying pan, heat oil over medium-high heat. Add lamb and quickly brown on both sides. Add garlic and onion; stir and cook for 5 minutes. Add vinegar, cilantro, kumquats, and satsuma juice; partially cover and simmer for 20 minutes, turning lamb once. Slit the thin slices of satsuma and twist them into fans to top each piece of lamb. Serve.

Lamb Medallions in Pumpkin Sauce

Thick, boneless medallions of lamb are especially good with this intriguing, peppery pumpkin sauce. Pureed winter squash is an excellent substitute when you don't want to cope with half a can of leftover pumpkin pulp. Carrots and parsnips echo the sweet-hot combination, their textures contrasting pleasantly with the tender, savory lamb. Serve broccoli or brussels sprouts braised in stock and sprinkled with grated Parmesan, and a glass of dry, smooth crimson rhubarb wine.

---

2 to 4 lamb medallions (8 to 12 ounces total)
2 fat carrots, peeled and sliced lengthwise into quarters
  (reserving a few curls for garnish)
2 fat parsnips, peeled and sliced lengthwise into quarters
2 to 3 teaspoons butter
2 cloves garlic, pressed
1¼ cups pumpkin pulp *or*
  1 10-ounce box frozen winter squash puree, thawed
2 to 3 teaspoons orange juice concentrate
½ teaspoon black pepper

●Rinse lamb, pat dry. In a saucepan, parboil carrots and parsnips in lightly salted water for 5 to 6 minutes. To make sauce, melt 1 teaspoon butter in a saucepan over medium heat. Press in 1 garlic clove; stir and cook for 3 to 5 minutes. Add pumpkin, orange juice, and pepper; heat through and keep warm over low. Press remaining garlic clove over medallions, a bit on each. In a heavy frying pan, heat remaining butter over medium heat until foamy. Put in lamb and sear quickly on both sides. Reduce heat and add drained, parboiled vegetables, stirring to coat with butter. Cook lamb for 6 to 7 minutes per side, turning once. Pour sauce on 2 plates, arrange meat and vegetables on top, garnish with carrot curls, and serve at once.

Zuñi Lamb Stew

This is a very old recipe from New Mexico, in which traditional Zuñi foods are simply combined in a thin stew or chunky soup. Spring lamb is cut small to cook quickly with the herbs, and the vegetables are added later to keep them crisp. If you grow wild celery (*Phellopterus* sp.) as the Zuñi do, use the greens fresh or dried; otherwise use the tops of ordinary celery or lovage. With dry herbs, use half the amount given below. Blue corn quesadillas are an appropriate side dish, and a clean, sturdy ale is equally complementary, though certainly less authentic.

---

8 ounces lean lamb
2 teaspoons oil *or* lard
1 medium onion, coarsely chopped
1 to 3 fresh green chiles, seeded (to taste) and thinly chopped
1 tablespoon chopped fresh mint (3 to 4 sprigs) *or*
   1½ teaspoons dried
1 tablespoon chopped fresh celery greens *or*
   1½ teaspoons dried
2 small summer squash, halved lengthwise, cut into
   ½-inch half-wheels
4 ounces green beans

●Rinse lamb, pat dry. Cut lamb into ½-inch cubes. In a large pan, heat oil (lard would be traditional) over medium-high heat. Add lamb and brown quickly on all sides. Add onion, chile(s), and herbs with enough water to cover. Bring to a rapid boil, lower heat, cover pan, and simmer 15 to 20 minutes, until lamb is just tender. Add squash and beans and continue cooking, partially covered, until vegetables are tender but still crisp, about 8 to 10 minutes.

*C*ured & Smoked Meats

169   *Cranberry-Gooseberry Ham*

170   *Ham with Chard and Capers*

171   *Avocado Ham Sauté*

172   *Spaghetti alla Carbonara*

173   *Pumpkin Tortellone all'Amatrice*

174   *Gorgonzola Pear Salad*

175   *Jicama Ham Salad*

176   *Green Eggs and Ham*

177   *Sorrel, Spinach, and Bacon Salad*

178   *Avocado Tzatziki Pita*

179   *Wensleydale Grill*

180   *Mixed Grill with Sausages*

181   *Sausage and Lima Casserole*

182   *Sausage Salad with Kasséri Cheese*

183   *Garbanzo Salad*

184   *Salami Salad*

185   *Smoked Chicken Salad*

186   *Smoked Turkey Salad in Poppy Seed Dressing*

187   *Smoked Chicken Tortillas*

Cranberry–Gooseberry Ham
(Serves 2 to 4)

The Northwest is one of the greatest cranberry producing areas in the world, as many displaced New Englanders are delighted to discover. Recent years have seen cranberries enjoying a vogue of sorts, so that people who never dreamed of eating them except during the winter holidays are now offering them with nonchalance during any season. This recipe pairs tart cranberries with gooseberry preserves (another Northwest specialty) and fresh orange in an exotic, citrus mélange with whispers of garlic and mustard. Even a mediocre ham is elevated by such treatment, and a good ham becomes exceptional. Serve steamed broccoli with tarragon vinegar, basmati rice or potato chunks, and perhaps a dry pear wine or any blush.

½ cup cranberries
2 tablespoons gooseberry jam or preserves
1 orange, juiced plus peel sliced into strips
1 fat clove garlic, mashed
1 tablespoon Dijon mustard
1 1-pound ham steak

● Rinse and pick over cranberries; drain. In a heavy saucepan, combine cranberries, jam, orange juice, several strips of peel, garlic, and mustard. Bring to a boil, stirring all the while. Reduce heat and simmer for 12 to 15 minutes, stirring occasionally, until cranberries pop, and mixture begins to thicken. Remove and discard garlic and orange peel. Put ham in a baking dish. Pour sauce over ham, covering it completely. Bake in 350 degree oven for 35 to 40 minutes.

Ham with Chard and Capers

Beautiful ham is worth searching for—not heavily salted or grossly saturated with liquid smoke, not puffy with injected water or thick with fat and gristle. Commercially, Cure 81 is the most reliable American ham on the market, but check out local smokeries as well for fresh, unadulterated ham, bacon, and sausages. This recipe calls for a thick ham steak, which, lightly glazed, then broiled, meets a savory down-home sauce of red-stemmed chard and capers. Serve it with cornbread, fresh fruit, a glass of stout, or a pinot noir.

---

1 pound ham steak
1 tablespoon olive oil
2 shallots, sliced
1 bunch fresh chard, trimmed and shredded
1 onion, chopped
2 tablespoons rosemary (or wine) vinegar
1 teaspoon capers

●Brush ham steak lightly with olive oil and grill or broil for 5 to 7 minutes on each side. While it cooks, brown shallots in remaining oil. Add chard and onions; stir and cook for 3 to 5 minutes, until greens begin to wilt. Add vinegar and capers, partially cover, and simmer, until ham steak is ready. Serve each portion of ham with a generous surrounding of chard and sauce.

Avocado Ham Sauté

Only the leanest ham, lightly smoked and not too salty, deserves this unusual treatment. The thick avocado slices warm only slightly, keeping texture intact while the flavor expands. The fluffy sauce, foamy green and flecked with almonds, has a pronounced onion flavor that emphasizes whatever the ham has to offer—so the better the ham, the better the result. Roasted potatoes and carrots, a salad of oakleaf and buttercrunch lettuce with a mustardy vinaigrette and a glass of grenache rosé are pleasant additions, as is a full-bodied ale.

---

1 pound ham steak
1 avocado, peeled, halved, and sliced into long, thin wedges
⅔ cup yogurt
¼ cup salted almonds, coarsely chopped
4 green onions
1 to 2 teaspoons almond oil *or* avocado oil
2 shallots, thinly sliced on diagonal
1 teaspoon chopped fresh tarragon *or*
 ½ teaspoon dried

●Rinse meat, pat dry, and cut in 2 equal pieces. Put half the avocado (reserving 6 wedges) into blender or food processor. Add yogurt, half the almonds, and 2 chopped green onions. Blend to smooth paste. In a frying pan, heat oil over medium heat. Add shallots and cook for 3 to 5 minutes. Increase heat, add tarragon and ham, browning meat quickly on both sides. Reduce heat, slide in remaining green onion, cut into long, thin strips, add avocado slices; heat through. Serve ham and avocado mixture. Spoon sauce over each portion and sprinkle on remaining almonds.

Spaghetti alla Carbonara

Coal miners' spaghetti is named for the chunky bits of black pepper that distinguish this simple peasant dish. In the original form, the sauce is made of unsmoked bacon, *pancetta*, which is rarely obtainable in this country. Mild ham or Canadian back bacon are both good substitutes, as they are closer to the taste and feel of the authentic dish than American bacon. The traditional fat spaghetti holds this sort of clingy, cheesy sauce best. Since the sauce relies on the stored heat in the pasta to cook, drain the pasta quickly, allowing a bit of the cooking water to return to the pan with the noodles. ON NO ACCOUNT should you commit the culinary crime of rinsing pasta with cold water. Horrors! Have side dishes of broccoli with lemon butter, gingery carrots or baby beets, and a glass of dolcetto or grignolino.

---

8 ounces fresh spaghetti (#8 or #9) *or*
    4 ounces dry
1 teaspoon olive oil
2 to 3 ounces mild ham or Canadian back bacon, finely diced
1 to 2 teaspoons whole black peppercorns
1 large or 2 small eggs
1 ounce grated Romano or pecorino cheese
1 ounce grated Parmesan cheese

•In a large pot, bring salted water to boil for spaghetti. As soon as spaghetti goes into the pot, start sauce. In a frying pan, heat oil over low heat. Add ham and peppercorns. Whisk eggs with a fork; add cheeses and stir well. When spaghetti is al dente, drain briefly, then return to pot. Add egg-cheese mixture at once, tossing the pasta with wooden forks if you have them. Sauce should be creamy. Add pepper and ham, mix well, and serve at once, spooning extra ham and pepper on each plate (it always falls to the bottom).

Pumpkin Tortellone all'Amatrice

Fini, the Italian fancy-food company, ships this fat pumpkin pasta stuffed with cheese frozen, and it gets from Modena to the supermarket in fine shape. Of course, any tortellini would do, and now most markets offer several varieties on a regular basis. These pumpkin ones are especially tasty, and because they are a bit oversized, they are called tortellone, "big dumplings," but they are just larger versions of the more familiar tortellini. The Amatrice sauce is always made with fresh tomatoes. It is full of smoky scraps of bacon, with subtle, tingling heat from the peperoncini (red-hot, dried Italian chiles). Start your meal with a simple green salad, just lettuce, shredded green onions, fresh dressing, and a scattering of herbed croutons on top. Next, the pasta, a bottle of Chianti Classico, and a bowl of ripe, local fruit. *Ottimo.*

---

250 grams pumpkin tortellone *or*
  ½ pound tortellini
4 slices smoked bacon
5 to 6 plum tomatoes, cut into chunks
1 to 2 peperoncini
1 teaspoon freshly ground black pepper *or* to taste
1 ounce shredded pecorino cheese

●In a saucepan, bring salted water to boil. Slice bacon into small pieces. Put bacon and peperoncini in a frying pan and cook over medium heat until brown and crisp. Remove and discard peperoncini. Drain off all but about 1 teaspoon of drippings. Add tomatoes to pan and cook for 2 to 3 minutes until bubbly. Put pasta in boiling water and cook for 6 to 8 minutes. Mash tomatoes a bit with fork, add black pepper. As soon as pasta is tender, drain and serve in 2 bowls. Put some sauce on each and top with half the cheese.

Gorgonzola Pear Salad

Northern Italians have been making Gorgonzola for nearly three thousand years. Special caves for aging the cheeses at the proper temperature and moisture levels have been made in the Italian alps, broadening the area in which it is produced to meet the increased demand from abroad for this rich cheese. Although it is mold ripened with the same strain used for Roquefort and other bleu cheeses (*Penicillium glaucum*), Gorgonzola has greener veins and a less pungent, salty flavor than all but the very best of the others. Here, it is matched with firm, tender-crisp fall pears—barely ripe Bartletts for choice—and lean, lightly smoked ham in a fall salad. Have warm rolls, a salad of mustard greens and shredded Chinese cabbage tossed with a mustard vinaigrette, and pour yourself a glass of dolcetto or a dry blush wine.

---

2 pears, cored and thinly sliced
4 ounces lean ham, thinly sliced
1 large avocado, peeled and thinly sliced
1 lemon, juiced plus grated peel
3 to 4 ounces Gorgonzola cheese, crumbled
½ cup walnuts, toasted and coarsely chopped
1 clove garlic

●Put pears, ham, and half the avocado slices into a salad bowl and toss gently. Sprinkle with 2 to 3 teaspoons lemon juice, 2 tablespoons Gorgonzola, and 2 tablespoons walnuts; set aside. Put remaining avocado into blender with garlic, 1 to 2 teaspoons lemon juice, ½ teaspoon peel, remaining nuts, and remaining Gorgonzola, adding 1 to 2 teaspoons water, if needed. Blend to thick sauce, pour over salad, toss gently, and serve.

Jícama Ham Salad

This is a hearty fall salad for a tailgate picnic. Strips of smoky ham and jícama are tossed with sharp Cheddar, red onion, salty almonds, and spiky romanesco broccoli shoots in a warm mustard vinaigrette. (You can also use broccoli side shoots from the garden, or florets broken off a big head from the supermarket.) Hot garlic bread or rolls, split and buttered, a basket of apples and pears, and a cold ale make a terrific fall feast.

---

1 head romanesco (or regular) broccoli
8 ounces lean ham, sliced into matchsticks
8 ounces jícama, sliced into matchsticks
4 ounces extrasharp Cheddar cheese, sliced into matchsticks
½ Bermuda (red) onion, halved and thinly sliced
¼ cup herbed vinaigrette or any garlic, herb oil-and-vinegar
   dressing
1 tablespoon Dijon mustard
¼ cup salted almonds

●Break broccoli into florets, steam for 3 to 4 minutes until barely tender. Gently toss together ham, jícama, cheese, and onion. In a saucepan, heat vinaigrette over medium heat. Stir in mustard until it steams, but don't let it boil. Drizzle dressing over salad, add almonds, toss, and serve. (For a picnic, put the hot dressing in a small thermos and the salad strips in a covered container. Pack the nuts separately to keep them crisp.)

jícama

Green Eggs and Ham

A foamy green sauce that tastes of spring envelopes strips of lean ham and hard-cooked eggs. This pretty mixture of greens, herbs, and walnuts is as good with chicken or fish as in salads like this one. Rinse, but don't spin-dry the greens; just shake them gently, for they cook in the steam from water that clings to their leaves. Pass a plate of thin watercress sandwiches, a basket of fruit, and a bottle of lemony weissbier, dry Orvieto, or hard cider.

---

1 bunch fresh spinach, rinsed and trimmed
1 bunch fresh sorrel, rinsed and trimmed
4 ounces lean ham, sliced into thin strips
3 hard-boiled eggs, quartered
2 tablespoons olive oil
1 bunch fresh watercress, rinsed and trimmed
1 small bunch fresh chives, rinsed and chopped
¼ cup walnuts, toasted

• Arrange a few leaves of spinach and sorrel on each plate; top with ham and eggs. In a small heavy saucepan, heat 1 teaspoon oil over medium heat. Add remaining spinach and sorrel, watercress and chives. Cover pan and cook over medium heat for 5 to 6 minutes, shaking pan several times. Greens should be limp but still bright green. Put greens in blender or food processor with remaining oil and half the walnuts, adding 1 to 2 tablespoons water as needed to make a smooth sauce. Pour over salads, top with remaining walnuts, and serve at once.

Sorrel, Spinach, and Bacon Salad

When the first young sorrel appears in the garden or market, this salad is an excellent way to enjoy it. Buttery, small spinach leaves and crisp, salty bacon provide a balanced counterpoint to the sour tang of sorrel. Chopped hazelnuts could be replaced with pine nuts, as they often are in Italian spring salads of this sort. The hot bacon dressing blends onions with a bit of curry and wine vinaigrette. Serve with hot rolls, sweet butter, perhaps a chunk of Gorgonzola, some aged Cheddar, and a smooth Jarlsberg. To drink, try an Italian white, a dry blush, or an imported ale.

---

4 strips lean bacon
1 medium yellow onion, chopped
½ teaspoon mild curry powder *or*
    ¼ teaspoon of a spicier blend
3 to 4 tablespoons vinaigrette (made with wine vinegar)
2 to 3 bunches young, fresh sorrel, rinsed and trimmed
1 bunch young, fresh spinach, rinsed and trimmed
¼ cup hazelnuts or pine nuts, toasted
3 hard-boiled eggs, quartered

●Put bacon in plastic bag and place in freezer. When bacon is cold, cut lengthwise into small strips. In a frying pan, cook bacon over medium heat until tender-crisp. Drain off all but 1 to 2 teaspoons drippings. Stir in onion and cook for 2 to 3 minutes until just soft. Add curry powder, stirring to make a smooth paste, then blend in vinaigrette and warm it gently. Pat greens dry, then heap into a salad bowl. Pour on dressing, add nuts and bacon, and toss well. Arrange eggs on top and serve.

Avocado Tzatziki Pita

Warm pitas, split and spilling a lush combination of ham,
walnuts, and olives bathed in garlic avocado tzatziki make
a welcome diversion when football levels approach the toxic.
A sturdy pilsner will complement this, as will that trenchant
Greek, red Demestica.

¼ cup walnuts, toasted
2 to 4 pitas
1 avocado, peeled and halved
4 ounces Cure 81 ham, sliced into 2- x ¼-inch strips
8 to 10 Greek olives, pitted and chopped
1 cup yogurt
2 to 4 cloves garlic, chopped
1 teaspoon oregano

●Loosely wrap pitas in foil, keep in warm oven. Cut half of
avocado into chunks and toss gently with ham, olives, and
walnuts. Put other half into blender or food processor with
yogurt, garlic, and oregano; buzz briefly to chunky blend. To
serve, split pitas and fill with ham mixture, then spoon tzatziki
over each.

Wensleydale Grill

Well into fall, there are warm nights when it is a pleasure to cook outdoors. This hearty mixed grill features a thick slab of lean ham—though beef is also delicious cooked in this combination—with vegetables and a sharp English cheese. Wensleydale is the Yorkshire version of Stilton; quite similar, though creamier, and more forceful in flavor. Less pronounced cheeses, such as Cheddar, ripe Asiago, or a well-aged California jack, can be substituted. Late plum tomatoes from the garden or supermarket will be full of flavor, but a touch of the grill brings out the best in any kind. Pile a platter with strips of sweet red peppers, florets of broccoli and celery—the fall crop is often fresh and local—adding a bowl of mustard dip. Have a bottle of Côtes du Rhône, an ale, or an oatmeal stout.

---

1 bunch fresh thyme, chopped *or*
  1 tablespoon dried
1 bunch fresh fennel *or* rosemary, chopped *or*
  1 tablespoon dried
Olive oil
2 cloves garlic, crushed
1 pound ham steak (as thick as possible)
2 to 3 tomatoes
Unsliced loaf bread *or* rolls
3 to 4 ounces Wensleydale cheese, sliced

●Fire up the coals, throwing a handful of fresh (or a couple of tablespoons dried) herbs onto the outer, cooler areas just before you start cooking. Reserve a few sprigs of each herb. In a pan, heat 3 to 4 tablespoons oil over low heat. Add garlic and herbs. Brush ham and tomatoes lightly with oil. Grill ham for 6 to 8 minutes on each side. Place whole tomatoes on outer part of grill and give them a quarter turn every couple of minutes. Cut thick slices of bread, 1 or 2 for each person, and brush one side of each piece with oil, or split rolls and brush insides with oil. Place bread on outer part of grill, oil-side down, for 2 to 3 minutes. While bread is grilling, slice strips off ham steak and cut tomatoes in thick slices. Layer ham and tomatoes on bread and top with cheese. Place open-face sandwiches on foil and grill for 1 to 2 minutes, until cheese is soft but not melted.

Mixed Grill with Sausages

The meat department of our local supermarket makes special sausages several times a week—potato; pork and tomato; apple-cinnamon; chorizo; bratwurst—without preservatives or fillers, and they sell for less than the commercial brands. Many larger stores are adding such special services, to the pleasure and benefit of the consumer. Here, a variety of fresh sausages are grilled with ripe vegetables to be made into do-it-yourself sandwiches. A basket of fruit, a few chunks of cheese—one sharp, one creamy, one smoked—will make a hearty and satisfying meal with very little effort. To drink, try rauchbier if you can find it; it is exposed to alder smoke during the open-pan mash boiling, so that it absorbs a wonderful, tangy flavor of woodsmoke.

---

2 tablespoons olive oil
1 tablespoon sherry or wine vinegar
1 pound mixed sausages (1 each of 2 or 3 kinds)
2 large, ripe tomatoes
1 large white onion, thickly sliced (keeping slices intact)
4 ounces large mushrooms
Mustard for sandwiches (offer several kinds)
Wheat rolls or bread for sandwiches (2 or more per person)

●Start coals in grill. Blend oil and vinegar in a jar and shake well. Prick sausages with a fork in several places. Brush tomatoes, onions, and mushrooms with oil and vinegar. (If mushrooms are small, thread them on skewers to keep them from falling through the grill.) Cook sausages on the central, hotter part of grill, turning several times. Larger ones will need 3 to 5 minutes a side, smaller ones as little as 2 to 3 minutes a side. Place vegetables on outer, cooler part of grill. The onions will take 4 to 6 minutes a side, the tomatoes, 3 to 5 minutes. Turn three or four times. The mushrooms should be the farthest from the heat. Grill only 1 to 2 minutes on each side, with extra basting at each turn. When all is cooked, have each person combine sausages, vegetables, mustard, and bread or rolls for sandwiches.

Sausage and Lima Casserole

Baby lima beans are tender and buttery, especially when fresh. If shelling them seems a chore, relax with a glass of wine, and get a friend to help. To use frozen limas, just separate them under running water, then add them to the casserole. For variety, try a spicy or savory sausage—fish; fresh summer; venison; smoked rabbit; or blood sausages. Look for local brands, made by small companies. These are often free of additives and made with extra care; the results have character rather than the lackluster sameness created by liberal use of liquid smoke and synthetic flavorings. Mix up a salad of spinach, beet and mustard greens tossed with a caraway-garlic vinaigrette, and serve pears, apples, and Gorgonzola for dessert. A dry blush wine or a heady microbrewed beer will go well with this meal.

---

8 ounces fresh sausage, chopped or broken up
1 medium white onion, chopped
4 ripe tomatoes, diced *or*
  1 15-ounce can diced
1 green sweet pepper, chopped
1 pound fresh baby lima beans, shelled *or*
  1 10-ounce box frozen
1 teaspoon fresh sage *or*
  ½ teaspoon dried
1 teaspoon fresh thyme *or*
  ½ teaspoon dried
½ cup dry red wine

●In a large skillet, cook sausage over medium-high heat until no longer pink. Add onion, green pepper, lima beans, and herbs. Stir well, then add wine and enough water to cover (about ¼ cup). Partially cover pan and simmer, until beans are tender, about 15 to 20 minutes. Remove cover and cook over medium-high heat until liquid is reduced by half. Serve hot.

Sausage Salad with Kasséri Cheese

Sharp, piquant kasséri cheese is usually found flaming in
restaurants that specialize in Peloponnesian foods. It adds
special snap to this sausage salad as well, though chunks of
mizíthra, Asiago, or pecorino are fine substitutes. Use summer
sausage or kielbasa, pepperoni or the local best for the main
event; in Montana, we made this with elk sausages poached in
beer. The tart, lemony dressing keeps the rich flavors separate
and clean. Serve hot rolls and a glass of Montepulciano
d'Abruzzo to round things out.

½ red onion, sliced into wheels
1 firm, unpeeled apple, King or Granny Smith, diced
2 ounces kasséri cheese, cut into chunks
4 ounces smoked sausages, cut into ¼-inch slices
1 lemon, juiced plus grated peel
1 tablespoon olive oil
1 teaspoon dried thyme
¼ cup walnuts, toasted

●Separate onion into rings and mound in a salad bowl. Add
apple, cheese, and sausage. Scatter some lemon peel over
salad. To make dressing, blend oil with lemon juice (tasting as
you go) and thyme. Pour dressing over salad, add walnuts, and
toss gently. Serve at once, before walnuts get soft.

Garbanzo Salad

This lively but simple salad relies on the excellence of just a few ingredients for its impact. Wine-cured, hard salami from Italy is showing up on a lot of supermarket shelves, but some of the best comes from San Francisco, where there is a long-established Italian community. Sun-dried tomatoes from California fields are just as sweet and chewy as the imported kind, and far less expensive; home gardeners can easily make their own for practically nothing. Serve with warm rolls, olives, and cheeses, Chianti or merlot.

---

6 to 8 sun-dried tomatoes, snipped
2 tablespoons garlic vinaigrette
4 ounces wine-cured salami, sliced into very thin rounds
1 cup garbanzo beans, cooked, rinsed, and drained
1 large cucumber, peeled and cut into ½-inch chunks
4 green onions, thinly sliced
⅔ cup yogurt

●In salad bowl, marinate tomatoes in vinaigrette. Add salami, beans, half the cucumber, and half the onions. Put other half of cucumber and remaining onion in blender or food processor. Add yogurt and 1 tablespoon of vinaigrette from salad bowl to blender; buzz to liquefy. Pour dressing over salad, toss gently, and serve.

green onion brooms, slivers, diagonals

Salami Salad

Bright with beets and root vegetables, this beautiful salad showcases wine-cured salami, either imported or made in San Francisco, where the Italian tradition has been lovingly continued for many years. Very few people can tell fresh beets from canned, nice to know when you are in a hurry. If you don't want the whole salad to turn pink, toss the beets with some vinaigrette in a separate container and add them at the last minute. If you can't get fine Gorgonzola, use Asiago, pecorino, or Romano, or jump across the channel and try Cheddar, Wensleydale, or double Gloucester. Heap a basket with warm herbed rolls or slices from a crusty baguette, and toss mixed greens with a few shreds of radicchio, peeled orange sections, red onion, and a garlic vinaigrette. Pull the cork on a zesty sangiovese with this one.

---

1 bunch small beets, rinsed and trimmed *or*
   1 16-ounce can whole cooked beets, diced
2 potatoes, cut into 1-inch cubes
2 carrots, halved lengthwise and cut into 1-inch pieces
2 tablespoons red wine vinegar
4 ounces wine-cured salami, thinly sliced
1 tablespoon chopped fresh flat Italian parsley
1 teaspoon green peppercorns
2 ounces Gorgonzola cheese, crumbled

●In a large saucepan, bring salted water to boil. Drop in beets and cook 15 to 20 minutes until fork-tender; cool and skin beets. Cut into ½-inch dice. In another saucepan, bring more salted water to boil. Drop in potatoes and carrots and cook for 12 to 15 minutes until just tender; drain and gently toss with vinegar. If salami is in large rounds, cut in half. Add salami, parsley, and peppercorns to potatoes and carrots, toss gently. Add beets and Gorgonzola, toss again, and serve.

Smoked Chicken Salad

This complex, savory salad is a study in contrasts, both of taste and of texture. Chewy, sweet snippets of sherried sun-dried tomatoes, smoky bits of chicken, crunchy pine nuts, and crisp, tart Granny Smith apples meet in splendid synergy. The dressing gentles the snap of mustard with smooth sour cream and a mellowing hint of honey. Use smaller apples for the best flavor. Try one of the all-dairy "alternative" sour creams; they can be extraordinarily good. In the spring, serve this salad on a bed of butter lettuce; in the summer, pile it into scooped-out tomatoes; in the fall or the winter, use it to fill ripe, red sweet peppers. The flavors are fresh and clean at any time of the year. Serve with rolls or hot garlic bread and a fumé blanc or sturdy ale.

---

1 tablespoon dry sherry
8 pieces sun-dried tomatoes, snipped
8 ounces smoked chicken, skinned, boned, and cut into chunks
2 Granny Smith apples, cored and diced
3 tablespoons pine nuts, toasted
⅔ cup sour cream
2 tablespoons Dijon mustard
1 teaspoon honey

●In a saucepan, heat sherry over medium heat. Add tomatoes; cover pan, turn off heat, and steep. Toss chicken, apples, and 2 tablespoons pine nuts with sherried tomatoes. Blend sour cream, mustard, and honey. Pour dressing over chicken mixture, toss again, and garnish with remaining pine nuts.

Smoked Turkey Salad in Poppy Seed Dressing

Smoked turkey is frequently found in the supermarket beside the Canadian bacon, the hard sausages, and other specialty meats. For the best flavor, choose a brand that is naturally smoked rather than those slathered with liquid smoke and pumped full of chemicals. Not only will it smell and taste better, the meat will be more tender as well. Here, smoked turkey chunks, pink grapefruit sections, and watercress meet in a sage-scented vinaigrette that is crunchy with pine nuts and grainy with poppy seeds. You can always substitute romaine or endive for the watercress, or use mixed greens with some shreds of arugula and green onion. A crusty baguette and a glass of dry chardonnay are all you need on the side.

---

2 bunches fresh watercress, chopped
8 ounces smoked turkey, cut into chunks
1 small pink grapefruit, peeled and sectioned
2 tablespoons vinaigrette
1 teaspoon minced fresh sage *or*
  ½ teaspoon dried
2 tablespoons fresh pine nuts, toasted
2 tablespoons poppy seeds

●Line a salad bowl with watercress. Gently toss together turkey and grapefruit and mound on watercress. Blend vinaigrette, sage, pine nuts, and poppy seeds; pour over salad, toss, and serve.

Smoked Chicken Tortillas

Nearly every town boasts a great barbecue joint, and most of them are fine sources for smoked chicken. Many supermarkets stock smoked turkey breast, which, when not overly salted and drenched in liquid smoke, can be an admirable substitute. This is not your average tortilla, perhaps, but the combination of flavors is remarkably delicious. Each ingredient is experienced individually, and each contributes severally. Chunks of smoky chicken and crunchy almonds meet spicy-hot salsa soothed with sour cream and buttery spinach. Juicy pieces of orange are, surprisingly, an addition one might encounter anywhere in central Mexican pueblo cooking. Just add beer, and you have a memorable and easily prepared meal in no time.

---

1 package large flour tortillas
½ to 1 pound smoked chicken (1 whole breast), skinned
   and boned
½ to 1 cup salsa
1 medium red onion, halved and sliced into strips
1 orange, peeled and cut into fans
1 bunch spinach, trimmed and coarsely chopped
2 to 3 tablespoons sour cream
¼ cup whole almonds, toasted and chopped

●Loosely wrap in foil as many tortillas as you think you can eat, keep warm in oven. Shred chicken into large pieces, wrap in foil, and warm in oven for 10 minutes. Heat salsa until hot but not boiling. To assemble, fill each tortilla with some chicken, onion strips, orange sections, and spinach. Top with salsa, sour cream, and almonds.

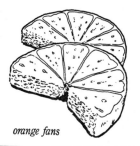

orange fans

$\mathscr{E}$ggs & Cheese

191   Corn-off-the-cob Soufflé

192   Double Gloucester Soufflé

193   Romanesco Broccoli Omelet

194   Sorrel Omelet

195   Almond and Gruyère Omelet

196   Mizíthra and Artichoke Omelet

197   Cheese and Pepperoni Omelet

198   Eggs with Eggplant

199   Oyster Mushroom Omelet

200   Leeks and Eggs in Balsamic Vinaigrette

201   Torta Verde

202   Cheddar and Hazelnut Torte

203   Peanut Pie

204   Bleu Cheese Blintzes

205   Fried Green Tomatoes and Mozzarella

206   Cheese Ravioli with Nut Sauce

207   Spaghetti with Gorgonzola Sauce

208   Cilantro Pesto Pizza

209   Gorgonzola Salad Soup

210   Marinated Fresh Mozzarella

211   Brazil Nut Tacos

Corn-off-the-cob Soufflé

When fresh corn gluts the market, cut it off the cob raw for this gilded, corn-studded soufflé. Tarragon and corn are complementary during any season, but when both are straight from the garden, the combination is unbeatable. The cheese can be sharp or mild; whatever you use yields a smooth, golden, custardy puff, which can wait in a warm oven for a few minutes without harm. If you've avoided making soufflés in the past, start with this one; it's nearly foolproof despite its ethereal texture.

---

3 eggs
1 cup corn, fresh or frozen
4 ounces Cheddar cheese, grated
½ cup sour cream
1 teaspoon chopped fresh tarragon *or*
  ½ teaspoon dried
½ teaspoon freshly ground black pepper
1 to 2 tablespoons butter

●Preheat oven to 350 degrees. Separate eggs, reserving whites. Put yolks in a bowl, add corn, cheese, sour cream, tarragon, and pepper, blend well. Butter a soufflé dish or a small straight-sided baking dish. Beat egg whites until soft peaks; fold into the corn mixture. Gently pour into soufflé dish, bake for 50 minutes. Serve hot or at room temperature.

Eggs and Cheese

Double Gloucester Soufflé

Gloucester is a firm English cheese, similar to Cheddar but more rich and less sharp; double Gloucester, more often on the supermarket shelves, is simply a thicker or taller wheel of the same cheese. Leicestershire, Wiltshire, and Derby are similar, and any can be substituted here, as can an aged Cheddar. Mustard and cheese have been found complementary for centuries, and not just in sandwiches—a dash of powdered mustard picks up the simplest cheese sauce, and a spoonful of prepared mustard enriches the flavor of any cheese soup or soufflé. Either tossed greens or broad beans drizzled with a mustard vinaigrette make tasty accompaniments. Have a chenin blanc or Taddy porter with your meal; a plate of pears and a bowl of nuts to shell by the fire after dinner.

---

1 cup cooked rice
8 ounces shredded double Gloucester
2 eggs
1 teaspoon Worcestershire sauce
½ cup milk *or* yogurt
2 teaspoons Dijon mustard
Whole nutmeg
1 to 2 tablespoons butter

•Preheat oven to 350 degrees. Mix rice with cheese. Divide eggs, adding yolks to rice; reserve whites. Add Worcestershire sauce, milk, and mustard to rice mixture; blend well. Butter a small soufflé dish or straight-sided baking dish. Beat egg whites until stiff but not dry; fold them into rice, pour gently into soufflé dish. Grate nutmeg over top. Bake for about 45 minutes until puffed and golden. For a drier soufflé, bake for an hour at 300 degrees. Serve at once.

Romanesco Broccoli Omelet

Italians love vegetables, and continue to grow a larger range than most Americans are accustomed to. Romanesco broccoli may look like the outer-space version of its ordinary cousin, but the flavor is similar, though slightly sweeter and milder. If you cook with gas, try roasting the peppers directly in the flame for a minute or two, then rubbing them gently in a tea towel to loosen the skin before slicing. Their sweet flavor gains a smoky undertone, and they become juicier than ever. Add a handful of toasted walnuts and slivered jícama to a green salad, dress it with walnut oil and wine vinegar, warm some fresh rolls, and open a bottle of Soave for a light evening meal.

---

2 tablespoons butter
1 small head romanesco broccoli, cut into spears
1 red sweet pepper, cut into strips
1 yellow sweet pepper, cut into strips
3 eggs, lightly beaten
1 teaspoon freshly ground black pepper
1 ounce Asiago cheese, coarsely grated
2 tablespoons crème fraîche *or* sour cream

●In a saucepan, heat 1 tablespoon butter over medium heat. Add broccoli and peppers, and sauté for 2 minutes. Cover pan, reduce heat, and steam in their own juices for about 6 to 8 minutes until tender. In an omelet pan or heavy frying pan, heat remaining butter over medium heat until foamy. Pour in eggs, tilting pan and lifting edges of omelet so liquid eggs run underneath. Add pepper and cook for 2 to 3 minutes, until eggs are set to your taste; fill with broccoli and pepper, sprinkle with cheese, and fold. Cut omelet in half and serve with a dollop of crème fraîche on each portion.

romanesco broccoli

Sorrel Omelet

Puffy and light, this celebration of sprouting involves the tenderest new shoots of garden herbs. If you don't like the tangy bite of sorrel, try a handful of mixed herbs; chives and parsley are another French classic. Salt toughens omelets, so perk up the flavor with a salty cheese instead. The secret to a perfect omelet is twofold: use a heavy iron pan and have the butter quite hot, foamy, and barely browning when the eggs are introduced. Cooked very quickly, the results will be smooth and airy, beautiful and delicious. Tossed oakleaf lettuce with a few shreds of mustard greens in a hot bacon and garlic dressing, warm rolls, and a white Côtes du Rhône or pear wine would complement this entreé well.

---

2 tablespoons butter
1 bunch fresh sorrel, chopped
2 tablespoons crème fraîche *or* sour cream
3 eggs, lightly beaten
2 tablespoons heavy cream
1 tablespoon grated Romano *or* Parmesan cheese
½ teaspoon green peppercorns, drained

●In a heavy saucepan, heat half the butter over medium heat until foamy. Add sorrel and cook over medium-low heat until limp. Stir in crème fraîche and remove from heat. Blend eggs, cream, cheese, and peppercorns. In an iron frying pan, heat 1 tablespoon butter over medium heat until foamy and barely brown. Add egg mixture, shaking pan to spread eggs and lifting edges to allow the runny part to slide under. Shake and lift for 20 seconds, then let it cook for 3 to 5 minutes until barely set. Spoon sorrel mixture onto half the omelet, fold over, and serve on warm plates.

Almond and Gruyère Omelet

This savory variation on the classic European dessert omelet
has a toasted coat of sliced almonds, golden and buttery. Salty
chopped nuts, Gruyère, garlic, and green peppercorns enliven
a traditional ricotta base, making it zippy rather than sweet.
Use more ricotta for a softer, creamier filling, less ricotta and
more Gruyère will make it thicker and richer. Serve with a
crisp salad of lettuce, mustard greens, and slivered cabbage,
a plate of fruit, and a sturdy young Beaujolais.

---

3 eggs
2 to 3 teaspoons butter
2 tablespoons sliced almonds
1 fat clove garlic, pressed
⅔ cup ricotta cheese
2 to 3 tablespoons chopped salted almonds
½ teaspoon green peppercorns in vinegar
2 to 3 ounces Gruyère cheese, diced

●Beat eggs gently with a fork, adding 3 tablespoons water.
In an omelet or a frying pan, heat butter over medium heat
until foamy. Add almonds, and cook for 1 minute. Pour eggs
over almonds; reduce heat to medium low. Add garlic, almonds,
peppercorns and their vinegar, and cheese to ricotta; stir.
Shake pan to loosen omelet, adding more butter if it sticks.
Spoon ricotta over half the omelet, cover pan, and cook until
filling is warm and Gruyère is soft. Fold omelet in half and
serve at once.

Mizíthra and Artichoke Omelet

Salty, pungent mizíthra cheese is made from aged sheep milk ricotta. This unusual Greek cheese lends its characteristic sharp flavor to this artichoke- and olive-stuffed omelet. If you can't find mizíthra, use a sharp kasséri, Asiago, pecorino, or any sharp, aged Cheddar; a mellow jack or mozzarella will give different but delicious results. Kalamata, Niçoise, or any flavorful olives may be used successfully. Serve with warm garlic bread, olives and cheeses, a green salad or plates of raw baby vegetables, a glass of red Demestica or Chianti.

Olive oil
1 medium onion, quartered and thinly sliced
4 to 6 black Greek olives, pitted and sliced
¼ cup artichoke hearts in olive oil, quartered
Freshly ground black pepper
3 eggs
1 tablespoon grated Parmesan cheese
1 to 2 ounces mizíthra cheese, coarsely grated or chopped

●In a small saucepan, heat 1 teaspoon oil over medium heat. Add onion and cook until soft, 4 to 5 minutes. Add olives, artichokes, and a lot of pepper; cover pan and reduce heat to warm. Beat eggs with Parmesan, adding 2 tablespoons water. In an omelet or frying pan, heat 2 teaspoons oil over medium heat. Pour in egg mixture and cook for 2 minutes. Sprinkle with mizíthra, reduce heat, and cook over low heat, until eggs are set to your taste. Spoon artichoke mixture over half the eggs, fold omelet, cut in half, and serve.

Cheese and Pepperoni Omelet

This simple, light omelet bursts with vegetables and pepperoni, and three cheeses. It is both tasty and good looking, just right for a midnight dinner after a play or the opera. Serve with a basket of warm rolls, a green salad with peppery shreds of arugula, and feathery red radicchio. Try a crisp sauvignon blanc or a dry blush with the meal.

---

2 eggs
½ cup ricotta cheese
1 ounce grated Parmesan cheese
1½ tablespoons butter
2 ounces pepperoni, thinly sliced
1 small zucchini, thinly sliced
1 small onion, thinly sliced
2 ounces fresh mozzarella cheese, thinly sliced

●Beat eggs with half the ricotta and 1 tablespoon Parmesan. In a small frying pan, heat 2 teaspoons butter over medium heat until foamy. Add pepperoni, zucchini, and onion; cook until vegetables are tender. Stir in remaining ricotta and remaining Parmesan. Turn off heat, but leave pan on burner. Top pepperoni mixture with mozzarella slices; cover pan. In omelet pan or second frying pan, heat 2 teaspoons butter over medium heat until foamy. Pour in egg/ricotta mixture; reduce heat, cover, and cook, until eggs are set (as soft or hard as you like). Shake pan to loosen omelet, spoon pepperoni mixture over half the eggs. Fold omelet, cut in half, and serve.

Eggs with Eggplant

This is an especially pretty dish when you don't peel the egg-plant, so buy the youngest you can find. The slender Japanese types are sometimes shaded while they ripen, so that their skin is a delicate, light lavender rather than the usual purple-black. Both are tender and colorful, and appear to advantage in this dish. If only larger eggplants are available, peel one and use about one cup of the flesh. The eggs bake in a name-sake nest; the timing of this depends on how firm or runny you like your eggs. Offer a mixed green salad tossed with a lively orange juice vinaigrette, a basket of warm rolls, and a glass of Frascati or a Valpolicella.

---

3 teaspoons olive oil
1 5- to 6-inch-long eggplant, cut into 1- x ½-inch strips
1 medium onion, chopped
2 ripe tomatoes, diced (reserve juice)
½ cup chopped flat Italian parsley
2 eggs
1 ounce grated pecorino or Parmesan cheese
Freshly ground black pepper

●In a heavy frying pan, heat 2 teaspoons oil over medium heat. Add eggplant and onion; stir and cook for 2 minutes. Add tomatoes and parsley with another teaspoon oil, if needed. Cook for 10 minutes until eggplant is tender. Mixture will be fairly dry. Reduce heat to medium low, make 2 shallow depressions in the sauce, break the eggs and gently drop them in the depressions. Grind on a lot of pepper (as much as 1 teaspoon) and sprinkle cheese thickly over eggs. Cover pan, reduce heat to low, and cook 3 to 5 minutes, until eggs are set, or for 6 to 8 minutes until firm. If your preference varies from that of your dinner partner, add egg to be softly cooked after first egg has been in pan for 3 to 4 minutes. Bring pan to the table and serve portions with a spatula.

Oyster Mushroom Omelet

Ruffled, cream-colored oyster mushrooms taste stronger and wilder than the usual button types, which are the meekest of all mushrooms when it comes to flavor. Omelets are a good way to showcase mushrooms of any kind—try substituting pungent shiitakes, woodsy cèpes, or slim, velvety enokis. This omelet uses a base of low-fat ricotta and relatively few eggs to make a puffy, creamy wrapper for the mushrooms and bacon. To cook bacon tender-crisp with as little fat as possible, the strips bake on a rack until golden but still flexible. Toss up a salad, pass a basket of warm scones, and pour out a glass of crisp, dry rhubarb wine, hard cider, or an earthy ale to complement this meal.

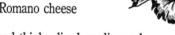
oyster mushrooms

4 strips bacon
¼ cup ricotta cheese
2 eggs
1 tablespoon grated Romano cheese
2 teaspoons butter
2 shallots, trimmed and thinly sliced on diagonal
6 to 8 fresh green beans, trimmed and thinly sliced
  on diagonal
3 oyster mushrooms, trimmed and halved lengthwise

●Preheat over to 350 degrees. Arrange bacon on a rack (the kind for cooling bread works well) and set on a baking sheet. Bake for 12 to 15 minutes; drain on paper towels when done. While bacon cooks, mash ricotta with eggs and cheese. In a small omelet pan or skillet, heat 1 teaspoon butter over medium heat until foamy. Pour in ricotta mix, turning pan to coat. Cover pan and reduce heat to low. In a small frying pan, heat remaining butter over medium heat until foamy. Add shallots, cook for 1 minute; add beans and mushrooms, stir to coat. Cover and cook for 3 to 4 minutes until just tender. Shake omelet pan to loosen omelet (eggs should be puffy and nearly dry); add vegetables, fold in half, and cut into 2 pieces. Transfer to plates, crisscross bacon over each, and serve.

Leeks and Eggs in Balsamic Vinaigrette

Milder than onions or garlic, raw leeks can be sliced thinly into salads. Their gentle bite is appreciated in late fall and again in early spring, when there isn't much else in the garden. Fall leeks are tender-crisp, growing sweeter with each nip of frost. In the past, spring varieties have been tough and harsh, but newer hybrids are both flavorful and tender. In Europe, leeks are highly admired and enjoyed in dozens of ways—marinated with steamed vegetables for cold summer salads, added liberally to soups and stews, braised in wine, sautéed in olive oil, or baked, as here, in vinegar. The astringency of the vinegar bakes out, leaving the food savory, tender, and fragrant. Bake your eggs as little or long as you like, warming herb rolls beside them as they cook. Toss a mixed green salad with toasted nuts, shredded carrots, and an orange-yogurt dressing, and pour out some dry Bartlett pear wine or a microbrewed ale.

---

2 tablespoons olive oil
2 large leeks, split lengthwise
2 tablespoons balsamic vinegar
2 eggs
1 tablespoon chopped chives
1 tablespoon chopped flat Italian parsley
2 tablespoons crumbled Roquefort cheese

●Lightly brush leeks with olive oil; set in a baking pan cut-sides down. Blend remaining oil with vinegar, pour over leeks, cover, and bake in 350 degree oven for 20 to 25 minutes, until leeks are tender. Break an egg into each end of pan. Sprinkle herbs and cheese over all, return to oven, and bake until eggs are cooked to your taste; 4 to 6 minutes for softly set eggs, 7 to 10 minutes for firm eggs. Bring the dish to the table to serve.

Torta Verde

This is an excellent vegetarian entrée—a glorious and golden puff of ricotta, spinach, and cheese substantial enough to satisfy the stoutest appetite, yet neither overly rich nor heavy. The key ingredient is the ricotta, and the larger curd works better than the creamed, though either skimmed or whole-milk ricotta is satisfactory. Mature Asiago, the pungent, flavorful skim-milk cheese used here, is crumbled or grated, much like Romano, which may be substituted. For a prettier presentation, slide the store-bought piecrust into one of your own pie pans and reflute the edge for that homemade look. In cold weather, serve this pie hot, or cool it to room temperature for a summertime supper. Serve with a leafy salad of greens, baby artichokes with a pesto and yogurt dip, and a dry Orvieto.

---

2 bunches spinach, chopped *or*
  1 10-ounce box, thawed and pressed dry
1 pound ricotta
2 eggs, 1 separated
5 ounces grated Asiago cheese
¼ cup whole wheat pastry *or* unbleached white flour
½ teaspoon grated nutmeg
1 9-inch piecrust
1 tablespoon butter

•Steam fresh spinach, press dry. Mash ricotta with 1 whole egg and 1 egg yolk, reserving egg white. Blend in ½ cup Asiago, flour, spinach, and nutmeg; set aside. Brush bottom and edges of piecrust with reserved egg white. Add filling, mounded in center and smoothed out to edge of pan. Dot with butter, sprinkle with remaining cheese, and bake in 350 degree oven for 35 to 40 minutes.

Cheddar and Hazelnut Torte
(Serves 6)

Cheese and hazelnut shortbread is filled with a peppery Cheddar and crème frâiche custard in a vegetarian recipe with nearly universal appeal, dieters excepted. A blend of whole wheat pastry flour and unbleached white flour makes a golden, flavorful crust. The torte tastes wonderful whether hot or at room temperature, and needs no other accompaniment than mixed greens with shreds of radicchio, slivered radishes, and red cabbage in a sharp vinaigrette. A white Burgundy or a fumé blanc would be complementary as well.

---

1 cup butter, softened
2 cups flour (up to half whole wheat pastry flour)
1 cup hazelnuts, toasted and chopped
1 to 2 ounces grated pecorino *or* Parmesan cheese
2 eggs
½ cup crème fraîche *or* sour cream
1½ teaspoons freshly ground pepper
12 ounces sharp Cheddar cheese, coarsely grated

●Blend butter and flour to soft dough. Stir in nuts and pecorino. Pat this mixture into 9-inch reversible tart mold. Bake on a baking sheet in 350 degree oven for 20 minutes. Remove (but leave oven on) and cool on rack upside down. Separate 1 egg, reserving about 1 tablespoon of the white. Combine yolk and remaining white with the other egg; beat gently. Add crème fraîche, pepper, and ½ cup Cheddar. Gently turn crust out of tin onto baking sheet. Brush bottom and sides with remaining egg white. Spoon in custard, smooth it out, sprinkle on remaining cheese, return to oven, and bake 20 to 25 minutes until set and golden. Remove from oven and let sit for 10 minutes before cutting.

Peanut Pie
(Serves up to 6)

This spicy-hot crustless pie comforts with the heat of sunnier places when the winter rains won't quit. Use fresh peanut butter if your store has a machine, or choose a commercial brand without sugar and hydrogenated fats for best flavor. The cheese can be Cheddar, jack, mozzarella—all work well in this recipe. Fresh chiles are available year-round in most places, but a can of chopped chiles (whatever heat you prefer) can be substituted. Serve a salad of shredded cabbage, grated carrots, and jícama with hot bacon dressing, corn muffins, and a sturdy beer.

---

6 strips bacon
1 pound ricotta cheese
⅓ cup peanut butter
3 eggs
1 medium onion, chopped
2 fresh chiles, seeded and chopped
2 to 4 tablespoons salsa
8 ounces grated Cheddar cheese

•Mash ricotta with peanut butter. Separate eggs, beating yolks into ricotta. Beat whites until stiff but not dry. Grease 9-inch pie pan with piece of bacon. In a frying pan, cook bacon over medium heat. Drain off all but 1 to 2 teaspoons drippings. Arrange bacon strips, undrained, radiating from center of pie pan (so each serving gets a piece). Add onions and chiles to frying pan, cook for 5 to 6 minutes until soft. Add salsa and remove from heat. Blend this mixture with ricotta and all but 2 to 3 tablespoons cheese. Gently fold in egg whites. Spoon into pie pan, sprinkle cheese over top. Bake in 350 degree oven for 35 to 40 minutes until puffed and golden brown.

Bleu Cheese Blintzes

Blue cheeses are American, bleu cheeses are French—in practical terms, the main difference is that the imported ones are less salty and more subtle in flavor than their American counterparts. In this offbeat entrée, the usual bland filling for Russian pancakes is jazzy with bleu (or blue) cheese. For further variety, try using Stilton, Roquefort, kasséri, or even Port-Salut—cheese fans can have a field day, for the creamy ricotta is the perfect background to set off the distinctive qualities of each. Yogurt (or buttermilk) gives the thin pancakes extra flavor, along with an especially tender texture. Drink hot tea (get out the samovar) from glass cups, with sugar cubes held between your teeth as you sip.

---

2 eggs
1 cup ricotta cheese
2 ounces bleu cheese, crumbled
2 shallots, thinly sliced
½ cup yogurt
½ cup unbleached white flour
1 to 2 teaspoons butter *or* walnut oil
2 to 3 tablespoons sour cream

blintzes

●Divide 1 egg into 2 bowls. Add ricotta and bleu cheese to yolk bowl. Stir in shallots; set mixture aside. Break second egg into egg white bowl; beat lightly with yogurt and fold in flour. Butter a 1½-quart baking dish or casserole; set aside. In a heavy frying pan, melt ½ teaspoon butter over medium-high heat until foamy. Pour in 2 to 3 tablespoons mixture, tilting pan so mixture runs to coat all or most of pan (it should make a more or less circular, thin pancake). Cook for about 1 minute on one side only, until edges of pancake are dry. Remove from pan to a plate, put 1 to 2 tablespoons filling on uncooked side, then fold, pulling up sides first, then tucking both ends under. It should look like a fat little pillow. Repeat this until you run out of either filling or blintz mixture, tucking blintzes snugly into buttered baking dish. Bake in 350 degree oven for 20 minutes, until warm through and pale golden brown. To serve, put 2 or 3 blintzes on each plate, top with sour cream.

Fried Green Tomatoes and Mozzarella

Cooks always need tasty recipes to use up the autumnal supply of unripe tomatoes. Once we admit they are never going to turn red, we can appreciate fat green tomatoes as a tangy ingredient in chili or chutney, curries or stir-fries. Here, cornmeal is blended with grated cheese and black pepper to make a crunchy, buttery jacket for the tomatoes. Thick slices of fresh mozzarella are similarly covered and cooked. The contrast between the delicate, melting cheese, the tart tomatoes, and the crisp coating is most pleasant. If you can find balls of mozzarella roughly the same size as the tomatoes, the dish will be even nicer to look at. This goes well with a very plain salad—greens or cole slaw—dressed with an anchovy or an orange juice vinaigrette, rough red table wine such as Magyar voros, and late fall sunshine.

---

2 eggs
½ cup finely ground cornmeal
1 teaspoon freshly ground black pepper *or* to taste
2 tablespoons grated Parmesan *or* Romano cheese
3 tablespoons butter *or* oil
8 ounces fresh mozzarella cheese, sliced into ½-inch wheels
2 green tomatoes, sliced into ½-inch wheels

●In a pie pan or other deep-sided, flat-bottomed dish, beat eggs. In another dish, combine cornmeal, pepper, and cheese. In a heavy iron skillet, heat butter over medium heat. Preheat oven to warm. When butter is foamy, dip tomato slices, both sides, into egg, and then into cornmeal. Fry quickly, 3 to 5 minutes on each side, adding more butter as needed. Transfer to foil-lined baking sheet, pat with paper towel to absorb grease, and hold in oven until all are cooked. Repeat process with cheese, frying until golden. Put some of each on 2 plates, serve hot.

Cheese Ravioli with Nut Sauce

Fresh or frozen, ravioli takes about twenty minutes to cook, just enough time to make a sauce. This one, based on walnuts and hazelnuts, has a grainy, coarse texture, with a delightfully smooth, complex flavor. It goes together quickly, but do read through the recipe and assemble the things you will need beforehand, so the ravioli isn't left waiting. If the ravioli are homemade or very small fresh ones, start the sauce when you put on the pasta water. Serve with a salad of butterhead lettuce and green onions with a mustard vinaigrette and croutons, a glass of verdicchio or white a crisp chardonnay.

---

8 ounces fresh cheese ravioli
2 to 3 teaspoons butter
1 clove garlic, crushed
¼ cup walnuts, coarsely chopped
¼ cup hazelnuts, coarsely chopped
½ teaspoon whole black peppercorns
2 ounces grated pecorino *or* Parmesan cheese
¼ cup crème fraîche *or* heavy cream

●In a saucepan, bring salted water to boil. Add ravioli and cook for 20 minutes. Meanwhile, make sauce by melting 2 teaspoons butter in a skillet over medium heat. Add garlic and cook until golden on all sides, then remove and discard garlic. Add walnuts and peppercorns and cook for 6 to 7 minutes, until walnuts are light brown. Put walnuts in blender or food processor with 1 tablespoon cheese and crème fraîche; blend briefly to a grainy paste. Return to pan and keep warm, until ravioli is done. When ravioli is done, drain and toss with remaining butter, spoon on sauce, and top with remaining cheese. Serve at once.

Spaghetti with Gorgonzola Sauce

Of all the forms of pasta, spaghetti has the greatest affinity for a clingy, cheesy sauce. This is a recipe to play with: a lesser amount of Gorgonzola yields a mild tasting sauce; more pepper gives it a pronounced bite, while less leaves just a warm undertone; dry sherry or a dry white wine can be used instead of vermouth. Include a green salad with a sharp dressing, steamed baby beets in orange vinaigrette, or a chunky tomato and onion salad.

½ cup dry vermouth
½ cup cream
½ to 1 teaspoon freshly ground black pepper
½ teaspoon nutmeg
8 ounces fresh spaghetti *or*
    4 ounces dry
3 to 6 tablespoons Gorgonzola
1 tablespoon Parmesan

•Heat water for pasta. In a saucepan, bring vermouth to rapid boil over medium-high heat. Cook, reducing by half, for 12 to 15 minutes. Let vermouth cool a bit, then gradually add cream. Add pepper and nutmeg and simmer for 10 minutes, stirring occasionally. Cook spaghetti until al dente. When spaghetti is ready, crumble 2 to 4 tablespoons Gorgonzola into sauce and stir in Parmesan. Drain spaghetti, spoon sauce over each portion and top with remaining Gorgonzola to taste.

Cilantro Pesto Pizza
(Serves up to 4)

This nontraditional pizza has a green sauce hot with chiles and cilantro. The zesty pesto is also wonderful on pork, chicken, or turkey; try adding a bit of coriander, cumin, and even caraway—many variations are delightful. Pizza crusts, fresh from the bakery or frozen, are available in most supermarkets. Keep a couple in the freezer for quick and different dinners like this one. Use any nuts you prefer—almonds, walnuts, pine nuts—with the possible exception of peanuts. Have a salad of chunky summer vegetables dressed with yogurt and herbs, and drink a glass of Chianti or beer.

---

1 9-inch pizza crust *or* sourdough baguette
2 tablespoons olive oil
2 bunches fresh cilantro, trimmed and chopped
2 fresh chiles (pasillas, hot wax, or any), seeded and chopped
2 cloves garlic, chopped
¼ cup pine nuts, almonds, *or* walnuts, coarsely chopped
2 ounces grated Parmesan cheese
8 ounces mozzarella cheese, sliced or grated

●Preheat oven to 425 degrees. Place crust on a baking sheet and brush with oil. Put cilantro in blender or food processor with chiles, garlic, nuts, 2 to 3 tablespoons Parmesan and 2 to 3 tablespoons oil, buzz to blend, adding more oil if needed to produce a thick paste. Scrape pesto out of blender (a narrow rubber spatula works very well), pour, and spread evenly over crust. Sprinkle on remaining Parmesan. Spread mozzarella over top; the greater amount will please fans of very cheesy pizza. Bake for 15 to 20 minutes until golden brown and bubby. Cut in pieces with scissors or pizza wheel. Serve at once.

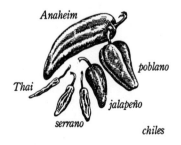

Anaheim

poblano

Thai

jalapeño

serrano

chiles

Gorgonzola Salad Soup

If you ever have too much of a marvelous salad, try this recipe. The soup is bubbly and fresh tasting, sharp with good dressing. Frothy white, flecked with carrots and cucumbers, it looks delightfully cool and pretty. The tang of buttermilk off-sets the creaminess of the Gorgonzola. Add the cheese to taste, starting with the smaller amount; a little goes a long way, and you don't want to eclipse the other flavors. As long as you don't tell how you made it, it is good enough for guests—even guests you like. Serve with fresh rolls, a pinot grigio or a brisk local ale, and peaches for dessert; a perfect summer meal in minutes.

---

3 cups leftover (dressed) salad*
2 cups buttermilk
1 ounce crumbled Gorgonzola cheese
Herbed croutons

●Put salad and buttermilk in blender or food processor; buzz briefly to liquefy. Pour into bowls, sprinkle on Gorgonzola, and pass the croutons.
*If your salad is a simple or plain one, add: ½ cucumber, peeled, seeded and chunked, and 1 carrot, scrubbed and sliced.

Marinated Fresh Mozzarella

Fresh mozzarella, once common in western markets, is enjoying a revival. Fresh mozzarella has a soft, tender curd that squeaks a bit as you chew it. The flavor is clean and delicate, gently tart. The smallest sort, fior di latte, is especially good—subtler and less salty than aged mozzarella. It comes in little four-ounce balls. Fresh mozzarella makes heavenly hot sandwiches, crumbles nicely into salads, and will do splendid things for your favorite pizza and pasta recipes. Briefly marinated in tomato-basil dressing, it brightens this pretty Italian summer salad. Carry it outside with a loaf of Italian bread or a basket or panini, a bowl of mixed greens, and a bottle of young Soave or a cheerful Spumante.

---

3 tablespoons vinaigrette
1 teaspoon fresh basil *or*
   ½ teaspoon dried
6 sun-dried tomatoes, snipped into strips
1 ounce grated pecorino cheese
3 tablespoons pine nuts
¼ cup walnuts, coarsely chopped
8 ounces fresh mozzarella cheese (2 balls), chopped into
   ½-inch cubes
1 yellow sweet pepper, chopped into ½-inch squares

●Put vinaigrette in blender or food processor with basil, 4 tomatoes, 1 tablespoon pecorino, 1 tablespoon each pine nuts and walnuts; blend. If mixture is too thick, add 1 to 2 table-spoons water and blend again. Toss mozzarella and pepper in dressing with remaining dried tomatoes; let marinate while you set the table. Spread remaining walnuts on baking sheet and toast in 350 degree oven for 8 to 10 minutes. If remaining pine nuts are not crisp, toast them for 5 to 6 minutes as well. When ready to serve, add toasted nuts to salad and top with remaining pecorino.

Brazil Nut Tacos

This unusual vegetarian taco recipe incorporates rich, meaty Brazil nuts with ricotta, salsa, and lime juice in a tart and spicy filling for your favorite kind of tortillas—even dedicated meat eaters have been known to eat large quantities of these in very short order. If Brazil nuts are too hard to slice, parboil them for a few minutes in boiling, salted water. Drain and cool them, and they will be soft enough to cut as thin as you like. Cashews, walnuts, pecans, or hazelnuts can be used also. Whole wheat flour tortillas are especially good, but any kind will do. Toss up a green salad, pour out some Mexican beer, and dig in.

1 package medium tortillas
1 cup ricotta cheese
2 cloves garlic, pressed
1 lime, juiced
1 to 2 sprigs fresh cilantro, chopped
½ cup whole Brazil nuts, toasted and sliced
1 medium Walla Walla sweet onion, halved and thinly
   sliced into rounds
¼ cup salsa

●Loosely wrap in foil as many tortillas as you think you can eat, keep warm in oven. Mix ricotta, garlic, and lime juice. Add cilantro and nuts and stir well. To assemble, put 1 to 2 tablespoons ricotta-nut mixture, some onions, and some salsa in each tortilla, fold. Serve at room temperature.

$\mathcal{V}$egetables & Fruits

215   Japanese Eggplant Parmesan

216   Glazed Eggplant Steaks

217   Black Beans with Two Potatoes

218   Spaghetti Caponata

219   Spaghetti Squash Caribbe

220   Peperonata

221   Leeks in Tuna Sauce

222   Gado Gado

223   Summer Berry Soup

224   Fresh Pea Soup

225   Spicy Mushroom Soup

226   Cucumber Soup

227   Tzatziki Soup

228   Yucatan Peanut Soup

229   Black Bean Soup

230   Caribbean Bean Salad

231   Satsuma Salad with Hot Cranberry Dressing

232   Orange and Hazelnut Salad with Hot Bacon Dressing

233   Insalata Russe

234   Summer Vegetable Salad

235   Yellow Finn Potato Salad

236   New Potato Pesto Salad

Japanese Eggplant Parmesan

The long, skinny eggplants hybridized by the Japanese are especially tender when young, and they are small enough to make a practical meal for two. Use a zucchini of the same size and then cut both into fat medallions to produce this lighter version of the Italian classic dish. Steamed runner beans or broccoli with garlic croutons, hot garlic bread, and a silky Orvieto or pinot bianco complete a great and easy meal.

---

1 7- to 8-inch-long Japanese eggplant, sliced into
   1-inch-thick medallions
1 7- to 8-inch-long zucchini, sliced into 1-inch-thick
   medallions
1 to 3 teaspoons olive oil
2 cloves garlic, mashed
1 to 2 ounces grated Parmesan cheese
4 to 5 plum tomatoes, diced (reserve juice)
4 to 6 ounces fresh mozzarella cheese, cut into thin slices
2 tablespoons chopped fresh basil *or*
   1 teaspoon dried

●In a heavy wide frying pan, heat 1 teaspoon oil over medium heat. Add garlic, brown on all sides. Fit medallions into pan; cook for 4 to 5 minutes, turn and cook for 2 more minutes, adding another teaspoon oil if needed. Set medallions with garlic in a baking dish in alternating circles; if they don't fit, overlap them slightly like fallen dominoes. If needed, add another teaspoon oil to frying pan, and cook tomatoes and basil, until juice is nearly gone, 5 to 6 minutes. Spoon a bit of tomato sauce on each medallion, cover each with a piece of mozzarella, sprinkle generously with Parmesan, and bake in 350 degree oven for 25 to 30 minutes until brown and bubbly.

Glazed Eggplant Steaks

Grill these thick, savory steaks for a vegetarian entrée with panache. The piquant teriyaki glaze gives rich, dark flavors to the eggplant, and the pale flesh, banded by the purple-black stripe of skin, looks attractively like an oversized sushi offering. Extra zip comes from paper-thin slices of sushi ginger, pickled with perilla, a deep purple herb with overtones of cinnamon and basil. Mitoku sushi ginger is outstanding and available in many supermarkets. Serve on pitas, whole wheat tortillas, sourdough, or more traditionally, with rice. Drink a crisp Canadian lager, a dark German beer, or your favorite stout.

---

1 fat eggplant, sliced lengthwise into ¾-inch steaks
¼ cup rice vinegar
¼ cup shoyu (Japanese soy sauce)
1 tablespoon honey
2 cloves garlic, minced
1 inch fresh gingerroot, peeled and grated or minced
1 to 2 ounces pickled sushi ginger with perilla

●Start coals in grill. Prepare eggplant, allowing 1 or 2 slices per serving. In a small bowl, blend vinegar, shoyu, and honey. Add garlic and gingerroot. Brush eggplant steaks with this mixture on both sides, repeating frequently as they cook. Place eggplant on grill that is set high off coals. Grill, turning at least twice, so that each side gets several coats of glaze. Allow 12 to 15 minutes per side; steaks should be soft but not mushy. To serve, transfer to plates and heap a spoonful of sushi ginger on each slice.

Black Beans with Two Potatoes

Dusky black beans contrast dramatically with vivid purple and orange potatoes in this delicious, decidedly unusual entrée. Perfect for an adult Halloween party, you will serve it again just to recapture the rich flavors and wonderful textures of the walnut sauce that surrounds the vegetables. Purple potatoes, though mystifyingly beautiful, taste exactly like their plain Jane counterpart. A brilliant confetti salad of shredded red cabbage, carrots, and romaine in a saucy, citrus dressing will play up the visual effect, though a somber one of butter lettuce, spinach, and green onions will do the same thing more subtly. That's all you'll need, except a nice nebbiolo or a clean ale.

---

1 15-ounce can black beans *or*
  1 cup cooked beans
2 large purple potatoes, sliced
2 small red-skinned sweet potatoes, sliced
¼ cup chopped walnuts
2 tablespoons butter
1 clove garlic, mashed
¼ cup sour cream
1 tablespoon minced fresh chives

•Rinse and drain beans. Arrange potato slices in a buttered 1½-quart dish, beginning with purple ones around the outside, then using orange ones for the next row, and ending with beans in the center. Dot with 1 tablespoon butter, sprinkle with 2 teaspoons chives, cover dish, and bake in 350 degree oven for 40 minutes. To make sauce, heat remaining butter in saucepan until foamy. Stir in walnuts and chives; cook and stir for 10 minutes, swirl in sour cream, and heat until bubbling. To serve, bring casserole dish and bowl of sauce to table. Spoon out beans and top with sauce.

Spaghetti Caponata

Fat spaghetti holds this chunky, emphatic eggplant mélange in the proper way, so that each strand becomes coated with the glossy sauce. Caponata is a Sicilian dish, of which there are many variations, most of them quite complex. This is a simplified version, which retains the essential agrodolce (sweet-and-sour) quality. If you can't find sweet pickled onions in the Italian food section at the supermarket, substitute cocktail onions pickled in vinegar, and add one to two teaspoons of sugar to the sauce, adjusting to taste. Italian, Greek, or Niçoise olives will give the right flavor to the dish, though any kind will do. Serve with a Chianti, a dolcetto, or a grignolino.

Olive oil
1 small unpeeled eggplant, sliced and cut into
   2- x ½-inch strips
8 to 10 pitted olives, sliced
1 teaspoon capers
1 to 2 anchovy fillets, mashed
½ cup Italian sweet pickled onions
1 15-ounce can diced tomatoes in sauce *or*
   3 to 4 ripe tomatoes, diced
8 ounces fresh spaghetti (#7 or #8) *or*
   4 ounces dry

●In a heavy saucepan, heat oil over medium-high heat. Add eggplant; stir and cook for 2 to 3 minutes. Add olives, capers, and anchovies, stirring well. Pour in onions and their vinegar (adjust as above) and tomatoes. Simmer for 12 to 15 minutes. Meanwhile, cook spaghetti until al dente. Serve spaghetti and top with sauce.

Spaghetti Squash Caribbe

The ancestors of our garden squashes are still running wild throughout tropical America, and many "new" types have been grown for centuries in the warmer countries to the south. Vegetable spaghetti is such a plant. Welcome in many dieters' kitchens, its long interior strands are pleasantly mild in flavor and much like pasta in texture, yet have very few calories. This tangy-hot West Indian sauce boosts the protein and adds considerable zip to the bland squash. Cut ripe tomatoes in thick slices, sprinkle them with chopped basil, and spritz with orange wedges for a refreshing summery salad. Iced tea, vinegar coolers, or cold ale will be equally complementary to the main event.

---

1 small spaghetti squash
2 teaspoons olive oil
1 medium onion, diced
6 tomatillos, husked and cut into wedges
1 small sweet potato, diced
1 to 3 fresh chiles, seeded and diced
3 ripe tomatoes, cut into wedges
¼ cup peanuts, toasted

●Cook spaghetti squash in steamer basket until soft, about 25 minutes. While it cooks, prepare sauce. In a heavy saucepan, heat oil over medium-high heat until sizzling. Add onion, tomatillos, potato, chiles, and tomatoes; stir and cook for 5 minutes, then cover pan and simmer until spaghetti squash is done. Split squash in half lengthwise, tease out strands until fluffy. Serve each person half the squash with the strands spilling out onto the plate. Heap sauce over each portion, and sprinkle with peanuts.

tomatillos

Peperonata

This Italian classic is among the most versatile of dishes and at its fragrant best when made with fresh, local ingredients. Here, the addition of eggs makes an elegant brunch, but you can also toss it with cheese ravioli, chill and serve with mixed greens for a hearty main-dish salad, or try it hot with vermicelli for a knockout pasta. By varying the kinds of peppers, you can radically change the character of the dish. Northern Italians make peperonata with white wine and sweet peppers. In southern Italy, vinegar and fiery little peperoncini take over until you end up in Calabria with tears in your eyes. Hot or mild, the basic recipe is the same.

---

2 tablespoons olive oil
2 cloves garlic
3 to 4 sweet peppers (any combination), seeded and sliced
  into thin strips
1 medium white onion, sliced into thin rings
4 plum tomatoes, diced
¼ cup dry white wine
2 eggs
1 ounce grated Parmesan cheese

●In a medium skillet, heat oil over medium heat. Add whole garlic; brown, then discard garlic. Add peppers and onions, stirring to coat, cover, and cook for 5 minutes. Add tomatoes with their juice and wine. Cook, uncovered, over medium-high heat until vegetables are just soft and juice is reduced by about half. Break in 2 eggs, cover, and simmer until eggs are firm, 6 to 8 minutes. Sprinkle with cheese and serve.

Leeks in Tuna Sauce

This is one of the few entrées that calls for canned fish, and certainly if you happen to have some leftover grilled tuna, it would be used to advantage here. Expensive tins of imported tuna in olive oil are a pleasant luxury, but really, plain old tuna, well drained, is going to taste fine in these elegant little casseroles. Warm, buttery rolls, a plain salad of winter greens zipped up with a mustardy vinaigrette, and a glass of chardonnay make for a snug little meal by the fireside.

---

2 large leeks, sliced lengthwise and cut into 1-inch chunks
3 teaspoons butter
2 teaspoons flour
⅔ cup half-and-half
3 ounces Gruyère cheese, diced into ½-inch pieces
1 6½-ounce can tuna fish, packed in oil or water
½ teaspoon freshly ground pepper *or* to taste
2 tablespoons coarsely chopped walnuts

●Steam leeks for 4 to 6 minutes until just tender. Place in 2 lightly buttered individual casseroles (or large custard cups). Hold in warm oven. For the cheese sauce, melt butter in a saucepan over medium heat. Stir in flour to make a paste. Cook, still stirring, for 2 to 3 minutes until faintly golden. Slowly add half-and-half, a little at a time, stirring well with each addition to keep the paste smooth. As the sauce thins, you will be able to pour half-and-half in more quickly. When all is added, continue stirring until sauce thickens; stir and cook for 2 more minutes, then reduce heat to low. Add cheese to sauce (reserving a few pieces for garnish), stirring gently. Drain tuna, flake it with a fork into small chunks, and add to sauce. Add pepper. When cheese begins to melt, spoon sauce over leeks. Finely chop remaining cheese and strew over each dish. Sprinkle walnuts over cheese, place casseroles under broiler for 3 to 4 minutes or until deep golden and bubbly.

Gado Gado

This spicy-savory Indonesian dish is based on seasonal steamed vegetables, usually root vegetables, and cauliflower. The accompanying gado gado sauce combines roasted and ground whole spices with toasted, crushed peanuts and a lot of garlic. There are quite a few bottled versions of this sauce available in the supermarkets, of which Java Sauce concentrate is noteworthy. For a quick substitute, combine a cup of toasted peanuts, four fat cloves of garlic, half a cup of canned coconut cream, and a can of diced green chiles in the blender and puree to a chunky liquid. Toss up a salad of raw slivered vegetables, perhaps peppery cabbage, black radishes and carrots with Oriental spiced vinegar and a dash of sesame oil. A side dish of firm bananas stir-fried with bok choy and mild chiles, big balls of sticky rice, and an icy pilsner beer would all be traditional accompaniments.

½ head cauliflower, cut into florets
4 ounces green beans, ends trimmed
6 green onions, 4 split lengthwise, 2 chopped
2 carrots, quartered lengthwise
1 red sweet pepper, cut into strips
1 small sweet potato, diced
⅓ cup gado gado sauce *or* make your own (see above)
¼ cup toasted, chopped peanuts

●Steam vegetables, reserving chopped green onions, for 10 to 12 minutes until barely tender. Stir 3 to 4 tablespoons boiling water into gado gado sauce and simmer for 3 to 5 minutes until hot through. Heap vegetables on a serving plate, pour hot sauce over them, and scatter peanuts and chopped onions on top. Serve hot.

Summer Berry Soup

Fruit soups are popular wherever there are Scandinavians. Many of these soups are quite sweet—almost dessert food— while others, like this one, have tart and savory undertones, which keep them firmly in the entrée category. Berries and soft stone fruits can be used, singly or in combination. Try cherries, raspberries, and loganberries; cantaloupe, strawberry, and lime (replace wine with fruit vinegar or orange juice); blackberry-rhubarb; apricot-peach; the list is as long as summer itself. Spice them with coriander, toasted cumin seeds, or caraway. Add bits of fennel bulb, shrimp, chopped nuts, or bacon for variety. To make lower calorie soups, replace sour cream or crème fraîche, the traditional creamy elements in such dishes, with yogurt or buttermilk. Serve a salad of buttercrunch lettuce and spinach with a mild curry-and-almond dressing, scones or hot biscuits, and a dry raspberry wine, a Beaujolais, or a fruity riesling.

---

1 cup raspberries
1 cup blueberries
1 cup strawberries, trimmed and sliced in half
1 cup white wine
2 cloves garlic, mashed
½ inch gingerroot, peeled and minced
½ teaspoon white pepper
2 tablespoons crème fraîche

•Put berries in a heavy saucepan with garlic and ginger. Pour in wine. Place over medium-high heat and bring to a boil. Reduce heat, partially cover pan, and simmer until berries are soft, about 8 to 10 minutes. Pour into a blender or food processor and blend briefly (soup should be slightly chunky). Return soup to pan. Add pepper and reheat. Serve in bowls with a swirl of crème fraîche.

Fresh Pea Soup

A far cry from the heavy "peas porridges" of winter, fresh pea soup is a delicate spring potage. The first tiny peas to appear in the market make the most satisfying puree. The mature peas of early summer, although fine for steaming, sautéing, or braising, develop a mealy texture and a coarser flavor than the fleeting children of spring; so soups like this can only be indulged in for a few short weeks in late spring. Serve this with wheat rolls, a plate of fruit and kasséri cheese, a spinach salad, and a sprightly white Orvieto.

---

6 to 8 red-skinned new potatoes (about 1 pound)
3 tablespoons butter
6 green onions, chopped in ½-inch pieces
1 pound fresh peas, shelled, reserving 6 whole peapods
    for garnish
1 pint heavy cream
2 tablespoons chopped fresh chives
1 teaspoon freshly ground white pepper

●Boil whole new potatoes in their jackets in lightly salted water just to cover. When fork-tender (about 12 minutes) skim off any foam and set aside, liquid and all. In a heavy saucepan, melt 2 tablespoons butter over medium heat. Add onions and peas and sauté for 5 to 7 minutes until just soft. Put onions, peas, and potatoes in blender or food processor, adding enough of the potato stock to cover. Blend briefly, so that mixture is flecked with small bits of vegetables. Pour mixture back into saucepan, adding cream, chives, pepper, and remaining butter. Heat soup gently until butter melts. Serve, garnished with reserved peapods.

Spicy Mushroom Soup

This soup cooks very quickly, so that the flavors remain fresh. Serve it hot or cold, depending on the weather; it's good either way. The lively blend of spices makes an intriguing combination without overwhelming the milder, woodsy taste of the mushrooms. The best sun-dried tomatoes taste much like dried apricots with a bright, warm tanginess. Other brands can be about as tempting as hay, so buy small amounts until you find one you enjoy. Serve this soup, hot or cold, with a basket of cornmeal muffins, coleslaw with a bit of orange peel grated into the mayonnaise, or a plate of small vegetables with a tangy dip. Garnish vegetables with pansies or bright nasturtiums with a few of their peppery leaves. Stout is always good with mushroomy food, and a nebbiolo would be nice also.

---

1 to 2 teaspoons walnut oil *or* olive oil
1 red onion, chopped
6 sun-dried tomatoes, snipped into small pieces
½ teaspoon coriander
½ teaspoon cumin
2 cups thickly sliced mushrooms
2 cups buttermilk
1 tablespoon salsa

•In a medium frying pan, heat oil over medium heat. Sauté onion and tomatoes with coriander and cumin for about 6 minutes until onion is soft and golden. Add mushrooms, stir to coat, and cover pan. Cook for 4 to 5 minutes, until mushrooms are tender. Add buttermilk and salsa, stir well. To serve immediately, heat quickly, stirring constantly, until very hot, but not boiling. Or, put in the refrigerator and serve chilled.

Cucumber Soup

Cucumber cool and interestingly pale—like a proper Victorian heroine—this chunky chilled soup makes a satisfying hot-weather entrée. Like most cold soups, this one is full-bodied; if the texture is too thick and creamy for you, thin it to taste with buttermilk, a fruit vinegar, strained chicken stock, or even water. Buttery cashews and slivered green onions make an attractive garnish, as do nasturtiums, pansies, or tiny English daisies. To complement the soup, serve thick bread sticks in a vase, a slab of sturdy double Gloucester or Cheshire cheese, and a pot of Provençal herb mustard. A full-bodied ale with a long, lingering finish is a pleasant adjunct as well.

---

2 cups yogurt
1 large *or* 2 small cucumber(s), peeled, seeded, and cut
  into chunks
3 green onions, trimmed and thinly sliced on diagonal
1 small bulb Florence fennel, trimmed and cut into chunks
1 yellow sweet pepper, trimmed and cut into chunks
2 to 3 tablespoons chopped fresh mint (6 sprigs)
1 ounce grated Romano cheese
2 tablespoons toasted, salted cashews, coarsely chopped

●Put yogurt and ½ large or 1 whole cucumber in blender or food processor. Add ⅔ green onions, ⅓ fennel, ½ pepper, and 2 to 3 tablespoons mint; add up to ½ cup water and blend until liquid. Add remaining cucumber and cheese to soup, stir gently. Refrigerate or pour into bowls. For garnish, scatter remaining onions and cashews on each portion just before serving.

Florence fennel

Tzatziki Soup

This is a spunky soup version of the salad one encounters in every taverna throughout Greece. Half the vegetables go into the blender, the rest are diced to provide the familiar texture, all mixed with a thick, sturdy tzatziki. Take it to the beach (in a wide-mouthed thermos) for a cool refreshment on a scorching day. Pack pitas, some salty feta or sharp kasséri cheese, pungent Greek olives, ripe figs, and a bottle of red Demestica for an easy, savory meal. Another thermos full of iced coffee with a good hit of Mavrodaphne or Saint Helena, both Greek dessert wines, makes a pleasant finale.

---

1 medium sweet onion (Walla Walla or Vidalia)
2 ripe tomatoes, peeled and halved
1 cucumber, peeled and halved
2 cups yogurt
2 cloves garlic
1 teaspoon chopped fresh oregano (3 sprigs) *or*
  ½ teaspoon dried
1 ounce feta cheese, crumbled
4 Greek olives, pitted and chopped

●Coarsely chop and put in blender or food processor ½ onion, 1 tomato, and ½ cucumber. Add yogurt, garlic, and oregano; blend to liquefy. Chop into dice remaining onion, tomato, and cucumber, add to soup. Add feta and olives. Chill or serve at once.

Yucatan Peanut Soup

This fiery soup originated in the Yucatan, but variations of it can be found all over Mexico. Fresh, real peanut butter makes a big difference, so splurge on the best you can buy. Some supermarkets and a lot of cooperative food stores have their own machines for grinding roasted peanuts without added oils, sugar, or salt. The resulting flavor is unbeatable. Try any kind or combination of fresh chiles, experimenting to find your favorite. Dieters will prefer to substitute yogurt for the heavy cream, but might want to cut back on the chiles, because the cream mellows the heat more than yogurt will. Have a few quesadillas or cornbread on the side, a salad of shredded cabbage, apples, and raisins with an orange-chile vinaigrette, and a Mexican beer or two.

---

1 teaspoon olive oil *or* peanut oil
1 pound yams, rinsed and cut into chunks
1 clove garlic, thinly sliced
1 to 3 fresh chiles, seeded and thinly sliced
¼ cup peanut butter
1 cup cream *or* yogurt
2 to 3 teaspoons chopped fresh cilantro
2 tablespoons peanuts, toasted and chopped

●In a saucepan, heat oil over medium heat. Add yams, garlic, and chiles, sauté for 5 minutes. Add 1½ cups water, cover, and simmer until yams are soft, about 20 minutes. Put mixture into blender or food processor and buzz to liquefy; return to pan. Stir in peanut butter and heat almost to the boiling point. Pour in cream, reduce heat, and cook just until hot through. Pour into bowls and sprinkle cilantro and peanuts over each serving.

Black Bean Soup

Smooth, rich black beans meet up with their Oriental cousins in the form of spicy hot black bean sauce. If you'd rather not use canned black beans, cook up a big batch on the weekend and freeze them in small quantities for this and other quickly made dishes, or cheat and buy ready-made canned black bean soup and gussy it up in the following manner. Plump out the meal with a basket of hot rolls, a plate of crudités, perhaps a wedge of good cheese, and a bottle of nebbiolo or a deep-chested stout.

---

1 teaspoon sesame oil
1 carrot, diced (reserve a few curls for garnish)
2 green onions, thinly sliced on diagonal
2 stalks bok choy, sliced
1 15-ounce can black beans, canned black bean soup, *or*
   2 cups cooked black beans
2 to 3 tablespoons black bean sauce
2 tablespoons sesame seeds, toasted

●In a heavy pan, heat oil over medium heat until sizzling. Add carrots, onions, and bok choy; stir-fry for 3 minutes. Add 1 cup water and simmer for 5 minutes. Rinse beans, drain, and puree in blender or food processor with vegetables and water, reserving 2 tablespoons of beans. Return puree to pan along with reserved beans over medium heat. Rinse black bean sauce before adding it to pan if it is the whole bean, extrasalty kind, otherwise just stir it into puree. Heat soup until very hot but not boiling. Stir in sesame seeds, and serve, garnishing each portion with carrot curls.

bok choy

Caribbean Bean Salad

This flavorful combination has a wonderful interplay of texture and aroma, the sweetness of citrus against garlicky vinegar; rich, chunky garbanzos with crunchy, salty peanuts; the sharp bite of Bermuda onion and capers mellowed by the olive oil in the dressing. When fresh beans are in the supermarket, try using fresh cranberry beans, scarlet runners, black turtles, or even baby limas. All may be shelled and quickly steamed until tender—a matter of minutes. Pass a plate of warm rolls with a smooth, creamy jack cheese. Cold beer, sangria, or fresh lemonade are traditional refreshments.

1½ cups cooked garbanzo beans *or*
   1 15-ounce can
1 medium red onion, chopped
12 ounces cooked shrimp
1 lime, juiced plus grated peel
1 orange, juiced plus grated peel
¼ cup garlic vinaigrette
1 teaspoon capers
¼ cup salted peanuts

●Drain garbanzos and toss with onion and shrimp. In a small bowl, blend lime and orange juices, ½ teaspoon lime peel, 1 teaspoon orange peel, vinaigrette, and capers. Toss bean mixture with dressing, garnish with peanuts, and serve.

Satsuma Salad with Hot Cranberry Dressing

Layers of semicircular satsumas, toasted almonds, savoy cabbage, and shallots tumble with a hot, dressing of cranberries and garlic. The shimmering red sauce fills the wrinkles of the crinkly savoy leaves, making a beautiful, glowing dish that is as pleasing on the palate as on the plate. Add the hot dressing just before serving and eat immediately, for the dressing cools quickly. Whole wheat baguettes, slices of Gorgonzola or Stilton, and a Soave Classico or a mellow Orvieto will complete this simple, knockout meal.

---

6 to 8 tender leaves savoy cabbage, trimmed
2 satsumas, peeled and cut into fans
½ cup walnuts, toasted
2 shallots, trimmed, thinly sliced, and cut into matchsticks
1 tablespoon walnut oil
2 cloves garlic, mashed
1 cup cranberries
2 to 3 tablespoons orange juice concentrate

●Chop cabbage leaves into narrow strips, then slice in half so each strip is about 1- x 2-inches long (should yield about 2 cups). Pile cabbage into salad bowl, scatter oranges, walnuts, and shallots on top. To prepare dressing, heat oil in a saucepan over medium heat. Add garlic and cook for 1 minute. Rinse and pick over cranberries. Add cranberries and ½ cup water to saucepan. Cover and cook over medium-low heat for 8 to 10 minutes. Remove lid and cook over medium-high heat for 3 to 5 minutes, stirring occasionally until liquid is nearly gone. Reduce heat, stir in orange juice, and heat until bubbling. Toss hot dressing with salad and serve at once.

orange fans

Orange and Hazelnut Salad with Hot Bacon Dressing

Oranges are peeled and sliced into translucent semicircles, beautiful and fragrant. Nuts, poppy seeds, oranges, bok choy, and green onions make colorful combinations with pleasantly contrasting textures echoed in the sizzling dressing of hot bacon, garlic, and lemon juice. The salad looks especially pretty layered in a glass bowl. Toss the salad with the hot dressing right at the table and serve at once. Hot rolls and a glass of verdicchio or a Soave Classico make it a light, bright meal.

---

4 green onions, trimmed
2 oranges, peeled and cut into fans
6 to 8 leaves bok choy
¼ cup hazelnuts, toasted and skins rubbed off
1 tablespoon poppy seeds
4 strips bacon, chopped into ¼-inch pieces
1 clove garlic, mashed
½ lemon, juiced plus peel sliced into strips

●Chop 2 onions into ½-inch pieces; thinly slice the other 2. Put sliced onions into a salad bowl. Heap oranges over them. Trim off bottoms of bok choy. Chop into narrow strips across leaves, so each has some of the thick white rib in the center (should yield about 2 cups). Arrange bok choy around edge of bowl. Scatter hazelnuts and poppy seeds over top. For dressing, put bacon, garlic, remaining green onions, and 2 to 3 strips of lemon peel into a frying pan; cook over medium heat, until bacon is crisp but still flexible. Add lemon juice to pan. Remove and discard lemon peel and garlic. Pour dressing over salad, toss, and serve at once.

Insalata Russe

In Italy, Russian salad is a summertime favorite. There are many versions of it, but some of the simplest are the tastiest. This one relies on the flavors of ripe summer vegetables for its subtle sweetness. If you can't find romanesco broccoli, substitute a young cauliflower or a young, fresh ordinary broccoli. The cheese is often a medium-sharp Asiago or pecorino, but small chunks of smoked provolone are also very good. Lemon juice and zest bring extra flavor and fragrance to bottled mayonnaise, making it closer to homemade. Serve this salad at room temperature or only slightly cool, for the most satisfying effect. A loaf of whole-grain bread, a jug of Orvieto, *e tu, eh*?!

---

1 large boiling potato, cut into 1-inch pieces
1 carrot, cut into 1-inch pieces
4 ounces green beans, cut into 1-inch pieces
1 small zucchini, cut into 1-inch pieces
1 small head romanesco broccoli
1 lemon, juiced plus grated peel
2 to 4 tablespoons mayonnaise
4 ounces cheese (pecorino, Asiago, or provolone), diced into
   ¼-inch cubes

●Prepare potato, carrot, green beans, and zucchini. Snap each long shoot off broccoli and leave it whole, trimming stems. Steam vegetables briefly, 5 to 7 minutes until tender but still firm. Add lemon peel and juice to taste to mayonnaise, making a thin but still clingy sauce. Drain vegetables and toss gently with cheese and dressing. Serve warm or chilled.

romanesco broccoli

Summer Vegetable Salad

This main-dish salad pairs summery vegetables with a mild anchovy dressing. If you aren't sure how you feel about anchovies, add the mashed fillets to the dressing one at a time, tasting as you go. It is worth trying several brands of anchovies; they are not expensive and vary greatly in taste, texture, and saltiness. The best are packed in good olive oil, often with a few capers thrown in (these are mildly flavorful and only moderately salty). Choose small new potatoes, about the size of the cherry tomatoes, and cook them whole in their little red jackets. Eat young sugar snap peas like snow peas, pods and all; both are juiciest and least stringy when under three inches long. Have crusty rolls, sweet butter, and a bottle of Cortese di Gavi on ice by your table beneath the grape arbor—summery food like this is always best when eaten out-of-doors.

---

1 to 3 anchovy fillets, mashed
¼ cup vinaigrette
1 small head buttercrunch or butterhead lettuce,
    torn into small pieces
1 pound new potatoes, well scrubbed
8 ounces cherry tomatoes, whole, trimmed of stems
4 ounces whole sugar snap or snow peas, trimmed
1 small Walla Walla or Vidalia sweet onion, thinly sliced
    into half-rounds
3 ounces pepperoni, thinly sliced

●Add anchovies to vinaigrette. Arrange lettuce in a salad bowl. Prick potatoes with a sharp fork and put in salted water to cover. Bring to boil, reduce heat, and simmer until tender, about 6 to 8 minutes; drain. Heap potatoes on lettuce with tomatoes. Sprinkle onions, peas, and pepperoni over all. Drizzle with dressing, toss gently, and serve at room temperature.

Yellow Finn Potato Salad

Fingerling yellow Finn potatoes are tender in a minute, so be careful not to overcook them, or the texture and flavor will be lost. Their delicate color and waxy, almost creamy flavor are wonderful with the buttery, nutlike flavor of Jarlsberg cheese. When tossed with vinegar while still hot, potatoes absorb the tangy vinegar aroma, but the sharpness is buffered by the addition of fruity olive oil. Flat Italian parsley is the most flavorful, but any kind will do. This salad is a great way to use up leftover fish, especially if grilled, but canned tuna packed in water or olive oil tastes nearly as good. Serve with cantaloupe and melon dressed with sage, fruit vinegar, and honey; fresh runner beans; and a cool ale or pilsner.

---

1 pound small yellow Finn potatoes, well scrubbed
3 to 4 tablespoons red wine vinegar
1 cup flaked, cooked fish *or*
  16½-ounce can tuna fish, drained
4 ounces Jarlsberg cheese, sliced into small strips
2 tablespoons chopped fresh flat Italian parsley
2 tablespoons olive oil
1 ounce grated Asiago *or* Parmesan cheese
1 teaspoon freshly ground black pepper or to taste

●In a large saucepan, bring salted water to boil. Add potatoes and cook for 8 to 10 minutes until just fork-tender. Drain and toss at once with vinegar; set aside. Add fish and Jarlsberg to potatoes. Add parsley to oil along with grated cheese. Add pepper, blend well, and drizzle over potatoes. Serve at room temperature or refrigerate, until you are ready to eat.

New Potato Pesto Salad

Lovers of pesto can never get enough of it. In this spring-time salad, hard-boiled eggs, new potatoes, and green onions blend with generous amounts of a slimmed-down version of the classic basil pesto, one which works equally well as a dressing for mixed greens, a sauce for fish, or an exceptional turkey sandwich spread. This salad will be most successful when the eggs and potatoes are freshly cooked and still warm, so that they absorb the flavor and scent of the dressing. Serve with a plate of fresh fruit, cheese, rolls, and stout or Chianti to stand up to the rich, vivid flavors of the pesto.

---

1 pound new potatoes (10 tiny)
2 hard-boiled eggs, quartered
4 green onions, sliced
1 bunch fresh basil, chopped
2 cloves garlic, halved
1 tablespoon olive oil
1 ounce pecorino *or*
  Parmesan cheese, grated
2 tablespoons pine nuts, toasted

●Place potatoes in a large saucepan, cover with salted water, and cook for 10 to 15 minutes until tender; cool enough to handle. Cut each in half and combine with eggs in a salad bowl. Scatter onions on top. Combine basil, garlic, oil, cheese, and 1 tablespoon pine nuts, along with ¼ cup water in a blender or food processor; buzz to a smooth paste. Pour over salad, toss very gently to cover, and garnish with remaining pine nuts. Serve at once at room temperature.

Toasting Nuts and Seeds

Spread nuts on a large baking sheet, add salt if desired, and toast in 350 degree oven: 5 to 7 minutes for cashews, pine nuts, pumpkin and sunflower seeds; 6 to 9 minutes for peanuts; 7 to 10 minutes for walnuts and pecans; 8 to 12 minutes for almonds; 10 to 12 minutes for hazelnuts; and 15 to 20 minutes for Brazil nuts.

Handling Fresh Chiles

The fiery oils of chiles can burn other tissue as well as your throat. Some people can actually get blisters from handling very hot ones. Be careful not to touch your eyes, mouth, or face while handling chiles. And if you are particularly sensitive, wear rubber or kitchen gloves. Always wash your hands carefully with soap after seeding or chopping chiles, for the oil clings to the skin unless properly removed.

To trim chiles or other peppers, cut the stem cap off and slit the chiles lengthwise. Scrape out the seeds and the inner membrane, and slice, sliver, or chop the flesh of the chile. The seeds often have the most concentrated hot quality, so if you want a dish to be intensely hot, leave in some or all of the seeds—but start with a few and work up, unless you are a confirmed fire-eater.

Tips and Techniques

Roasting mellows and enriches the flavor of both sweet peppers and chiles. Use a gas stove, a barbecue grill, or an oven. To roast chiles over an open flame, thread them, whole, on a long skewer or toasting fork. Hold them close to the flame, turning often, until the skins are charred. To grill, place whole chiles near the hottest part of the fire and sear, turning several times until the skins are charred. In an oven, place chiles on a rack a few inches from the heat and broil 1 to 2 minutes per side. Once you have charred the chiles, wrap them loosely in a hand towel or tea cloth and set aside for 10 to 15 minutes until cooled. Rub them gently to remove skins.

Cracking Whole Peppercorns

Place whole peppercorns in a zip-lock or other sturdy bag; whack with a rolling pin, hammer, bottle, or the handle of a heavy knife.

Salad Dressings

Basic Vinaigrette I

1 to 2 parts oil
1 part vinegar

●Mix oil and vinegar with any of the variations listed below; store in a glass jar.

Basic Vinaigrette II

1 part vinegar
3 parts buttermilk, yogurt, sour cream, *or*
  crème fraîche.

●Mix vinegar and buttermilk with any of the variations listed below; store in a glass jar.

Herbed Dressing

½ cup Basic Vinaigrette I *or* II
A few leaves tarragon, sage, fennel, *or* lovage, chopped
(for a strong flavor) *or*
up to 1 teaspoon chopped marjoram, chervil, *or*
parsley (for a mild flavor)

●Combine ingredients well.

Garlic Dressing

½ cup Basic Vinaigrette I *or* II
1 to 2 cloves garlic, lightly mashed
Pinch grated cheese
Pinch freshly ground black or white pepper, nutmeg, *or*
coriander

●Combine ingredients well.

Citrus Dressing

½ cup Basic Vinaigrette I *or* II
½ to 1 teaspoon finely grated fresh orange, tangerine, lemon
or grapefruit peel
1 clove garlic (optional)
Freshly ground black or white pepper
¼ to ½ teaspoon chopped fresh tarragon, fennel, *or*
sage (or a combination) *or*
⅛ teaspoon dried (optional)

●Combine all or a combination of ingredients well.

Mustard Dressing

½ cup Basic Vinaigrette I *or* II
1 teaspoon to 1 tablespoon prepared mustard

●Combine ingredients well.

Pesto Dressing

½ cup Basic Vinaigrette I *or* II
1 tablespoon to ¼ cup pesto (basil, cilantro, dill, sage, *or* parsley)

● Combine ingredients well.

Salsa Dressing

½ cup Basic Vinaigrette I *or* II
1 teaspoon to 1 tablespoon salsa

● Combine ingredients well.

Curry Dressing

¼ cup oil
1 clove garlic, sliced
½ to 1 teaspoon curry powder, garam masala *or* other spice blend
¼ cup vinegar

● Warm oil. Add garlic and curry and blend. Add vinegar, blend well.

Chutney Dressing

½ cup Basic Vinaigrette II
1 tablespoon or more chutney (any kind)

● Mix vinaigrette and chutney well.

Index

Almond(s)
  chicken livers with wild rice
    and, 105
  and Gruyère omelet, 195
  veal with peaches and, 142
Almond oil
  in avocado ham sauté, 171
  in veal with peaches and
    almonds, 142
Anchovy(ies)
  in rabbit in balsamic
    vinegar, 136
  in spaghetti caponata, 218
  in summer vegetable salad, 234
Apples
  pork with, and yams, 119
Apricots
  in turkey El Café, 107
Artichoke(s)
  with lamb chop with baked
    garlic, 160
  mizíthra and, omelet, 196
  veal with, 141
Arugula (rocket)
  description, 9
Asiago
  description, 9
  in aglio-oglio with bay
    shrimp, 62
  in insalata Russe, 233
  in oyster stew, 85
  in romanesco broccoli
    omelet, 193
  in Roquefort crab with green
    peppercorn sauce, 68
  in squid and shrimp salad, 88
  in torta verde, 201
  in yellow Finn potato salad, 235
Asparagus
  Chilean, description, 8
Avocado(s)
  fajitas with, sauce, 159

ham sauté, 171
  in hot scallop salad with blood
    oranges, 79
  in Mexican shrimp salad, 64
  pork strips with hot potato-,
    salad, 128
  in prawn and jícama salad, 59
  tzatziki pita, 178
Avocado oil
  in avocado ham sauté, 171

Bacon
  with beef in merlot, 151
  Canadian, *in* spaghetti alla
    carbonara, 172
  in chicken in white
    burgundy, 96
  in clam chowder, 75
  in game hens Perugino, 114
  game hens with, and beans, 113
  liver, shrimp, and, in pepper
    sauce, 104
  orange and hazelnut salad with
    hot, dressing, 232
  in oyster mushroom omelet, 199
  in peanut pie, 203
  in pumpkin tortellone
    all'amatrice, 173
  rabbit with, and
    mushrooms, 132
  in raspberry game hens, 112
  in skewered scallops, 76
  sorrel soup with shrimp and, 63
  sorrel, spinach, and, salad, 177
  veal with leeks, and
    tomatoes, 143
Balsamic vinegar (see Vinegar)
Bananas
  red, *in* chicken Caribbe, 93
  red, *in* Thai banana chicken, 95

Basmati rice
    in scallops with cardamom
        orange rice, 77
Beans
    black, see Black bean(s)
    broad, *in* pork with
        sunburst squash, 125
    garbanzo, see Garbanzo bean(s)
    green, *in* gado gado, 222
    green, *in* insalata Russe, 233
    green, *in* oyster mushroom
        omelet, 199
    green, *in* Zuñi lamb stew, 166
    lima, *in* sausage and lima
        casserole, 181
    purple, *in* summery beef sauté,
        157
    runner, *in* game hens with
        bacon and, 113
    runner, *in* pork with
        sunburst squash, 125
    snap, *in* lamb and beans, 163
Beef (see chapter contents for list
        of recipes), 149
    do pyaza, 155
    ground, *in* burgers in bitter
        beer, 156
    in merlot, 141
    in squash blossom stew, 158
    summery, sauté, 157
Beer
    burgers in bitter, 156
Beets
    in salami salad, 184
Black bean(s)
    prawns in, sauce, 56
    soup, 229
    with two potatoes, 217
Bleu cheese
    blintzes, 204
Blintzes
    bleu cheese, 204

Blood oranges
    hot scallop salad with, 79
Blueberries
    in summer berry soup, 223
Bok choy
    description, 9
    in black bean soup, 229
    in orange and hazelnut salad
        with hot bacon dressing, 232
    in prawns with sushi ginger, 57
Brazil nut
    tacos, 211
Brie
    description, 9
Broccoli
    romanesco, *in* insalata Russe,
        233
    romanesco, *in* jícama
        ham salad, 175
    romanesco, omelet, 193
Burgers
    in bitter beer, 156
Buttermilk
    veal in, 146

Cabbage
    Napa, *in* chile cream
        chicken, 101
    savoy, *in* satsuma salad with hot
        cranberry dressing, 231
Capers
    description, 13
    in Caribbean bean salad, 230
    in gold fish, 32
    ham with chard and, 170
    in rabbit piccata, 137
    in spaghetti caponata, 218
    in steamed mussel soup, 83
    in summery beef sauté, 157
    veal with, 145

Index

Cardamom
  description, 13
  in pods, *in* grilled turkey breast
    with rhubarb sauce, 108
  pods, *in* veal with peaches
    and almonds, 142
  scallops with, orange rice, 77
  spicy, chicken, 97
Cashews
  in cucumber soup, 226
Casserole
  camarónes Bolivianos, 60
  crab, 66
  sausage and lima, 181
Catfish
  in cornmeal with black
    butter, 52
  with three butters, 51
Cauliflower
  in gado gado, 222
Chard
  ham with, and capers, 170
Cheddar
  (English, description), 9
  (Tillamook, description), 9
  in crab and clam pie, 65
  and hazelnut torte, 202
  in peanut pie, 203
Cheese (see also individual
    cheeses or chapter contents
    for a list of recipes), 189
  and pepperoni omelet, 197
  ravioli with nut sauce, 206
Cherries
  in chicken in cherry ale, 99
Chervil
  poached perch with, 50
Cheshire
  description, 9
Chestnuts
  pork roast with, 118
  sherried, with rabbit, 134

Chicken (see chapter contents for
    a list of recipes), 89
  Caribbe, 93
  in cherry ale, 99
  chile cream, 101
  coconut, with two
    corianders, 102
  jícama and, soup, 103
  mushroom-stuffed, breasts, 92
  orangerie, 100
  with plums and ginger, 98
  roasted lemon, 91
  smoked, see Smoked chicken
  spicy cardamom, 97
  Thai banana, 95
  tomatillo, 94
  in white burgundy, 96
Chicken livers
  shrimp, and bacon in pepper
    sauce, 104
  vermicelli with, and
    pine nuts, 106
  with wild rice and almonds, 105
Chile(s)
  description, 13
  in aglio-oglio with bay
    shrimp, 62
  in camarónes Bolivianos, 60
  in catfish in cornmeal with
    black butter, 52
  in fresh tomato curry with
    halibut, 45
  green, *in* chile cream
    chicken, 101
  green, *in* Zuñi lamb stew, 166
  in grilled turkey breast with
    rhubarb sauce, 108
  in halibut mixed grill, 44
  handling fresh, 237
  Japanese, description, 13
  in lamb and cucumber
    sauté, 161

Chile(s), *continued*
  pasillas, *in* cilantro pesto
    pizza, 208
  pasillas, *in* halibut mixed
    grill, 44
  in peanut pie, 203
  in pork with fresh mango
    chutney, 122
  in prawns in black bean
    sauce, 56
  with prawns in green salsa, 58
  in pueblo rabbit stew, 140
  red, *in* chile cream chicken, 101
  red, *in* squash blossom
    stew, 158
  serraños, *in* chicken Caribbe, 93
  in sizzling walnut rabbit, 133
  in spaghetti squash
    Caribbe, 219
  in spicy cardamom chicken, 97
  in stars and stripes snapper, 37
  Thai, *in* Thai banana
    chicken, 95
  in Yucatan peanut soup, 228
Chili oil
  in pork kebabs with three
    peppers, 130
  in spicy cardamom chicken, 97
Chutney(s)
  description, 13
  dressing, 240
  pork with fresh mango, 122
Cilantro
  in black cod in pine nut
    sauce, 40
  in Brazil nut tacos, 211
  in camarónes Bolivianos, 60
  in catfish with three butters, 51
  in chicken Caribbe, 93
  in coconut chicken with two
    corianders, 102

in grilled turkey breast with
    rhubarb sauce, 108
in lamb and cucumber sauté,
    161
in lamb with emerald satsumas
    and kumquats, 164
in Mexican shrimp salad, 64
in mussels gratinée, 81
pesto pizza, 208
in prawn and jícama salad, 59
in squash blossom stew, 158
in stars and stripes snapper, 37
in tomatillo chicken, 94
in Yucatan peanut soup, 228
Citrus dressing, 239
Clam
  butter, hash, 73
  capelli d'angelo with, sauce, 74
  chowder, 75
  crab and, pie, 65
  prawns in, clouds, 55
Coconut (milk)
  in camarónes Bolivianos, 60
  chicken with two
    corianders, 102
  in spicy cardamom chicken, 97
Coconut cream (see Coconut)
Cod
  black, in pine nut sauce, 40
  black, in tuna Lampedusa, 17
  black, muscadet, 41
  black, with Chinese mustard
    sauce, 39
  in fish chowder, 42
  honey-glazed, 38
Coriander(s)
  coconut chicken with two, 102
  in saffron haddock, 43
  in spicy cardamom chicken, 97
Cornmeal
  blue, *in* pueblo rabbit stew, 140

Index

Crab
    bisque, 71
    casserole, 66
    and clam pie, 65
    with enoki mushrooms, 69
    grilled Dungeness, 67
    red peppers stuffed with, 70
    Roquefort, with green
        peppercorn sauce, 68
    salad, 72
Cranberry(ies)
    gooseberry ham, 169
    satsuma salad with hot,
        dressing, 231
Cucumber
    soup, 226
Cured and smoked meats (see
        chapter contents for a list
        of recipes), 167
Currants
    perch with, and walnuts, 49
Curry
    dressing, 240
    fresh tomato, with halibut, 45

Eggplant
    eggs with, 198
    glazed, steaks, 216
    Japanese, Parmesan, 215
    in spaghetti caponata, 218
Eggs (see chapter contents for a
        list of recipes), 189
    baked, with smoked salmon, 22
    with eggplant, 198
    green, and ham, 176
    leeks and, in balsamic
        vinegar, 200
    omelets, see Omelet
    soufflés, see Soufflé
    torte(s), see Torte

Enoki mushrooms
    (see Mushrooms)
Escarole
    description, 9

Feijoa
    scallop and, salad, 80
Fennel
    in crab bisque, 71
    Florence, *in* cucumber
        soup, 226
    Florence, *in* hunter's rabbit, 131
    fresh tuna with, 19
    fresh, *in* Wensleydale grill, 179
    in lemon fettuccine with
        scallops and three peppers, 78
    in stars and stripes snapper, 37
Feta
    in tzatziki soup, 227
Filet mignon
    in pepper steak, 153
Fish (see individual fish
        or chapter contents for
        a list of recipes), 15
Fontina
    in smoked salmon
        sandwiches, 27
Fruits (see individual fruits or
        chapter contents for a list of
        recipes), 213

Gado Gado, 222
Game hens
    with bacon and beans, 113
    gooseberry-glazed, with sage
        stuffing, 111
    Perugino, 114
    raspberry, 112
Garam masala
    in beef do pyaza, 155
    in curry dressing, 240

Garam masala, *continued*
  in fresh tomato curry with
    halibut, 45
  in lamb with mint raita, 162
Garbanzo bean(s)
  in Caribbean bean salad, 230
  salad, 183
Garlic dressing, 239
Garlic tips
  in hunter's rabbit, 131
Gin
  squid in, with ginger, 86
Ginger
  chicken with plums and, 98
  in honey-glazed true cod, 38
  pickled, *in* glazed eggplant
    steaks, 216
  pickled, *in* prawns with
    sushi, 57
  in pork with sunburst
    squash, 125
  root, *in* beef do pyaza, 155
  root, *in* glazed eggplant
    steaks, 216
  root, *in* pork kebabs with
    fresh pineapple, 129
  root, *in* summer berry soup, 223
  squid in gin and, 86
Gloucester
  description, 9
  double, soufflé, 192
Goat cheese
  description, 9
  Gooseberry(ies)
  cranberry, ham, 169
  glazed game hens with sage
    stuffing, 111
Gorgonzola
  pear salad, 174
  in salami salad, 184
  spaghetti with, sauce, 207
Grapefruit

pink, *in* smoked turkey salad
  in poppy seed dressing, 186
Green peppercorns
  in crab bisque, 71
  in crab casseroles, 66
  in crab with enoki
    mushrooms, 69
  in game hens Perugino, 114
  in gooseberry-glazed game
    hens with sage stuffing, 111
  in mussels gratinée, 81
  in pork with sunburst
    squash, 125
  Roquefort crab with, sauce, 68
  in salami salad, 184
  in salmon butter and peas with
    fettuccine, 25
  in sorrel omelet, 194
  in tuna noodle casserole, 20
Green salsa
  prawns in, 58
  red snapper in, 34
Green tomatoes
  fried, and mozzarella, 205
  in green snapper, 36
  sole and, in cornmeal, 33
  in squash blossom stew, 158
Gruyère
  almond and, omelet, 195
  in crab casseroles, 66
  in leeks in tuna sauce, 221
  in mussels gratinée, 81
  in smoked salmon
    sandwiches, 27

Haddock
  in fish chowder, 42
  saffron, 43
Halibut
  fresh tomato curry with, 45
  mixed grill, 44

Ham (see chapter contents for a
    list of recipes), 167
  avocado, sauté, 171
  with chard and capers, 170
  cranberry-gooseberry, 269
  Cure 81, *in* avocado
    tzatziki pita, 178
  in Gorgonzola pear salad, 174
  green eggs and, 176
  jícama salad, 175
  in spaghetti alla carbonara, 172
Hazelnut(s)
  cheddar and, torte, 202
  orange and, salad with
    hot bacon dressing, 232
  toasting, 237
Herbed dressing, 239
Horseradish
  root, *in* turkey cutlets
    with, cream, 109

Jalapeños
  in halibut mixed grill, 44
  in Thai banana chicken, 95
Jarlsberg
  in yellow Finn potato salad, 235
Jícama
  and chicken soup, 103
  ham salad, 175
  in hot scallop salad with
    blood oranges, 79
  prawn and, salad, 59
Juniper berries
  in pueblo rabbit stew, 140
  in rabbit grilled over
    alderwood, 138

Kasséri
  sausage salad with, cheese, 182
Kumquats
  lamb with emerald satsumas
    and, 164

Lamb
  description, 12
  and beans, 163
  chops with baked garlic, 160
  and cucumber sauté, 161
  with emerald satsumas and
    kumquats, 164
  medallions in pumpkin
    sauce, 165
  with mint raita, 162
  Zuñi, stew, 166
Leeks
  and eggs in balsamic
    vinegar, 200
  in tuna sauce, 221
  veal with, bacon, and
    tomatoes, 143
  in veal stew with
    cocktail onions, 147
Liver (see Chicken livers)
Lovage
  in capelli d'angelo with
    clam sauce, 74

Mango
  pork with fresh, chutney, 122
Marsala
  in veal Marsala, 144
Masa harina
  in pueblo rabbit stew, 140
Merlot
  beef in, 151
Mirin
  in black cod with Chinese
    mustard sauce, 39
  in crab salad, 72
Mizíthra
  and artichoke omelet, 196
Mozzarella
  description, 9
  in cheese and pepperoni
    omelet, 197

Mozzarella, *continued*
 cilantro pesto pizza, 208
 fried green tomatoes and, 205
 in Japanese eggplant
  Parmesan, 215
 in jícama and chicken soup, 103
 marinated fresh, 210
 in red peppers stuffed
  with crab, 70
Muscat grapes
 in black cod muscadet, 41
Mushroom(s)
 enoki, crab with, 69
 enoki, with shrimp
  and sanbai-su, 61
 in mixed grill with
  sausages, 180
 oyster, omelet, 199
 rabbit with bacon and, 132
 spicy, soup, 225
 stuffed chicken breasts, 92
Mussel(s)
 gratinée, 81
 in pesto sauce, 82
 steamed, soup, 83
Mustard
 Dijon, *with* broiled steak
  with tomato coulis, 154
 Dijon, *in* cranberry-
  gooseberry ham, 169
 Dijon, *in* double Gloucester
  soufflé, 192
 Dijon, *in* gooseberry-glazed
  game hens with sage
  stuffing, 111
 Dijon, *in* jícama ham salad, 175
 Dijon, *in* smoked chicken
  salad, 185
 dressing, 239
Mustard greens
 description, 8
 in crab salad, 72

 scallop and feijoa salad, 80

Napa cabbage (see Cabbage)
Nuts (see individual types)
 toasting, 237

Olives
 in camarónes bolivianos, 60
 Greek, *in* avocado tzatziki
  pita, 178
 Greek, *in* mizíthra and
  artichoke omelet, 196
 Greek, *in* tzatziki soup, 227
 in prawns in green salsa, 58
Omelet
 almond and Gruyère, 195
 cheese and pepperoni, 197
 mizíthra and artichoke, 196
 oyster, 84
 oyster mushroom, 199
 romanesco broccoli, 193
 sorrel, 194
Onions
 veal with cocktail, 147
Orange
 and hazelnut salad with hot
  bacon dressing, 232
Organic meats
 description, 12
Oriental vegetables
 description, 9
Oyster
 omelet, 84
 stew, 85
Oyster mushrooms
 (see Mushrooms)

Papaya
 in pork Palau, 123
Parmesan
 description, 9
 in cheddar and hazelnut
  torte, 202

Parmesan, *continued*
   in cheese and pepperoni
      omelet, 197
   in cheese ravioli with nut
      sauce, 206
   in cilantro pesto pizza, 208
   in eggs with eggplant, 198
   in fried green tomatoes
      and mozzarella, 205
   Japanese eggplant, 215
   in mizíthra and artichoke
      omelet, 196
   in new potato pesto salad, 236
   in peperonata, 220
   in sorrel omelet, 194
   in spaghetti alla carbonara, 172
   in spaghetti with Gorgonzola
      sauce, 207
   in turkey cutlets with
      horseradish cream, 109
   in veal with artichokes, 141
   in yellow Finn potato
      salad, 235
Parsley
   Italian, *in* butter clam hash, 73
   Italian *in* eggs with
      eggplant, 198
   Italian, *in* leeks and eggs
      in balsamic vinaigrette, 200
   Italian, *in* trout with
      green sauce, 47
   Italian, *in* yellow Finn
      potato salad, 235
Parsnips
   with lamb medallions, 165
Pasta
   capelli d'angelo with clam
      sauce, 74
   cheese ravioli with
      nut sauce, 206
   lemon fettuccine with scallops
      and three peppers, 78

linguine *in* aglio-oglio
   with bay shrimp, 62
pumpkin tortellone all'
   Amatrice, 173
rosemary, *in* rosemary
   rabbit, 139
salmon butter and peas with
   fettuccine, 25
shell, *in* mussels in
   pesto sauce, 82
spaghetti alla carbonara, 172
spaghetti caponata, 218
spaghetti with Gorgonzola
   sauce, 207
squid rings with rotini, 87
tuna noodle casserole, 20
vermicelli with liver and
   pine nuts, 106
Pea(s)
   fresh, soup, 224
   sugar snap, *in* summer
      vegetable salad, 234
Peaches
   veal with, and almonds, 142
Peanut
   pie, 203
   Yucatan, soup, 228
Pear
   Gorgonzola, salad, 174
Pecan(s)
   pork, 127
   toasting, 237
Pecorino
   description, 9
   in broiled tuna with pine
      nuts and dill, 18
   in Cheddar and hazelnut
      torte, 202
   in cheese ravioli with nut
      sauce, 206
   in eggs with eggplant, 198
   in fresh tuna with fennel, 19

Pecorino, *continued*
  in gold fish, 32
  in insalata Russe, 233
  in new potato pesto salad, 236
  in pumpkin tortellone
    all'Amatrice, 173
  in red peppers stuffed with
    crab, 70
  in spaghetti alla carbonara, 172
Peperoncini
  description, 13
  in beef in merlot, 151
  in lamb chops with baked
    garlic, 160
  in liver, shrimp, and bacon in
    pepper sauce, 104
  in pumpkin tortellone
    all'Amatrice, 173
  in veal stew with cocktail
    onions, 147
  in vermicelli with liver and
    pine nuts, 106
Peppercorns
  cracking, 238
Pepperoni
  cheese and, omelet, 197
  in summer vegetable salad, 234
Peppers
  Hungarian hot wax, *in*
    pork Palau, 123
  pork kebabs with three, 130
  red, stuffed with crab, 70
  sweet, *in* lemon fettuccine with
    scallops and three peppers, 78
  sweet, *in* peperonata, 220
  sweet red, *in* gado gado, 222
Perch
  with currants and walnuts, 49
  poached, with chervil, 50
Pesto
  cilantro, pizza, 208

dressing, 240
  mussels in, sauce, 82
  new potato, salad, 236
Pie
  peanut, 203
Pine nut(s)
  black cod in, sauce, 40
  broiled tuna with, and dill, 18
  in cilantro pesto pizza, 208
  in crab salad, 72
  in marinated fresh
    mozzarella, 210
  in mussels in pesto sauce, 82
  in new potato pesto
    salad, 236
  in smoked chicken salad, 185
  in smoked turkey salad
    in poppy seed dressing, 186
  in sorrel, spinach, and
    bacon salad, 177
  toasting, 237
  in veal Marsala, 144
  vermicelli with liver and, 106
Pineapple
  pork kebabs with fresh, 129
  turkey kebabs with fresh, 110
Pineapple oranges
  pork with, 117
Pita
  avocado tzatziki, 178
Pizza
  cilantro pesto, 208
Plums
  chicken with, and ginger, 98
Poppy seed(s)
  in orange and hazelnut salad
    with hot bacon dressing, 232
  in smoked turkey salad
    in, dressing, 186
Pork
  description, 12

Pork, *continued*
  with apples and yams, 119
  broiled, chops with potatoes
    and sauerkraut, 124
  chops with pears and
    ginger, 120
  chutney, chops, 121
  cutlets with sorrel, 126
  with fresh mango chutney, 122
  kebabs with fresh
    pineapple, 129
  kebabs with three peppers, 130
  Palau, 123
  pecan, 127
  with pineapple oranges, 117
  roast with chestnuts, 118
  strips with hot potato-avocado
    salad, 128
  with sunburst squash, 125
Potato(es)
  broiled pork chops with,
    and sauerkraut, 124
  new, *in* fresh pea soup, 224
  new, pesto salad, 236
  pork strips with hot, avocado
    salad, 128
  purple, *in* black beans with
    two potatoes, 217
  sweet, *in* black beans with
    two potatoes, 217
  sweet, *in* sizzling walnut
    rabbit, 133
  sweet, *in* spaghetti squash
    Caribbe, 219
  yellow Finn, salad, 235
Poultry (see chapter contents
    for list of recipes), 89
Prawn(s)
  in black bean sauce, 56
  in clam clouds, 55
  in green salsa, 58

and jícama salad, 59
  with sushi ginger, 57
Provolone
  in insalata Russe, 233
Pumpkin
  lamb medallions in,
    sauce, 165
  in pueblo rabbit stew, 140
  tortellone all'Amatrice, 173
Pumpkin seeds
  in pueblo rabbit stew, 140
  in red snapper in
    salsa verde, 34
  toasting, 237

Rabbit
  description, 12
  with bacon and mushrooms, 132
  in balsamic vinegar, 136
  with green peppercorns, 135
  grilled over alderwood, 138
  hunter's, 131
  piccata, 137
  pueblo, stew, 140
  rosemary, 139
  with sherried chestnuts, 134
  sizzling walnut, 133
Radicchio (chicory)
  description, 9
Raspberries
  in summer berry soup, 223
Raspberry vinegar (see Vinegar)
Red snapper
  with green tomatoes, 36
  poached in orange juice, 35
  in salsa verde, 34
  stars and stripes, 37
Rhubarb
  grilled turkey breast with,
    sauce, 108
Rice vinegar (see Vinegar)

Index

Ricotta
  in almond and Gruyère
    omelet, 195
  in bleu cheese blintzes, 204
  in cheese and pepperoni
    omelet, 197
  in oyster mushroom omelet, 199
  in peanut pie, 203
  in torta verde, 201
Roast beef (see Beef)
Romanesco broccoli (see Broccoli)
Romano
  description, 9
  in cucumber soup, 226
  in fried green tomatoes
    and mozzarella, 205
  in oyster mushroom omelet, 199
  in oyster omelet, 84
  in skewered scallops, 76
  in sorrel omelet, 194
  in spaghetti all carbonara, 172
Roquefort
  crab with green
    peppercorn sauce, 68
  in leeks and eggs in
    balsamic vinaigrette, 200
  in red snapper poached
    in orange juice, 35
Rosemary
  rabbit, 139

Saffron
  description, 13
  haddock, 43
Sake
  in black cod with Chinese
    mustard sauce, 39
  in pork kebabs with fresh
    pineapple, 129
Salad
  Caribbean bean, 230
  crab, 72

dressings, 238-240
fresh salmon, 26
garbanzo, 183
Gorgonzola pear, 174
hot scallop salad with
  blood oranges, 79
insalata Russe, 233
jícama ham salad, 175
Mexican shrimp, 64
new potato pesto, 236
orange and hazelnut, with hot
  bacon dressing, 232
pork strips with hot
  potato-avocado, 128
prawn and jícama, 59
salami, 184
satsuma, with hot cranberry
  dressing, 231
sausage, with kasséri
  cheese, 182
scallop and feijoa, 80
smoked chicken, 185
smoked turkey, in poppy seed
  dressing, 186
sorrel, spinach, and
  bacon, 177
squid and shrimp, 88
summer vegetable salad, 234
tuna *in* fresh salmon salad, 26
Salami
  salad, 184
  wine-cured, *in* garbanzo
    salad, 183
Salmon
  description, 10
  butter and peas with
    fettuccine, 25
  fresh, salad, 26
  with herbed barbecue sauce, 24
  with herbed mustard sauce, 23
  masked, 21
  smoked, see Smoked salmon

Index

Salsa
in Brazil nut tacos, 211
dressing, 240
green, in fajitas with
avocado sauce, 159
in jícama and chicken soup, 103
in Mexican shrimp salad, 64
in peanut pie, 203
in prawn and jícama salad, 59
in smoked chicken tortillas, 187
in tomatillo chicken, 94
in turkey El Café, 107
Sanbai-su
enoki mushrooms with shrimp
and, 61
Sandwiches
avocado tzatziki pita, 178
smoked salmon, 27
Satsuma(s)
lamb with emerald, and
kumquats, 164
in pork kebabs with three
peppers, 130
salad with hot cranberry
dressing, 231
Sauerkraut
broiled pork chops with
potatoes and, 124
Sausage(s)
and lima casserole, 181
mixed grill with, 180
salad with kasséri cheese, 182
Savory
in game hens with bacon
and beans, 112
in lamb and beans, 163
Savoy cabbage (see Cabbage)
Scallop(s)
with cardamom orange rice, 77
and feijoa salad, 80
hot, salad with blood
oranges, 79

lemon fettuccine with, and
three peppers, 78
skewered, 76
Seafood (see individual seafood or
chapter contents for a list
of recipes), 53
Sesame oil
in black bean soup, 229
in black cod with Chinese
mustard sauce, 39
in enoki mushrooms with
shrimp and sanbai-su, 61
in honey-glazed true cod, 38
in pecan pork, 127
in squid in gin and ginger, 86
in tomatillo chicken, 94
Sesame seeds
in black bean soup, 229
Sherry
oloroso, in crab bisque, 71
oloroso, in rabbit with
sherried chestnuts, 134
in veal with artichokes, 141
Shoyu
in black cod with Chinese
mustard sauce, 39
in crab with enoki
mushrooms, 69
in glazed eggplant steaks, 216
in honey-glazed true cod, 38
in pecan pork, 127
in pork kebabs with
fresh pineapple, 129
in pork kebabs with
three peppers, 130
in prawns in black bean
sauce, 56
in prawns with sushi ginger, 57
in sizzling walnut rabbit, 133
in squid in gin and ginger, 86
Shrimp
aglio-oglio with bay, 62

Shrimp, *continued*
  in camarónes Bolivianos, 60
  in Caribbean bean salad, 230
  enoki mushrooms with, and
    sanbai-su, 61
  Liver, and bacon in pepper
    sauce, 104
  Mexican, salad, 64
  sole with, meringue, 31
  sorrel soup with, and bacon, 63
  squid and, salad, 88
Smoked chicken
  salad, 185
  tortillas, 187
Smoked salmon
  baked eggs with, 22
  sandwiches, 27
Smoked turkey
  salad in poppy seed
    dressing, 186
Snow peas
  in prawns in black
    bean sauce, 56
  in summer vegetable salad, 234
Sole
  gold fish, 32
  and green tomatoes in
    cornmeal, 33
  in rosé sauce, 29
  with shrimp meringue, 31
  with spinach and curried
    cashews, 30
  Veronique, 28
Sorrel
  description, 8
  in green eggs and ham, 176
  omelet, 194
  pork cutlets with, 126
  soup with shrimp and bacon, 63
  spinach and bacon salad, 177
Soufflé
  corn-off-the-cob, 191

double Gloucester, 192
Soup
  black bean, 229
  clam chowder, 75
  crab bisque, 71
  cucumber, 226
  Gorgonzola salad, 209
  jícama and chicken, 103
  sorrel, with shrimp and
    bacon, 63
  spicy mushroom, 225
  steamed mussel, 83
  tzatziki, 227
  Yucatan peanut, 228
Spinach
  in green eggs and ham, 176
  in Mexican shrimp salad, 64
  in smoked chicken tortillas, 187
  sole with, and curried
    cashews, 30
  sorrel, and bacon salad, 177
  in Thai banana chicken, 95
  in torta verde, 201
  in trout with green sauce, 47
Squash
  acorn, *in* turkey El Café, 107
  blossom stew, 158
  Danish, *in* turkey El Café, 107
  pattypan, *in* summery beef
    sauté, 157
  spaghetti, Caribbe, 219
  summer, *in* blossom stew, 158
  summer, *in* Zuñi lamb stew, 166
  sunburst, with pork, 125
  sunburst, *in* rosemary
    rabbit, 139
  winter, *in* pueblo
    rabbit stew, 140
Squid
  in gin and ginger, 86
  rings with rotini, 87
  and shrimp salad, 88

Star fruit
  with fish sticks, 46
Steak (see also Beef)
  broiled, with tomato coulis, 154
  in fajitas with avocado
    sauce, 159
  pepper, 153
  sirloin, with pan-fried
    tomatoes, 152
Stilton
  description, 9
Strawberries
  in summer berry soup
String cheese
  in jícama and chicken soup, 103
Sun-dried tomatoes (see
  Tomatoes)
Swordfish
  in fish sticks, 46

Tacos
  Brazil nut, 211
Tahini
  description, 10
  in honey-glazed true cod, 38
Ti leaves
  in Thai banana chicken, 95
Tomatillo(s)
  chicken, 94
  in jícama and chicken soup, 103
  in prawns in green salsa, 58
  with red snapper in
    salsa verde, 34
  in spaghetti squash
    Caribbe, 219
Tomatoes
  sun-dried, *in* marinated
    fresh mozzarella, 210
  sun-dried, *in* smoked chicken
    salad, 185

sun-dried, *in* spicy mushroom
  soup, 225
sun-dried, *in* veal in
  buttermilk, 146
veal with leeks, bacon, and, 143
Torte
  torta verde, 201
  cheddar and hazelnut, 202
Tortellone
  pumpkin, all'Amatrice, 173
Tortillas
  blue corn, *in* prawns in
    green salsa, 58
  blue corn, *in* stars and
    stripes snapper, 37
  in Brazil nut tacos, 211
  in fajitas with avocado
    sauce, 159
  smoked chicken, 187
Triple sec
  with flaming trout, 48
Trout
  flaming, 48
  with green sauce, 47
Tuna
  with fennel, 19
  in fresh salmon salad, 26
  grilled, Lampedusa, 17
  leeks in, sauce, 221
  noodle casserole, 20
  with pine nuts and dill, 18
  in yellow Finn potato salad, 235
Turkey
  description, 12
  cutlets with horseradish
    cream, 109
  El Café, 107
  grilled, breast with
    rhubarb sauce, 108
  kebabs with fresh
    pineapple, 110
  smoked, see Smoked turkey

Index

Turnip(s)
in poached perch with
chervil, 50
in pork roast with
chestnuts, 118

Veal
with artichokes, 141
in buttermilk, 146
with capers, 145
with leeks, bacon,
and tomatoes, 143
Marsala, 144
with peaches and almonds, 142
stew with cocktail onions, 147
Vegetables (see individual
vegetables or chapter contents for a list of recipes), 213
Vermouth
in spaghetti with
Gorgonzola sauce, 207
Vinaigrette
basic, 238
Vinegar
balsamic, rabbit in, 136
balsamic, in catfish in cornmeal
with black butter, 52
balsamic, in hot scallop salad
with blood oranges, 79
balsamic, in hunter's rabbit, 131
balsamic, in leeks and eggs in,
vinaigrette, 200
balsamic, in liver, shrimp, and
bacon in pepper sauce, 104
balsamic, in mushroom-stuffed
chicken breasts, 92
raspberry, in lamb with emerald
satsumas and kumquats, 164
raspberry, in liver, shrimp,
and bacon in pepper
sauce, 104

raspberry, in raspberry game
hens, 112
rice, in glazed eggplant
steaks, 216
rice, in pecan pork, 127
rice, in pork kebabs with
fresh pineapple, 129
Walnut(s)
sizzling, rabbit, 133
toasting, 237
Walnut oil
in rabbit with green
peppercorns, 135
in satsuma salad with
hot cranberry dressing, 231
Watercress
in green eggs and ham, 176
with trout with green sauce, 47
Wensleydale
description, 9
grill, 179
White burgundy
chicken in, 96
Wild rice
chicken livers with,
and almonds, 105

Yams
pork with apples and, 119
Yellow Finn potatoes
(see Potatoes)

Zucchini
in cheese and pepperoni
omelet, 197
in insalata Russe, 233
in Japanese eggplant
Parmesan, 215